The Liberal Order and its Cont

The notion that we are experiencing a change in times, whereby an old global order is giving way to a new one, has been gaining legitimacy in international debates. As US power is waning, the argument goes, so is the set of liberal norms, rules and institutions around which the United States organised its global supremacy. Ideational contests, power shifts, regional fragmentation, and socio-economic turmoil paint a broad picture of complex and often interrelated challenges that fuel contestation of the liberal order, both as a normative project and as an emanation of US power. Major players – China and India, Europe and Russia, and the United States itself – are all engaged in a process of global repositioning, most notably in areas where the liberal project has only fragile roots and order is contested: Eastern Europe and the Caucasus, the Asia-Pacific and the Middle East. This volume aims to provide critical frames of reference for understanding whether geopolitical and ideational contestations will eventually bring the US-centred liberal order down or lead to a process of adjustment and transformation.

The chapters in this book were originally published in a special issue of *The International Spectator*.

Riccardo Alcaro is Research Coordinator and Head of the Global Actors Programme at the Istituto Affari Internazionali of Rome, Italy. He has been a Visiting Fellow at the Brookings Institution, Washington, DC, and is a European Foreign and Security Policy Studies Fellow. He holds a PhD from the University of Tübingen, Germany.

The Liberal Order and its Contestations

Great Powers and Regions Transiting in a Multipolar Era

Edited by
Riccardo Alcaro

Routledge
Taylor & Francis Group

LONDON AND NEW YORK

First published 2019
by Routledge
2 Park Square, Milton Park, Abingdon, Oxon, OX14 4RN, UK

and by Routledge
52 Vanderbilt Avenue, New York, NY 10017

First issued in paperback 2020

Routledge is an imprint of the Taylor & Francis Group, an informa business

British Library Cataloguing-in-Publication Data
A catalogue record for this book is available from the British Library

ISBN 13: 978-0-367-58770-3 (pbk)
ISBN 13: 978-1-138-61771-1 (hbk)

Typeset in Minion Pro
by codeMantra

Publisher's Note
The publisher accepts responsibility for any inconsistencies that may have arisen during the conversion of this book from journal articles to book chapters, namely the possible inclusion of journal terminology.

Disclaimer
Every effort has been made to contact copyright holders for their permission to reprint material in this book. The publishers would be grateful to hear from any copyright holder who is not here acknowledged and will undertake to rectify any errors or omissions in future editions of this book.

Contents

CONTENTS

Citation Information

The chapters in this book were originally published in the journal *The International Spectator*, volume 53, issue 1 (March 2018). When citing this material, please use the original page numbering for each article, as follows:

Chapter 1
The Liberal Order and its Contestations. A Conceptual Framework
Riccardo Alcaro
The International Spectator, volume 53, issue 1 (March 2018) pp. 1–10

Chapter 2
Diversity Management: Regionalism and the Future of the International Order
Giovanni Grevi
The International Spectator, volume 53, issue 1 (March 2018) pp. 11–27

Chapter 3
Present at the Destruction? The Liberal Order in the Trump Era
John Peterson
The International Spectator, volume 53, issue 1 (March 2018) pp. 28–44

Chapter 4
The EU and the Global Order: Contingent Liberalism
Michael H. Smith and Richard Youngs
The International Spectator, volume 53, issue 1 (March 2018) pp. 45–56

Chapter 5
Global Reordering and China's Rise: Adoption, Adaptation and Reform
Shaun Breslin
The International Spectator, volume 53, issue 1 (March 2018) pp. 57–75

Chapter 6
Russia's Neorevisionist Challenge to the Liberal International Order
Tatiana Romanova
The International Spectator, volume 53, issue 1 (March 2018) pp. 76–91

For any permission-related enquiries please visit:
http://www.tandfonline.com/page/help/permissions

Notes on Contributors

Riccardo Alcaro, PhD, is Research Coordinator and Head of the Global Actors Programme at the Istituto Affari Internazionali of Rome, Italy. He has been a Visiting Fellow at the Brookings Institution, Washington, DC, USA and is a European Foreign and Security Policy Studies Fellow. His main areas of expertise are US and European policies in Europe's surrounding regions.

Shaun Breslin is Professor of Politics and International Studies at the University of Warwick, Coventry, UK. He is an Associate Fellow of the Asia Research Centre based at Murdoch University, Perth, Australia and an Honorary Professorial Fellow at the Centre for European Studies at Renmin University, Beijing, China. He is Co-Editor of the *Pacific Review*.

Laure Delcour is Research Fellow at the Fondation Maison des Sciences de l'Homme, Paris, France. Her research interests focus on the diffusion and reception of European Union norms and policies as part of the European Neighbourhood Policy, as well as region-building processes in Eurasia.

Giovanni Grevi is Senior Fellow at the European Policy Centre, Brussels, Belgium. His research interests include EU foreign and security policy, strategic affairs, global governance, US foreign policy and foresight and EU politics.

John Peterson is Professor of International Politics at the University of Edinburgh, UK. His research interests include transatlantic relations, European integration and public policy. He is currently a Visiting Fellow at the Centre for European Policy Studies in Brussels, Belgium.

Tatiana Romanova is Associate Professor in the Department of European Studies, Saint Petersburg State University, Russia. Her main areas of expertise are EU-Russian relations, normative competition, resilience, legal approximation, sanctions, energy markets and security, Russian foreign policy, EU institutions and decision-making.

Paul Salem is Senior Vice President for Policy Analysis and Research at the Middle East Institute in Washington, DC, USA. He focuses on issues of political change, transition and conflict as well as the regional and international relations of the Middle East.

Samir Saran is President at the Observer Research Foundation, New Delhi, India. He writes on issues of global governance, climate change, energy policy, global development architecture, artificial intelligence, cyber security, internet governance and India's foreign policy.

Michael H. Smith is Professor in European Politics at the University of Warwick, Coventry, UK. His research seeks to combine awareness of historical processes with a focus on institutions and norms as key shaping forces in EU external policy-making and external relations.

Richard Stubbs is Professor Emeritus in the Department of Political Science at McMaster University, Hamilton, Canada. His main research interests are international relations and the politics of the Asia-Pacific region. His current research centres on political economy and security issues in the Asia-Pacific.

Richard Youngs is Senior Fellow in the Democracy and Rule of Law Program at Carnegie Europe, Brussels, Belgium and Professor of International Relations at the University of Warwick, Coventry, UK. He is author of twelve books on issues related to democracy, the EU and international affairs.

The Liberal Order and its Contestations. A Conceptual Framework

Riccardo Alcaro

The notion that we are experiencing a change in times whereby an old 'order' of the world is giving way to a new era has been gaining legitimacy in international debates among experts, policymakers and practitioners. Such debates are as animated as they are inconclusive in their outcomes. The contours of the upcoming era remain vague, its structure and contents undefined, its direction uncertain. Grim predictions of renewed great power competition as we have not seen since the end of the Cold War or even World War II or of an increasingly fragmented and ungovernable world abound. They co-exist though with less disheartening expectations of future global re-alignments eventually providing order. In the face of such divergent opinions, imagining the future at times looks like an act of divination.

Whereas opinions differ as to what the world of tomorrow will be, greater consensus exists as to what it will not be. Two assumptions, in particular, seem relatively uncontroversial: it will be post-, or less *liberal*, and it will be post, or less *American*. It is no coincidence that experts have singled out these two features, often in connection with one another. Liberal discourse and American power have, after all, profoundly shaped the world that is ostensibly waning. International Relations theorists have in fact long recognised the combination of these two factors as systemic in nature, capable in other words of producing and defining a distinctive historical order: the *liberal international order*.

Contestation, both on an ideological level and in geopolitical terms, has been a constant of the liberal international order since its inception – usually set at 1945, the year of the crushing defeat of the Axis powers by the Allies-Soviet coalition and the creation of the United Nations. As long as communism had appeal, particularly during decolonisation, liberalism was hardly the dominant ideological framework for many countries. As for geopolitics, the Soviet Union was a formidable opponent severely limiting US power for over forty years. Academics, experts and practitioners are aware of this, as they know that the liberal order has come out on top of the many challenges it faced in the past. Yet, a pervading sense that the liberal order is waning persists, as if the challenges the order is confronted with today are of a different and ultimately more damaging nature.

This Special Issue of *The International Spectator* identifies and dissects this new set of challenges. It looks at the internal fissures and examines the external pressure points that are making the liberal order edifice reel, with a view to providing some more conclusive arguments about what we may expect in the future.

The liberal project

Historically, the liberal international order was born of three failures: the failure to ensure peace among great powers, the failure to bind national economies together along a mutually beneficial pattern, and the failure to provide representation for huge sectors of the world's population, particularly in non-Western countries. Two world wars, the most serious global economic depression of modern times, and the moral and practical fraying of empires powerfully attested to the inability of unrestrained sovereignty, protectionism and imperialism to provide guarantees against international instability. These are not ex-post reflections by historians. They were lessons deeply rooted in the minds of the policymakers who, as World War II was drawing to a close, tended to the task of laying the foundations of the world that would come after that greatest of conflagrations. The result of their work was the set of norms and institutions that make up the liberal order.

The liberal international order is thus, first, an *ideational* and *normative project*. Underlying the values that states should take inspiration from, the norms they should enforce, the rules they should abide by, the institutions they should participate in, and the practices they should follow, is the ultimate goal of taming international anarchy. Driving this view of international politics is the liberal proposition that interstate relations are not competitive by nature because state interests are not mutually exclusive. Theorists who identify themselves as 'liberals' do not claim that anarchy can be permanently overcome and continue to believe that foreign policy is ultimately driven by 'self-help'. Yet they insist that cooperation is not only possible, but the one pattern of international conduct that best serves each country's national interest.

This theoretical minimalist approach has been heavily criticised by thinkers who contend that anarchy is not an immutable condition but the result of social interaction among states. They also claim that interests are not given but again a social product inseparable from the formation of collective identities. These are legitimate and, in many cases, well grounded criticisms. However, this is not the place to discuss the merits of the theoretical premises of the liberal international order. What matters here is to establish that liberalism as a normative project has had an immense impact on the structure of interstate relations since the end of World War II. And even if liberalism's theoretical premises remain widely contested, several of its conclusions are not. The logic of absolute gains underlying the generation of collective interests, the fact that state interests extend well beyond considerations of security and power, and the recognition that norms and institutions can drive state action as much as strength does are just the most prominent ones. Paramount is also the notion that foreign policy can hardly be explained if domestic politics are not brought into the picture. Liberalism has articulated these notions in specific ideational-normative frameworks, on which it is therefore necessary to dwell, even if briefly.

The first of such frameworks is *internationalism*, that is, the notion that all states are members of an international society rather than isolated units. With some partial exceptions, the liberal international order has remained firmly anchored in state sovereignty, thereby acknowledging that international politics cannot be organised around a formally superior legal authority. From this however it does not follow that states can act as they please. Their interaction creates mutual responsibilities and an obligation to respect their sovereignty, protect their citizens, and ensure that economic development is environmentally sustainable. Internationalism is thus inseparable from human rights and environmentalism.

The second normative framework articulating the liberal order is multilateralism or, to be more precise, *institutionalism*. If internationalism is about values, institutionalism is about norms and rules. It is not by chance that the conventional date of birth of the liberal order coincides with the establishment of the United Nations. The UN was no historical novelty – the failed experiment of the League of Nations preceded it by twenty-five years. However, it was the most radical attempt to harness the destabilising forces of interstate competition by way of an institutionalised framework for peaceful conflict resolution or, failing this, cooperative crisis management. In the years that followed 1945, the UN evolved into a large framework of international organisations and agencies, creating an exceptionally dense network of intergovernmental interactions.

Faulting the UN with failing to bring enduring peace and security to the world is a legitimate, yet irresponsibly narrow criticism. The formation of the UN has created the conditions for a massive expansion of international law doctrine and practices. Human rights covenants, agreements prohibiting or containing the proliferation of weapons of mass destruction, arms control treaties and climate change conventions have reduced the risk of war and mitigated the effects of heavily polluting industrial development. The liberal order has even extended to criminal justice in the attempt to prevent or punish mass atrocities committed by individual rulers against civilians, although this step remains deeply contested and so far largely ineffective. Besides such macro-issues, institutionalism has unfolded in a myriad of treaties, regimes and institutions regulating sectorial aspects of international politics, ranging from the law of the sea to aviation safety to protection of the cultural heritage of humankind.

Multilateral institutions suffer from many shortcomings, ranging from frustratingly cumbersome decision-making processes to a scarcity of resources. Yet it is undeniable that they have injected a high degree of predictability into international politics and created a widespread expectation that states are accountable to one another.

The third normative framework articulating the liberal order is *regionalism* or *regional communities*. In a way, this is nothing other than internationalism and institutionalism on a smaller scale. It draws from the same premises, namely that of turning competitive patterns of interaction into cooperative ones. Actually, regionalism carries significant additional advantages, as geographic proximity has traditionally been a source of deeper and more bitter competition, with countries vying for the same land or the same resources developing deep-rooted national, cultural and political rivalries. Hence, as regions become more stable, so does the broader international system. At its best, regionalism is capable of greater achievements than global intergovernmentalism, as the cultural affinity, reciprocal knowledge and common history of regional states can become the bedrock of more ambitious processes of interstate cooperation, eventually extending into regional integration – as the case of the European Union attests.

The fourth normative framework of the liberal order is *interdependence*, understood not so much as a fact of life (otherwise there would be nothing normative about it) but rather as an obligation to pursue economic welfare in a non-discriminatory fashion (in fact, a more accurate name for it would be the *liberal economic system*). The promoters of the liberal order deliberately rejected both mercantilism and protectionism as bad practices that impoverished people and states while widening political divides. Aware that political internationalism could by no means be detached from its economic base, they were determined to turn interdependence, which had been so destructive in the late 1920s and 1930s, into an engine of development and a mechanism for distributing gains more evenly among nations.

They set up an International Monetary Fund to ensure financial stability and lend money to heavily indebted countries, and a World Bank to sustain infrastructure and economic development in poor countries. They also agreed progressively to open the world economy by reducing tariffs and eliminating quotas. Eventually, global trade negotiations, rules and disputes became the responsibility of a World Trade Organisation. In the meantime, other dimensions grew in importance, such as capital flows, foreign direct investments, transfers of knowledge and technology. Increasingly, the liberal international order has concerned regulations, the rules disciplining production, the testing of goods and provision of services. All these links tie the states' economic fortunes to one another, creating incentives to regulate competition and avoid potentially disruptive trade and currency wars.

It is not only trade or capital flows that link countries to one another. There are a number of challenges, and threats, that affect states transversally, so much so that we refer to them as transnational rather than international problems. They range from climate change to organised crime, from terrorism to regional crises, from resource and food scarcity to internet management and cyber security.

The complexity of these challenges has long outstripped the ability of international institutions to provide adequate management. States have increasingly been cooperating in informal settings, such as the G7 or the G20, to facilitate consensus on major issues of international concern and lay the ground for policy responses. Sometimes they act on an *ad hoc* basis in the context of contact groups or coalitions of the willing to address urgent issues in a more flexible and speedy fashion. As intergovernmentalism unfolds on various levels (multilateral or minilateral, formal and informal), cooperation also occurs below the intergovernmental level. Transgovernmental networks of regulators supplement polit-ical-diplomatic exchanges at various levels, ranging from banking to police cooperation. Non-governmental actors, be they corporations, business groups or civil society organisa-tions, participate in international policymaking processes.

Governance is what we call this multilevel, multi-actor management of problems. And even if governance cannot be considered a normative framework, liberalism informs it as well. After all, governance, and particularly global governance, is a legitimate notion only if one assumes a perspective that subsumes the particular national interest of individual states to a superior interest of the international society as such – this most liberal of ideas.

The last liberal normative framework is *democracy*. The liberal order is premised on the assumption that all states, the rich and powerful as well as the poor and weak, have a right to representation and participation in international decision-making. This soft form of democratisation concerns relations between states and not their internal organisation. Yet it would be disingenuous to ignore the powerful role that democracy, both as a concept and as a reality of a multiplicity of states, plays in sustaining the liberal order. That order assumes states to be respectful of the rule of law, protectors of human security, accountable for their actions, capable of solving conflict without force, and promoters of individual and corporate potential. Democracy is historically and conceptually deeply associated with all this, whereby the liberal order has an inbuilt bias towards democracies as the polities struc-turally best suited to perform the role of responsible members of the international society.

American hegemony

Internationalism, institutionalism, regionalism, interdependence and governance, as well as democracy, are the normative frameworks into which the liberal order breaks down. For its implementation, a normative project of such ambitions presupposes a relatively high degree of subjective adherence to its values, principles and rules. Countries around the world do share, then, a sense of ownership of the liberal order (or at least the order if not its liberal core). Yet no order can exist without authority or, absent that, a guarantor with sufficient power to promote the order, defend its institutions and enforce its rules. The one country that has framed its international role accordingly is of course the United States. To be sure, the US has shared the task of ensuring a degree of world order with partners and even rivals. Yet it is undeniable that, thanks to its superior power, the US is the country that has, more than any other, promoted the liberal order's values, laid down its institutional grounds and expanded its reach. In these terms, the liberal order cannot be seen but in conjunction with US power.

The above warrants some elaboration. A constitutional authority presiding over an order is itself part of that order – the two cannot be separated. But the relationship between a guarantor and an order is more nuanced. The guarantor has an interest in sustaining the order, but how much capital (political, financial or military) it is willing to invest in it depends on its own autonomous considerations and resources. In a constitutional system, authority is a manifestation of the order. In global politics, the order is an emanation of power. In these terms, the liberal order is the expression of US power – in discourse, norms and institutions. Conceiving of the liberal order as a specific geopolitical configuration of power involves understanding how this power works and what nexus there is between its main components and the mentioned normative frameworks.

American hegemony underlies the liberal order, whose reach has largely coincided with the extension of US power. Beyond that, areas of contestation have emerged, characterised by a high potential for political instability and insecurity. That said, US power has been such that no region in the world has remained untouched by it. American clout has in fact been felt, one way or another, everywhere. The magnitude of its power has made the US a systemic 'pole', the hub around which global state interactions revolve. This has been true regardless of whether US pre-eminence has been sternly challenged (as during the Cold War), uncontested (as during the unipolar moment that followed the collapse of the Soviet Union), or simply resisted (as in the nascent multipolar system).

At no point throughout the period since US policymakers opted for global engagement, and especially since the end of the Cold War, have rival 'poles' mastered the resources necessary to replace the US-centred order with one of their own making, although they might have been able to resist its advancement or consolidation, both geographically and functionally. This asymmetric balance of power, all its oscillations notwithstanding, has worked as a strong deterrent against great power conflict. This is perhaps the most important dividend in terms of international stability that American hegemony has brought with it. Yet it has not been the only one. The US has also provided protection of the global commons, most notably freedom of navigation, and leadership in the management of transnational challenges. No wonder American thinkers love to speak of enlightened leadership or, at times, 'benign' hegemony – a notion that leads directly to the next point.

US power has endured and expanded through a system of *alliances and partnerships*. Unlike traditional hegemonic powers, the US exerts influence over other countries less through coercion and pressure – which it usually applies to rivals or enemies – than through co-optation, persuasion and inspiration. The US is not a despot that uses force to quell dissent and ensure compliance with its desiderata in satellite countries. The US relationship with its allies in Europe and East Asia, however, is one between leader and followers, wherein the latter voluntarily accept a subordinate position because they define their interest largely in agreement with that of the leader.

Partnerships with the US facilitate processes of *regional consolidation*. The relatively light touch with which the US exerts its hegemonic power over its partners and allies leaves them ample leeway to make inroads into regional governance along patterns of cooperation that reflect, complement and supplement the nature of their partnership with the US. Europe provides the main example. European nations have embarked on an integration process that has paid off massively in terms of continental security, stability and prosperity. They have thus contributed to the stability of the order centred on US power, on which they continue to rely through membership in NATO. Regional consolidation has proceeded less in other regions under US influence, yet the point stands that US hegemony creates a more forthcoming environment for US allies living in the same geographical area to interact cooperatively.

Another feature of the US-centred order and arguably the ultimate source of US power is *free market capitalism*. America's hegemony is sustained by its economy, in turn driven by its entrepreneurial culture as well as the capacity of its major corporations to achieve dominance in technological and financial innovation. Size and dynamism make the US economy the main engine of globalisation, whereby the economic development of other countries have become dependent on access to US markets and technologies.

The final feature of US hegemony is what inextricably ties US power to the liberal order, namely its *liberal-democratic constitutional regime*. Support for democracy has been a constant in US foreign policy and a critical source of legitimacy for its hegemony. The US commands loyalty not least because it inspires emulation and provides its partners with access to its political leadership. No amount of US arrogance and hypocrisy can change the fact that a hegemonic power whose political system is transparent, predictable and open to foreign lobbying is preferable to a regime that exhibits the opposite characteristics.

Tracing the normative instances of liberal internationalism back to their geopolitical foundations adds nuance to our understanding of the liberal order. The exercise validates the assertion that American hegemony and the liberal order are mutually constitutive. The US not only moves *in* the system but moves *the* system – indeed, what we have here is an instance of an almost symbiotic relationship between system (the liberal order) and agency (the US).

Comparing the normative dimensions with the geopolitical foundations of the liberal order also serves the purpose of highlighting the *inherent tension between US power and the order that emanates from it*. The US has always retained the 'right' to derogate from the rules and accepted practices of the liberal order. Recently, it has often taken steps in contrast with the principles of internationalism. Its commitment to multilateral institutionalism has been intermittent, its support for liberalism and democracy ambivalent (going so far as to claim to 'export' democracy by way of arms, or openly supporting authoritarian regimes for the sake of its alleged geopolitical and economic interests), its version of free market capitalism has been aggressive, inflexible and disrespectful of the specific needs of other countries.

While supportive of regional consolidation, it has been careful not to let such processes undermine its influence. And in areas where its hegemonic power was or is contested (or simply not accepted), such as Latin America in the 1970s and 1980s or the Middle East since the 1980s, the US has hardly been a force for peace and democratic development. If anything, the opposite is the case: the US has been a disruptive force, fomenting instability and supporting autocracies.

More broadly speaking, the US has always retained the right to derogate from the norm of multilateral cooperation if that suits its interests, more often than not defined in full autonomy. The upshot is a paradox: US power is what has enabled the liberal international order and at the same time the ultimate obstacle to its most complete realisation.

Multi-dimensional contestations

Today, US power is declining relative to that of other powers. Concomitantly, the liberal project the US has espoused for decades has lost some of its traction, not only in countries that have traditionally placed themselves outside the US' reach but also in the Western core of the US-centred order. As a result, a number of fault lines have emerged that threaten the endurance of that order.

First comes a *contest of ideas*. Liberalism does not face a global challenge from a rival ideology comparable to communism. However, some of its most fundamental ideas are increasingly contested. Nationalism, often underpinned by nativist instincts, has staged a sudden comeback in Western politics. To be sure, this kind of nationalism is not the aggressive version European nations developed during the age of imperialism. Today's nationalists do not aim for conquest and world domination. Instead, they have a narrow, defensive understanding of sovereignty, which they consider incompatible with the principle of internationalism. Nationalists question the proposition that multilateral commitments can serve the national interest and perceive interdependence as a force disempowering individual citizens and governments of the ability to be in control of their destiny. Demands for protectionism and closed borders have grown louder than ever in the last decades.

Even representative democracy is under pressure, from within as well as from without. The challenge from within is populism, the proposition that owes its electoral fortunes to the radical 'othering' of political opponents. Populists claim to represent 'the people' against an undefined 'other', which may alternately take the form of unaccountable, corrupt elites or impersonal international forces. This tactic magnifies polarisation, which in turn augments mistrust of political leaders and fuels doubts that representative democracies are adequately equipped to manage and solve domestic as well as international problems. The challenge from without stems from the illiberal regimes where democracy is demeaned to controlled plebiscites legitimising the rule of semi-authoritarian or authoritarian leaders.

The second fault line in the liberal order is a *clash of power*. With US power declining relative to that of rising and resurgent states, such as China, India and Russia, the sustain-ability of American hegemony is very much in question. The United States' diminished standing is partly the result of imperial overreach by the US itself, which has embarked on drawn-out and largely inconclusive military interventions that have consumed political capital and immense financial resources for little or no returns.

The US has proven unable to ensure a political order – the main 'duty' of a hegemon – in several regions of the world, ranging from the Middle East and Eastern Europe to, increasingly, East Asia. Rival or non-aligned powers have become more effective at frustrating American objectives and pushing back against its influence, at least on a regional level: China in East and Central Asia; Russia in Eastern Europe, Central Asia and to some extent the Middle East; Iran in the Middle East.

The shift in the strategic focus away from Europe to the Asia-Pacific, the Middle East and Southern Asia has led the US to tighten links with countries with which it shares little cultural and political affinity. Transatlantic relations remain strong but the sense of common purpose across the ocean is fading. The US system of international relations' gradual rebalancing towards opportunistic alliances, particularly with the Sunni Arab states of the Gulf, may well have a long-term systemic impact. Alliances based on long-term strategic interests *and* values, such as the alliance with Europe, perform a critical supplementary task in defending, sustaining and expanding the liberal order. Patron-client relationships with regimes espousing little commitment to liberal norms and discourse do not.

Another critical fault line is *regional fragmentation*. A distinctive feature of contemporary international politics is the increase of areas in which state power has collapsed (Somalia, Libya, Yemen), is violently contested by domestic actors (Syria, Ukraine, Iraq), or is extremely limited (the Sahel countries). These crises have a considerable destabilising potential. Local conflicts easily spill over into neighbouring states, spreading instability as a contagion. Internally displaced persons join migrants from other countries in swelling migration flows, which in turn can create social or political disruptions in the countries of transit or destination. Illicit trafficking, including of human beings, flourishes, enriching local and foreign criminal networks. Armed militias proliferate and extremist groups find fertile ground for recruitment, training and planning of attacks both within and outside the area in which they are based. Regional players are invariably drawn into such crises, as are global actors, with the frequent result of war by proxy, increased regional instability and more acute global tensions.

A final set of challenges resides in the *ills of globalisation*, whether real or perceived. The liberal order was associated, for a while, with a period of financial stability and economic growth, with traditionally liberal economic propositions such as free trade and market-oriented policies moderated by the state through redistribution policies and the provision of welfare benefits. The end of the dollar's convertibility to gold and the oil price shocks of the 1970s put an end to this period of financial tranquillity, steady growth and social advancements. It was followed by the neoliberal counter-revolution of the 1980s that continued, unabated and triumphant, in the 1990s. The dominance of supply-side economics, particularly in the financial industry with the removal of capital controls, has gone hand in hand with that unprecedented acceleration in economic activity, movement of people and technological advances (particularly in communications) that we refer to as globalisation. Contrary to the great moderation, the era of turbo-capitalism has been associated with financial turbulence, loss of jobs due to a mix of automation and delocalisation, wage stagnation and rising income inequality.

The exposure to sudden financial shocks and the continuing deterioration of living standards have put Western middle classes under severe pressure and contributed to eroding support for those responsible for economic governance – whether national governments, international organisations, banks or multinationals. Massive industrialisation and urbanisation in fast-growing developing countries have created huge income disparities. The result is a demand for protecting domestic markets and, particularly (but not only) in authoritarian regimes, securing state control of national champions, thus raising the risk of trade fragmentation and market distortions.

The power of agency

Ideational contests, power shifts, fragmentation, socio-economic turmoil draw a broad picture of complex and often inter-related challenges. This nurtures contestation of the liberal order, both as a normative project and as an emanation of US power (in some way the 'ideology' of US power). Balances of power, distribution of resources and ideological contests are powerful systemic drivers. Yet they do not deterministically set countries on a specific course of action. Agency is an equally potent force, particularly of the international players whose cooperative or competitive interaction has the greatest potential to shape systemic dynamics. Contestation is not necessarily a prelude to demise, as revival or adjustment and transformation are also possible outcomes.

The power of agency is why this Special Issue concentrates on *global* actors: the US, Europe, China, Russia and India. Granted, for anyone but the US the definition of 'global actor' may be generous or at least premature. Their inclusion in this study is nonetheless very much legitimate, for two reasons. The first is that they are all powerful players whose clout extends beyond their immediate neighbourhood and may then have systemic implications. The second reason is that they all play a part in one or more regions of the world where the liberal project has only weak roots and order is very much a contested thing: Eastern Europe, the Asia-Pacific and, of course, that inexhaustible source of turmoil that is the Middle East. These three *areas of contested order* make up the second focus of this Special Issue.

The five articles on the global-systemic players elaborate on the role of each player in the liberal order. Specifically, they consider the extent to which the player in question is committed to the liberal project, whether it shares all of its components, accepts only some of them, or rejects them altogether, and why. They also examine, and it could not be otherwise, the systemic position of the player in the configuration of power underlying the liberal order – whether they contribute to upholding it or oppose it, and why and how they do so. Bowing to the liberal argument that all foreign policy is domestic politics, the analyses look into the internal processes producing state interests and policies. They identify the main actors – political forces, government officials, interest groups, business lobbies and civil society organisations – that may have a stake in participating in or contesting the liberal order, thus tracing foreign policy back to its domestic roots.

The articles on the three areas of contested order investigate the nexus between the liberal order and the region in question from two complementary perspectives. The first is an 'outside-in' perspective. They measure the extent to which regional interstate relations reflect the principles and practices of liberal internationalism. They look into regionalisation or fragmentation dynamics to find out whether norms, institutions and practices of the liberal order have contributed to either process. And they assess the impact on regional dynamics of broader, global geopolitical balances. They then examine the contested order from an 'inside-out' perspective. They appraise whether regional arrangements and institutions support the liberal order or espouse alternative forms of intraregional interaction. They inquire into the ideological premises of the competing visions of order in the region, and elaborate on the possible geopolitical constellations of power that could support these alternative visions. Finally, they consider the question whether the liberal international order can accommodate regional sub-systems defined by different normative frameworks.

This body of analysis is preceded by an article that traces the liberal order to its historical roots, reconstructing in greater detail its institutional configurations at the global as well as the regional level. The study ends with a final reflection, based on the results of the individual contributions, on what we may expect in the future.

Diversity Management: Regionalism and the Future of the International Order

Giovanni Grevi

ABSTRACT

The ongoing redistribution of power on the international stage points to a more decentred international system featuring a multiplication of governance arrangements. A larger range of pivotal countries have the capacity and the confidence to pursue different priorities, a development that questions the prevalent post-Cold War expectation that the liberal international order would grow both wider and deeper. The central challenge for the future of the international order is managing diversity in ways that minimise conflict and leverage the benefits of interdependence. The evolution of regionalism and regional orders will be a critical dimension of the realignment of power, interests and normative agendas at the global level. Both more competition and more cooperation are likely to take place at the regional level, with the mix changing in different parts of the world. Provided that it is not merely a cover for coercive hegemonic aspirations and that it is designed to complement other levels of cooperation, regionalism can play an important role in preventing a more polycentric world from becoming a more fragmented and unstable one.

After four decades of bipolar confrontation, many expected that the end of the Cold War would herald the disappearance of credible alternatives to the Western-led liberal international order. The latter would progressively expand worldwide on the heels of economic globalisation, with more and more countries embracing open markets and liberal democracy. In short, modernisation would by and large equal Westernisation. That expectation was to some extent fulfilled. The liberal international order expanded its reach to a number of countries emerging from the Soviet empire and to others, such as China, that joined global and regional institutions. The order became deeper too, with new norms and multilateral frameworks emerging on issues ranging from climate change to international criminal justice and the 'responsibility to protect'.

Alongside this expansion, however, the order also grew more contested and uneven. A number of countries proved reluctant to commit to new principles and norms reaching further into the sphere of domestic affairs. While their motivations differed, the common denominator was their concern to preserve national sovereignty in the face of more intrusive multilateral regimes. Emerging countries contested the distribution of power in existing multilateral institutions, notably the United Nations (UN) and the Bretton Woods bodies, as reflecting a bygone era of Western predominance. As their economic and political weight grew, they called for greater representation in leading fora and aimed to take a bigger role in setting the terms of international cooperation.

With the international order growing both wider and more contested, new forms and formats of cooperation have been developing in the last 20 years to accommodate greater diversity. Weakly institutionalised, flexible minilateral initiatives have brought together like-minded partners to work on issues of shared concern, such as non-proliferation or global health. In parallel to this evolution, some of the existing regional cooperation frameworks, such as the Association of Southeast Asian Nations (ASEAN), have been strengthened and new ones created, such as the Shanghai Cooperation Organisation (SCO) or the Union of South American Nations (UNASUR), with regional powers often leading these efforts.

Multiple factors, endogenous and exogenous to each region, have driven investment in regionalism throughout the world. These include managing power politics at regional level, balancing external powers, fostering economic integration, coping with shared trans-national challenges and acquiring more influence on the global stage. The outcome of regional cooperation has been very uneven in different parts of the world, whether in terms of effectiveness, degree of institutionalisation or policy scope. However, the evolution of regional orders reflects a variety of developments common to several regions: for instance, the growing influence of some regional powers and the aim of their neighbours to tame that influence, while setting cooperation on firmer, more predictable grounds; or the need felt by regional actors to equip themselves better to be able to compensate for the shortcomings of global multilateral institutions or regimes on issues such as trade and security.

The evolution of regional cooperation will be a key variable affecting the shape of the international order. From this standpoint, the question is whether regionalism will exacerbate or mitigate competition in a polycentric strategic environment, and whether it will complement or weaken the multilateral frameworks that have been the pillars of the liberal international order. This article looks at the origins and main features of the liberal international order, appraises how the emergence of a polycentric international system challenges that order and reviews different prospects for its evolution. In particular, it gauges the approach of major powers towards regional order-building and addresses how cooperation at the regional level can enhance or undermine global governance in a more competitive world.

The article concludes that regionalism is likely to gain relevance both as a level of governance and as an arena for power politics, but that this evolution and the interplay between these two dimensions of regional orders will feature different characteristics in different parts of the world. On balance, multiple factors, such as the density of multiple layers of global governance, complex interdependence and the projection of big powers and regional ones within and beyond respective regions militate against the prospect of a world segmented in regional spheres of influence or closed blocs. The ongoing redistribution of power points, rather, to a more asymmetric international order where relative economic openness co-exists with different and sometimes conflicting value systems and power strategies. In this context, regionalism can be an important tool to manage diversity and reconcile the priorities of pivotal countries with the need for collective action in a post-hegemonic order.

From the hegemonic liberal order to a decentred world

The distribution of power among states, the strategies by which the biggest powers seek to achieve their goals, and the extent to which norms and values are shared or contested are the main variables determining the features of international orders. Orders can therefore be embedded in multipolar, bipolar or unipolar international systems and can be more or less codified and institutionalised. Depending on the nature of the relationship between the more powerful and less powerful states, orders can range from imperial forms of dominance to rule-based multilateralism predicated on common principles of conduct and diffused reciprocity. Various forms of order can co-exist within the international system, whether informed by different norms and principles (such as at the time of the bipolar confrontation), or corresponding to different regions, or both.[1] The relationship between different orders can be confrontational, competitive or cooperative, which carries profound implications for the scope and quality of cooperation at the global level.

The end of World War Two saw an unprecedented order-building effort principally driven by the United States. As Ikenberry points out, the US was the leading architect of new multilateral deals and frameworks. However, the shape of what would become the liberal international order was not simply the subject of a master plan concocted in Washington. It was rather the product of the progressive adaptation of the American approach to a shifting strategic context, as relations between the US and the Soviet Union deteriorated.[2] The emergence of the Cold War undermined prospects for a concert of powers sharing responsibility for global stability through the United Nations (UN) system and required the much more direct engagement of the US in supporting its partners and allies. The framing of the liberal international order therefore owed much to both the vast resources that the US commanded and Washington's choice to channel its unparalleled power through a set of institutions and practices that would simultaneously multiply and delimit American power. In other words, the order was both liberal and hierarchical.[3]

Not least given the large influence of the US relative to that of other partners in the negotiation of the UN Charter, universalist aspirations prevailed at the time over envisaging greater responsibilities for regional cooperative frameworks. Under Chapter VIII, the Charter envisaged that regional arrangements could deal with the peaceful settlement of disputes and also carry out enforcement action under the authority of the Security Council. Some thought that regions could play an important role in peace and security matters to tame anarchy and confront aggression. Others were concerned that regions could again become vehicles for discriminatory economic practices and platforms for geopolitical competition. In the course of the Cold War, with the exception of the distinctive experience of European integration, attempts at regional cooperation proved relatively ineffective given both the limited engagement or scarce capacity of participating countries and the constraints that the rivalry between the two superpowers imposed on all regions.

The pillars of the liberal international order were economic openness and non-discrimination, collective security arrangements between like-minded partners and multilateralism. While ultimately resting on US power, and encompassing political differences and occasional tensions among its main stakeholders, the order was not based on coercion

---

[1]Flockhart, "The coming multi-order world"; Kissinger, *World Order*.
[2]Ikenberry, *Liberal Leviathan*. 162-9.
[3]*Ibid.*, 297.

but on the acceptance of American leadership by US partners. This was due to a variety of factors, chief among them the shared threat posed by the Soviet bloc, the relative affinity of values and political systems among Western democracies and the distinctive features of the order, which opened opportunities for influence for weaker states and bound the US to common institutions. The US performed a hegemonic role within this order, in the sense that its dominant position was recognised by others and that the American and more broadly Western liberal political tradition informed the principles underpinning the order itself. In addition, the US was willing and able to provide public goods at the global and regional level, including the stability of the international trade and monetary systems and the freedom of the commons. According to the hegemonic stability theory, the provision of these goods by the leading power is critical to the functioning and preservation of the order, as it meets the interests of participating states and offers predictability.[4]

The US and its allies played a pivotal role in shaping the liberal international order but the latter did not amount to a global one. Under a relatively thin umbrella of shared principles and institutions, such as the principle of sovereignty and the UN, the bipolar confrontation generated two antagonistic orders – the liberal international order and the Soviet-led order – with alternative norms and structures.[5] The demise of the Soviet Union appeared to remove any serious competition to the US' hegemonic role and to unleash the worldwide expansion of the liberal international order. Progressively, the latter would coincide with the world order. With hindsight, however, the uncontestable success and expansion of the liberal order contained the seeds of the crisis that it is facing today and of the evolution towards a more decentred international system. Over the last twenty years, the liberal order has been growing simultaneously larger and more contested.

First, by encompassing new countries and global regions, the order also grew shallower. Some of the countries that joined or became more engaged in multilateral cooperative frameworks did not fully subscribe to their normative foundations or agree with the distribution of power within them. They did not feel any ownership of an order that they had not contributed to shaping. Second, by evolving to include principles and regimes that would delimit national sovereignty in the name of 'universal' values, as in the case of responsibility to protect or human rights, the order also became more contested.[6] A number of countries only reluctantly accepted or outright refused constraints on their sovereignty, not least out of concern that Western powers would use them to interfere in their domestic affairs. Third, in the economic domain, globalisation and regionalisation have proceeded in parallel, with regionalism mobilised alternatively to fit global flows better, to mitigate their impact or to counter the prevalent neoliberal agenda, depending on different regions and bodies.

The core structural trend that has unleashed the multidimensional and controversial evolution of the liberal international order is the redistribution of power away from established powers as well as from states to non-state actors such as large multinational companies, trans-national civil society coalitions or criminal and terrorist networks. One of the primary manifestations of this trend is the rise of countries, notably China, bearing different conceptions of order and often dissonant priorities on the multilateral stage. This development

---

[4] Kindleberger, "Dominance and Leadership"; Krasner, "State Power".
[5] Flockhart, "The coming multi-order world".
[6] Ikenberry, "Three Faces of Liberal Internationalism"

clearly challenges America's hegemonic role and points to the paradox whereby the liberal international order reached its peak at a time when its structural foundations began to shift.

Debates on the decline of American hegemony date back to the 1970s and revolve today around three basic questions. The first concerns the sustainability of multilateral cooperation at a time when the leading power is no longer willing or able to take principal responsibility for the stability of the system.[7] The second question is about whether the ongoing transition of power from the West to the rest will amount to a succession of hegemonies, in particular from the US to China.[8] The third question, which somehow bridges the other two, is about what the approach of the US will be to a multilateral order that becomes more contested and less amenable to influence from Washington. This is about whether the US will continue to invest in the grand milieu-shaping strategy that has informed much of its foreign policy during and after the Cold War, or whether it will adopt a narrower definition of national interests and downscale its engagement in multilateralism, partnerships and alliances.

This question is central to the current strategic debate in the US.[9] The Obama administration upheld the narrative about the indispensable role of the US to support collective action and problem-solving at the global level and aimed to embed American influence in various cooperative formats. However, it also acknowledged that US power faced increasing constraints and that trade-offs and compromises would be needed to deal with emerging powers. President Trump and many in his administration see the liberal international order as no longer fitting American national interests, disproportionately benefitting others and imposing undue restrictions on American sovereignty. They have advocated an 'America first' foreign policy that is inflicting serious damage on the global standing of the US as the ultimate guarantor of a broadly rule-based, open international order.[10]

Despite the rhetoric of the Trump administration and the uncertainty currently surrounding US foreign policy, the prospect of a succession of hegemonies appears remote. First of all, it seems very unlikely that the US will durably reverse its extensive investment in international cooperation and forego the influence that stems from that. Secondly, others do not appear prepared to generate and implement an alternative vision of global order. The so-called BRICS,[11] in particular, may take issue with various aspects of the liberal international order and are likely to play an increasingly important role in shaping regional orders but, so far, do not form a common front when it comes to promoting a different set of values and institutions.[12]

The defining features of the emerging international system are its diversity and its connectedness. For the first time in history, powers carrying different conceptions of order are also deeply interdependent, with their dense interactions processed, at least in part, through a thick, if contested, framework of cooperative institutions and regimes.[13] This points to the central challenge for the future of the international order, namely managing diversity in ways that minimise conflict and leverage the benefits of interdependence in a more polycentric international system. Whether regionalism can contribute to overcoming this challenge or will rather compound geopolitical polarisation is a central issue in the current strategic debate.[14]

---

[7]Keohane, *After Hegemony*.
[8]Clark, "China and the United States".
[9]Grevi, *Lost in transition*.
[10]Burns, "Risks of the Trump administration".
[11]Brazil, Russia, India, China and South Africa.
[12]EU Institute for Security Studies and National Intelligence Council, *Global Governance 2025*.
[13]Kupchan, *No One's World*.
[14]Telò, *Regionalism in Hard Times*.

Where to from here?

The debate on the shape and future of the international order in a post-hegemonic environment encompasses a variety of positions. Some believe that the progressive downsizing of the US global role heralds an age of geopolitical competition in a multipolar world. The latter will see the 'return of history' in the form of ideological struggles, if not outright conflict, among the largest powers.[15] In this view, it is a mistake to conflate the end of the Cold War with the end of power politics: ideological alternatives to Western liberalism may have disappeared, but geopolitics are in full swing.[16] The liberal order will retrench or break down under the pressure of revisionist powers and that will engender the crisis or collapse of multilateral cooperation. A frequent corollary of this thesis is that the US and its allies should counter the growing influence of authoritarian powers like China or Russia by adopting a more robust strategic posture and mobilising a coalition of like-minded allies and partners.

Others recognise that a more multipolar world will be harder to manage but do not draw a direct correlation between multipolarity and conflict. While power shifts point to a multipolar configuration of the system, that says little about the nature of the relationship between different power centres.[17] The latter will depend in part on the degree of normative affinity or disconnect between major powers, on prospects for their convergence around shared priorities or divergence over time, as well as on the impact of deep interdependence on their national interests and strategic calculations.

Daniel Deudney and John Ikenberry maintain that despite current tensions and normative antagonism, emerging powers are actually taking part in multilateral arrangements and modernising their economies and societies.[18] The liberal order is flexible enough to accommodate powers and regions holding political traditions, worldviews and priorities that do not coincide with those of the US and the West at large, but which are bound by the requirements of cooperation. Joseph Nye recently argued that the liberal international order will prove more resilient than many expect even in the face of the possible disengagement from multilateral cooperation of the Trump administration. The biggest challenge to the current order will not come from revisionist powers, who have a major stake in it, but from the diffusion of power to non-state actors and the political crises in Western democracies.[19] Barry Buzan and George Lawson observe that ideological divisions between great powers persist but are smaller than in the past. Capitalism and restraint on the use of force, in particular among major powers, provide a common ground for their interaction. This is why, in the view of these authors, geopolitical and geo-economic competition are likely to take softer forms than outright conflict.[20]

The relationship between power, interdependence and conflict has long been at the centre of reflections on the shape and stability of the international order. Interdependence entails both mutual vulnerabilities and mutual benefits. It can be instrumentalised in zero-sum games but also jointly managed for shared gains. It can prove a platform for

---

[15]Kagan, *The Return of History*.
[16]Russel Mead, "The Return of Geopolitics".
[17]Grevi, *The Interpolar World*; Acharya, *End of American World Order*.
[18]Deudney and Ikenberry, "The Myth of Autocratic Revival"; Ikenberry, "The Illusion of Geopolitics".
[19]Nye, "Will the Liberal Order Survive?".
[20]Buzan and Lawson, *The Global Transformation*.

cooperation or an arena for competition. Some assessments have put the accent on the potential mitigating effects of interdependence on sheer geopolitical confrontation in a so-called 'inter-polar' world.[21] Others have emphasized that various dimensions of interdependence, from trade to migrations, can be used as weapons to gain leverage over rivals.[22]

The question of how the US and other major powers will respond to (and seek to shape) structural shifts such as the de-concentration of power and deepening interdependence finds no definitive answer at this stage. What is clear is that a larger number of important countries will have more say on the shape of the future international order. That puts the relationship between the US and the future of the international order in a new perspective. In short, the correlation between the future of American power and the sustainability of a cooperative international order seems to become less direct. Washington's approach to the international order remains of course a defining variable for the future of international cooperation, but other factors, namely the priorities and preferences of other actors, have become more relevant.

Ikenberry and Amitav Acharya have captured this point, even though they draw different conclusions from it. The former argues that the fact that the order becomes less hierarchical, due to the relative decline of the West and the relative rise of others, raises serious challenges but does not necessarily entail the waning of its liberal character. The current order delivers important benefits to rising powers too. Acharya feels that the liberal order (which he defines the 'American world order') is coming to an end whether or not the US is declining because the international system is growing more heterogeneous and different actors feature different norms and interests.

Acharya shares with a number of other authors the central insight that managing pluralism and diversity in a more decentred international system will be the defining challenge for reforming the international order or building a new one. Andrew Hurrell calls for recognising the emergence of a more pluralistic liberal order, beyond the dichotomy between the Western-led order and revisionist challengers.[23] Charles Kupchan believes that "the world is fast headed toward multiple versions of modernity", which is the reason why, if "a new rules-based order is to emerge, the West will have to embrace political diversity".[24] Henry Kissinger argues that the challenge is "how divergent historic experiences and values can be shaped into a common order".[25] In particular, many scholars and observers point to the emergence of a more regionalised international system. The shape of regional orders will, from this standpoint, be a key variable in determining whether a more decentred system will also be a more fragmented and unstable one.

Regional orders between cooperation and competition

The ongoing de-concentration of power and de-decentring of the international system has given more voice and options to more countries. In a more diverse and pluralistic environment, international cooperation has taken new forms. A variety of formal bodies and informal frameworks have been set up, leading to articulate regime 'complexes' in policy

---

[21]Grevi, *The Interpolar World*.
[22]Leonard, "Introduction: Connectivity wars".
[23]Hurrell, "Power Transitions".
[24]Kupchan, *No One's World*, 205 and 187.
[25]Kissinger, *World Order*, 10.

fields such as the environment,[26] development and health, among others. This development reflects both the different priorities of the various countries aiming to shape multilateral agendas and the expansion of the range of influential actors beyond states to non-state actors and networks. In other words, the de-concentration of power is accompanied by the gradual de-concentration of governance frameworks well beyond the traditional global and regional Western-led multilateral institutions established during the Cold War. This trend has also created more political space for regional powers to shape regional orders, as a component of the larger ongoing process of redefinition of power balances and governance arrangements.

The strength and features of regional orders are likely to be increasingly important variables in determining the shape and stability of the post-hegemonic international order. The relationship between the global order and regional orders, or between 'one world' and 'many worlds', can be assessed from different standpoints, focusing on power, governance or identity issues.[27] In a polycentric world, pivotal countries may face fewer constraints to project their influence in some regions, while competing regional initiatives may intersect in others. In a more connected world, the management of deep interdependence may require complementing global institutions with regional ones (as well as other governance formats such as minilateral groupings). In a more heterogeneous world, regional identities and historically embedded norms and values may come to play a more relevant role in shaping distinct regional orders. These three levels of assessment need not be seen as mutually exclusive, since they carry more or less explicative value depending on the mix of factors driving regional cooperation in different parts of the world at different times. Just like the liberal international order, regionalism has evolved in response to both structural trends and the deepening of interdependence, following different patterns that fit different regional contexts. In particular, the end of the Cold War has created the conditions for the proliferation of regional cooperative frameworks and for the revamping or reform of existing ones.

Aside from the unique case of supranational integration pioneered by the European Union, the so-called 'new regionalism' of the 1990s was regarded as departing from previous attempts at regional cooperation in various ways.[28] The policy remit of regional bodies expanded beyond economic or traditional security issues to include the environment, human rights and non-traditional security challenges, among other matters. Furthermore, new regionalism was driven not only by states but also by the input and priorities of a variety of non-governmental actors and networks. As such, new regionalism encompasses both formal and informal modes of governance and is more inclusive of business and civil society.

Assessments of 'new regionalism' rooted in international political economy and new institutionalism have framed it as one dimension of broader developments in multilateral governance. Larger institutional agendas shaped by a wider set of stakeholders emerged alongside the spread of economic globalisation in the relatively benign post-Cold War strategic environment. At the same time, however, the evolution of regionalism has always reflected power considerations and distinct political agendas. Both internal variables, such as the nature of domestic political regimes and the preferences of national elites, and external ones contribute to accounting for the design and multiplication of regional governance frameworks.

---

[26]Keohane and Victor, *Regime complex for climate change.*
[27]Hurrell, "One world? Many worlds?".
[28]Hettne *et al., Globalism and the New Regionalism.*

In some cases, such as with the establishment of the African Union (AU) and of the New Partnership for Africa's Development (NEPAD) in the early 2000s and with the launch and subsequent multilateralisation of the Chiang Mai initiative following the financial crisis in Asia, regional frameworks have been set up to help deliver regional solutions to regional problems. Diminishing trust in the ability of global multilateral institutions to address regional challenges, concerns with the influence of extra-regional powers therein and the assertion of distinct regional preferences motivated these institutional undertakings.

Competing designs for regional cooperation have reflected different visions of order and different perceptions of regional identities and interests in various parts of the world. In Asia, for example, East Asia-centred projects have long co-existed with initiatives encompassing the Asia-Pacific, mainly promoted by the US, such as the Asia-Pacific Economic Cooperation forum (APEC).[29] In Latin America, some countries have supported regional cooperation on the hemispheric level (including all the Americas), while others, such as Brazil, have favoured cooperative initiatives limited to South America or Latin America, thereby excluding the US.[30] Eastern Europe features a competition between the neighbourhood policy of the EU and Russia's attempts to shape alternative regional frameworks to assert its influence in the post-Soviet space.

The ways in which regional powers relate to their neighbours and approach cooperation in their respective regions is a key variable for the future of regionalism and for the connection or disconnection between regional orders and the international order. To be sure, not all regional arrangements result from the initiative of powers that stand out among their neighbours because of their power assets and political influence. Where this is the case, however, Sandra Destradi has pointed out that the strategies of regional powers can vary in two basic dimensions, namely the means they use to advance their interests and the extent to which these interests are shared, or not, by other countries in their region.[31] On this basis, strategies range from overt coercion, including through military means, to the institutionalisation of rule-based cooperation at the service of common interests. In between these extremes lie various forms of regional hegemony, from harder to softer ones. Hegemonic strategies are those most commonly used by regional powers and include a mix of material incentives and disincentives (such as offering or withdrawing market opening, development finance and security cooperation), institution-building and value- or identity-based narratives.

Since the turn of the century, various regional powers have increasingly sought to channel their influence through institutional vehicles. This has been the case of, for example, South Africa, Nigeria and other important African countries when setting up the AU in 2002, of Nigeria in the context of the Economic Community of West African States (ECOWAS), of Brazil with the launch of UNASUR and the Community of Latin American and Caribbean States (CELAC), and of China, as illustrated below. That said, regional powers may invest in regional institution-building and simultaneously use other means, including coercive ones, to protect and advance their interests. As increasingly happens on the global stage, relations between main countries in the same region can feature a mix of competition and cooperation.

---

[29]Higgott, *Regional Economic Institutionalisation of East Asia?*
[30]Bianculli, "Latin America".
[31]Destradi, "Regional powers and their strategies".

East Asia provides a particularly interesting laboratory of these countervailing trends. Beijing has adopted a muscular posture towards some of its neighbours over territorial disputes in the East and South China Seas, while at the same time making a growing effort to embed its power in cooperative structures. China's regional engagement is motivated by multiple factors, including reaping the economic benefits of free trade, building new value chains centred around China, securing transport routes and access to raw materials, projecting a benign image, lowering the suspicion of neighbouring countries and mitigating their efforts to balance China's rise, and progressively delimiting the influence of the US in Asia.

The last few years have also seen a shift in China's regional strategy from joining or striking deals with existing regional structures to setting up new ones, in which Beijing's influence is more pronounced. After joining APEC in 1991, China deepened its partnership with ASEAN after 1997 (including the China-ASEAN free trade agreement in 2010), largely drove the creation of the SCO in 2001, played a key role in the launch of the East Asia Summit in 2005, and has promoted negotiations towards the Regional Comprehensive Economic Partnership (RCEP) free trade deal since 2012, fleshed out the very ambitious if ill-defined transregional One Belt One Road (OBOR) strategy since 2013 and set up the Asian Infrastructure Investment Bank (AIIB) in 2015. This pattern shows China's growing institutional entrepreneurship at the regional level, which is framed today by a narrative of community-building based on historical and cultural bonds throughout Asia.[32]

China's approach to Asian regionalism is pragmatic but not transient: it seems to be a lasting feature of its foreign policy.[33] Investment in regional cooperation does not dilute Beijing's emphasis on national interests and sovereignty; it is instrumental to promoting China's rise amidst geopolitical tensions and does not exclude coercive tactics *vis-à-vis* its neighbours. On the other hand, it shows that China is prepared to invest in rule-based regional structures and mobilise adequate resources behind its initiatives. It also shows that Beijing aims to diversify its investment through a variety of regional structures, so as to be able to shift the focus of its engagement in accordance with changing political circumstances.

Like China, although on a different scale and in less polarised strategic environments, countries like Brazil and South Africa have promoted regional cooperation as a way both to reassure their neighbours and boost their credentials as rising powers within and beyond respective regions.

Russia's approach differs in that its investment in regionalism appears more shallow and discontinuous and its use of hard power more pronounced. Russia sees itself as a great power, is keen to be recognised as one and calls for a multipolar international order in which major powers run international affairs in concert, while respecting respective spheres of influence.[34] Moscow's approach to regional order-building is apparently hierarchical and power-based, centred on the delivery of material benefits (low energy prices, financial assistance, remittances) to much weaker neighbours, as well as on (diplomatic, economic or military) coercive tools and tactics. Moscow has for years sought to lock in its influence through regional bodies, most notably the Eurasian Economic Union (EAEU) launched

---

[32]Zhang and Li, "China's Regionalism in Asia".
[33]Thung-Chieh and Liu, "Whither East Asian Regionalism?".
[34]Lo, *Russia and New World Disorder*, 38-67.

in 2015, but the latter remains a weak and ineffective institution thus far.[35] Russia clearly privileges asymmetrical bilateral relations with individual neighbours over the constraints of regional rule-making and multilateral governance.

The different approaches of pivotal powers to regional cooperation and order-building carry considerable implications for the future of the international order and its liberal features. As noted above, regionalism can be considered a layer of cooperation contributing to multi-level global governance or an expression of power politics. In practice, given the intimate connection between power and governance, the two dimensions cannot be delinked: they co-exist and their balance changes in different regions. Some believe that, while the international system has entered a post-hegemonic phase, hegemonic rule may well resurface at regional level.[36] Others find little evidence of emerging regional hegemonic orders and observe that many regional powers are in fact struggling for recognition and legitimacy in their respective regions.[37]

Overall, the more regional powers seek to assert their spheres of influence over their neighbourhoods through hierarchical orders, the more regionalism becomes a vehicle of geopolitical competition. In a world of blocs or 'competitive regionalism', large powers disinvest from global governance bodies in favour of regional arrangements that they can control better.[38] Conversely, the more regionalism is codified through rules of general application and inclusive decision-making frameworks, the more it can fuel multilateralism within and beyond individual regions. A culture of cooperation develops within regions and can inform other levels of governance. Large powers that choose to set rules with their neighbours and work through them are also likely to be more inclined to work through multilateral bodies to address global challenges. That said, multilateralism at the regional level is no guarantee of effective multilateralism at the global level. The quality of coordination between different institutions – global and regional, formal and informal ones – and the compatibility of their agendas are going to be important factors for the future of the international order.

The regionalism-global governance nexus

Multilateralism is becoming simultaneously more contested and more messy. In a contested multilateral system, countries or coalitions of countries unsatisfied with the principles, mandates or procedures of any given institution can decide to support other fora or create new frameworks that reflect their priorities better. This has been the driver behind a variety of initiatives by the US and European countries in policy areas ranging from non-proliferation to global health and energy.[39] Oliver Stuenkel notes that rising powers, and notably China, can be expected to emulate this practice and compound the trends towards competitive multilateralism both to deflect pressures and channel their influence through institutional vectors that they can steer more effectively.[40] At the same time, the proliferation of governance structures and, in particular, of informal, *ad hoc* minilateral groupings,

---

[35]Dragneva and Wolczuk, *The Eurasian Economic Union*.
[36]Buzan and Lawson, *The Global Transformation*, 293 and 303.
[37]Acharya, *End of American World Order*, 101-5.
[38]Telò, *Regionalism in Hard Times*, 8-15.
[39]Morse and Keohane, "Contested Multilateralism".
[40]Stuenkel, *Post-Western World*.

is making multilateralism messier and challenging traditional institutions.[41] Common to both developments is the risk of increasing forum-shopping, namely the prospect of countries or groups of countries picking and choosing the formats and institutions that fit their immediate interests the best, with little consideration for the overall coherence of global governance. This illustrates why the future of the international order will depend in part on coordination between different institutions and levels of governance.

From this standpoint, the development of new forms of regional cooperation is part of a larger trend towards the multiplication and diversification of governance arrangements. The connections between regional and global governance are critical for the functioning of a post-hegemonic international order that is growing more diverse. Fostering these connections will require strong political investment in partnership diplomacy among major powers alongside institutional innovation to develop operational links between different institutions. If approached this way, regionalism can help prevent a decentred international system from becoming more fragmented and polarised. The record so far is mixed and changes depend on different policy areas.

In the security field, for example, cooperation between the UN and regional organisations in peacekeeping and crisis management at large has made significant progress since the end of the Cold War. Different multilateral actors have joined forces in a number of theatres, such as sub-Saharan Africa and the Balkans, whether through simultaneous or sequential engagements. The partnerships between the UN and the AU, as well as the UN and the EU, are among the most advanced, while cooperation between regional bodies such as the EU and the AU has also made considerable strides to strengthen the so-called African Peace and Security Architecture (APSA).[42] The relationship between these and other organisations is far from spotless, not least because regional bodies may have different threat assessments and capability levels, for example to plan and run military operations. On balance, however, the work of the UN and regional bodies such as the EU and the AU has proven that coordination and cooperation among different institutions can deliver added value.

Economists have long debated whether regional or plurilateral trade agreements enhance or divert trade, thereby boosting or undermining the overall effectiveness of the trade governance system.[43] While there seems to be no conclusive evidence on this point, the last 20 years have seen a proliferation of these agreements within and between regions. The content of many of them goes well beyond the policy scope of the agreements concluded in the framework of the World Trade Organisation (WTO), whether including more ambitious commitments than those taken in the WTO framework or addressing issues not dealt with by the WTO, such as non-tariff barriers to trade and investment or labour and environmental standards. Because of this evolution, the international trade regime has become more complex and risks fragmentation.[44] Different countries or groups promote competing arrangements such as the China-sponsored Regional Comprehensive Economic Partnership (RCEP) negotiations and the (pre-Trump) US-driven Trans-Pacific Partnership (TPP) accord in the Asia-Pacific. Preferential trade agreements can help fill governance gaps and regulate new dimensions of international trade, but they also risk marginalising the rule-making function of the WTO and, in perspective, challenge its dispute settlement mechanism.

---

[41]Haass, "The Case for Messy Multilateralism"; Patrick, "The New 'New Multilateralism'".

[42]Williams, *Global and Regional Peacekeepers*.

[43]*World Trade Report 2011*, 164-95.

[44]Kim *et al.* "Regional Trade Governance"; Bown, *Mega-Regional Trade Agreements*.

In the area of development finance, the World Bank and regional development banks have long cooperated by jointly supporting projects on the basis of a broadly shared normative platform. Since the turn of the century, however, new donors have been contributing increasing resources to finance development while openly challenging aspects of the approach of traditional Western donors, in particular the so-called 'conditionality' attached to aid.[45] As rising powers have shifted from recipients to providers of development aid, they have also sought to join forces and set new agendas through bodies such as IBSA, which brings together India, Brazil and South Africa.

China's institutional entrepreneurship stands out in this field, reflecting both its financial critical mass and its distinct priorities, such as infrastructure building throughout Asia and beyond as part of the broader One Belt One Road Initiative. Beijing has led the creation of the New Development Bank with other BRICS countries and of the AIIB, which today gathers together 80 countries from Asia and other continents. The early years of operation of these new bodies suggest that the new multilateral development banks complement rather than undermine traditional ones. The AIIB, in particular, has launched various projects in cooperation with the World Bank, the Asian Development Bank and the European Bank for Reconstruction and Development, among other partners.[46]

This brief overview of some key areas of multilateral cooperation shows that regionalism and global governance intersect in multiple and sometimes countervailing ways. On the one hand, regionalism can bring a positive contribution to global governance, including additional resources (whether for peacekeeping, development finance or credit lines for countries in financial crisis, as in the case of the European Stability Mechanism) or local knowledge, enhancing the legitimacy of multilateral initiatives and spurring governance innovation and experimentation (as in the fields of trade and development).[47] On the other, the development of more robust regional arrangements with larger remits and resources can trigger inter-institutional competition and fragmentation within increasingly cumbersome multilateral regimes. It can also compound normative divergence, for example through regional trade deals promoting different standards.

The interplay between regionalism and global governance concerns the bargaining tactics of both rising and incumbent powers in global fora.[48] These actors can use regional arrangements as platforms to boost their negotiating power or the legitimacy of their claims in settings such as the WTO or global climate negotiations. They can also leverage regional cooperation as an 'exit option' to show that they can pursue alternative avenues if multilateral negotiations do not meet their priorities. Lastly, regionalism can affect and sharpen differences between regions, whether because regional institutions can be much more effective in some regions than in others or because of the different strategies of regional powers in shaping regional orders.

Conclusion

The core trend in contemporary global governance is the multiplication of governance arrangements. This trend matches the structural development in the international system

---

[45]Castillejo, *New donors, new partners?*
[46]Wang, New Multilateral Development Banks.
[47]Kahler, *Regional Challenges to Global Governance*.
[48]Kahler, "Rising powers and global governance".

towards the redistribution of power and the emergence of a polycentric world. In this decentred system, a growing number of pivotal states and non-state actors express a range of often dissonant interests and normative preferences. Different conceptions of order are emerging or re-emerging in different regions, alongside a renewed emphasis on identity politics and resurgent nationalism in both incumbent and emerging powers. This evolution challenges the sustainability of the liberal international order established against the bedrock of American hegemony. The international order is therefore facing a fluid and highly uncertain transition towards an unknown destination. Whether this transition will lead to a world of unbounded power politics or to new cooperative arrangements will ultimately depend both on the future of US power and on the approach of a wider set of important powers to the reform or transformation of governance structures.

The US will have to adapt to a post-hegemonic environment where its leadership is contested and its room for manouvre smaller. The Trump administration's narrowly transactional approach to international cooperation shows the risk of Washington disinvesting from an order it cannot influence as much as before. Trump's harsch attacks on global governance may prove a passing distortion, followed by renewed American commitment to multilateral cooperation and partnerships. However, gone are the days in which the West could aim to shape the rest.

Emerging powers are deeply embedded in the international economic order and their prosperity depends on geopolitical stability, all the more so given the serious domestic challenges that many of them face. Some have argued that they take issue less with the core tenets of the liberal order than with the hierarchy within it, namely the traditionally predominant position of the US and the West more generally.[49] Emerging powers operate both through established multilateral channels and through new institutions, which they lead to enhance their influence. Their posture ranges from confrontational to collaborative depending on the issues at stake and their perceived core interests. This foreshadows an international context where relations between big powers are going to be more compartmentalised, featuring competition and cooperation at once. In an increasingly interconnected but competitive world, major actors will both seek grounds for cooperation and exploit mutual dependencies to gain leverage, while struggling for political influence in contested regions.

The evolution of regionalism and regional orders will be an important dimension of the realignment of power and interests at the global level. As the global influence of the US is in relative decline, and no other power can aspire to a worldwide hegemonic role, it can be expected that more cooperation as well as more competition will take place at the regional level. Given the density of global connections across different regions and of multilateral governance structures, this is unlikely to lead to a world of separate regional spheres of influence or closed blocs. Besides, there are significant differences between the regional strategies of major powers, along a continuum from sheer coercion to multilateral milieu shaping. It is plausible, however, that regional cooperation will become a more important vehicle for, depending on the issues, voicing differences, deflecting unwelcome initiatives, advancing shared solutions and providing resources within the emerging global governance patchwork.

When assessing the impact of regionalism on the liberal features of the international order, the variety of drivers of regional order-building and of the shape, tasking and capabilities of regional arrangements makes the identification of any single pattern elusive.

---

[49]Stuenkel, *Post-Western World*.

What can be argued is that forms of 'competitive regionalism' that reflect the dissonant agendas of regional or global powers are today more prominent than in the past.[50] From this standpoint, regionalism can be seen as one of the vectors of growing political and economic contest, with detrimental effects on the openness and normative fabric of the liberal order. While this scenario cannot be excluded, the relationship between regionalism and the liberal international order is to be assessed not against the expectations of the 1990s of an ever expanding and deepening liberal order, but with reference to the central challenge for cooperation and stability in today's international affairs. This is about how to reform the international order to manage diversity without undermining its basic liberal features, namely economic openness, rule-based cooperation and the rejection of the use of force as a means to resolve international disputes.

The evolution of the international order and the preservation of the broad liberal features that define it will depend on domestic developments in major powers, on building confidence among them and a wider range of influential actors and on fostering cooperation between different institutions within complex governance regimes. Regionalism can be an important component of this effort, provided that it is not simply a thin cover for coercive hegemonic aspirations and that it is designed in such a way as to complement other formats or levels of cooperation. In other words, regionalism can be one of the tools enabling the difficult transition from a hegemonic liberal order to a post-hegemonic one that corresponds to a decentered international system.

References

Acharya, A. *The End of the American World Order*. Cambridge: Polity Press, 2014.

Bianculli, A. "Latin America". In *The Oxford Handbook of Comparative Regionalism*, edited by T.A. Börzel and T. Risse: 154–77. Oxford: Oxford University Press, 2016.

Bown, C.P. *Mega-Regional Trade Agreements and the Future of the WTO*, Discussion Paper Series on Global and Regional Governance. New York: Council on Foreign Relations, September 2016.

Burns, W.J. "The risks of the Trump administration hollowing out American leadership". *Washington Post*, 19 April 2017.

Buzan, B., and G. Lawson. *The Global Transformation. History, Modernity and the Making of International Relations*. Cambridge: Cambridge University Press, 2015.

Castillejo, C., ed. *New donors, new partners? EU strategic partnerships and development*, European Strategic Partnerships Observatory Report no. 3. Brussels: FRIDE and Egmont Institute, 2014.

Clark, I. "China and the United States: a succession of hegemonies?". *International Affairs* 87, no. 1 (January 2011): 13–28.

Destradi, S. "Regional powers and their strategies: empire, hegemony and leadership". *Review of International Studies* 36, no. 4 (2010): 903–30.

Deudney, D., and G.J. Ikenberry. "The Myth of the Autocratic Revival. Why Liberal Democracy Will Prevail". *Foreign Affairs* 88, no. 1 (January/February 2009): 77–93.

Dragneva, R., and K. Wolczuk. *The Eurasian Economic Union: Deals, Rules and the Exercise of Power*, Chatham House Research Paper. London: Chatham House, May 2017.

---

[50]Telò, "Globalization, New Regionalism".

EU Institute for Security Studies and National Intelligence Council. *Global Governance 2025: At a Critical Juncture*. December 2010.

Flockhart, T. "The coming multi-order world". *Contemporary Security Policy* 37, no. 1 (2016): 3–30.

Grevi, G. *Lost in transition? US foreign policy from Obama to Trump*, EPC Discussion Paper. Brussels: European Policy Centre, December 2016.

Grevi, G. *The interpolar world. A new scenario*, EUISS Occasional Paper no. 79. Paris: EU Institute for Security Studies, 2009.

Haass, R.N. "The Case for Messy Multilateralism". *Financial Times*, 2 January 2010.

Hettne, B., A. Inotai and O. Sunkel. *Globalism and the New Regionalism*. Basingstoke: Macmillan, 1999.

Higgott, R. *Towards the Regional Economic Institutionalisation of East Asia?*, CSGR Working Paper no. 280/16. Warwick: Centre for the Study of Globalisation and Regionalisation, 2016.

Hurrell, A. "Power Transitions, Global Justice, and the Virtues of Pluralism". *Ethics and International Affairs* 27, no. 2 (2013): 189–205.

Hurrell, A. "One world? Many worlds? The place of regions in the study of international society". *International Affairs* 83, no. 1 (2007): 127–46.

Ikenberry, G.J. "The Illusion of Geopolitics. The Enduring Power of the Liberal Order". *Foreign Affairs* 93, no. 3 (May/June 2014): 80–91.

Ikenberry, G.J. *Liberal Leviathan: The Origins, Crisis and Transformation of the American World Order*. Princeton and Oxford: Princeton University Press, 2011.

Ikenberry, G.J. "The Three Faces of Liberal Internationalism". In *Rising States, Rising Institutions*, edited by A.S. Alexandroff and A.F. Cooper: 17–47. Waterloo, Ontario; Washington DC: Centre For International Governance Innovation; Brookings Institution Press, 2010.

Kagan, R. *The Return of History and the End of Dreams*. London: Atlantic Books, 2008.

Kahler, M. *Regional Challenges to Global Governance*, Discussion Paper Series on Global and Regional Governance. New York: Council on Foreign Relations, September 2016.

Kahler, M. "Rising powers and global governance: negotiating change in a resilient status quo". *International Affairs* 89, no. 3 (2013): 711–29.

Keohane, R.O. *After Hegemony: Cooperation and Discord in the World Political Economy*. Princeton: Princeton University Press, 1984.

Keohane, R.O., and D.G. Victor. *The regime complex for climate change*, Discussion Paper no. 10-33. Cambridge, MA: Harvard Project on Climate Change Agreements, January 2010.

Kim, Y., E.D. Mansfield and H. Milner. "Regional Trade Governnace". In *The Oxford Handbook of Comparative Regionalism*, edited by T.A. Börzel and T. Risse: 323–50. Oxford: Oxford University Press, 2016.

Kindleberger, C. "Dominance and Leadership in the International Economy: Exploitation, Public Goods and Free Rides". *International Studies Quarterly* 25, no. 2 (1981): 242–54.

Kissinger, H.A. *World Order*. New York: Penguin Press, 2014.

Krasner, S. "State Power and the Structure of International Trade". *World Politics* 28, no. 3 (1976): 317–43.

Kupchan, C.A. *No One's World. The West, the Rising Rest and the Coming Global Turn*. New York: Oxford University Press, 2012.

Leonard, M. "Introduction: Connectivity wars". In *Connectivity wars. Why migration, finance and trade are the geo-economic battlegrounds of the future*, edited by M. Leonard: 13–27. London: European Council on Foreign Relations, 2016.

Lo, B. *Russia and the New World Disorder*. London and New York: Chatham House and Brookings Institution Press, 2015.

Morse, J.C., and R.O. Keohane. "Contested Multilateralism". *The Review of International Organizations* 9 (2014): 385–412.

Nye, J.S. "Will the Liberal Order Survive? The History of an Idea". *Foreign Affairs* 96, no. 1 (January/February 2017): 10–6.

Patrick, S. "The New 'New Multilateralism': Minilateral Cooperation, but at What Cost?". *Global Summitry* 1, no. 2 (2015): 115–34.

Russel Mead, W. "The Return of Geopolitics. The Revenge of Revisionist Powers". *Foreign Affairs* 93, no. 3 (May/June 2014): 69–79.

Stuenkel, O. *Post-Western World: How Emerging Powers and Remaking Global Order*. Malden, MA: Polity Press, 2016.

Telò, M. *Regionalism in Hard Times. Competitive and Post-Liberal Trends in Europe, Asia, Africa and the Americas*. London and New York: Routledge, 2017.

Telò, M. "Globalization, New Regionalism and the Role of the European Union". In *European Union and New Regionalism*, edited by M. Telò: 1–22. Farnham: Ashgate, 2014.

Tung-Chieh, T. and T.T. Liu. "Whither East Asia Regionalism? China's Pragmatism and Community Building Rhetoric". *Japanese Journal of Political Science* 14, no. 4 (December 2013): 543–66.

Wang, H. *New Multilateral Development Banks: Opportunities and Challenges for Global Governance*, Discussion Paper Series on Global and Regional Governance. New York: Council on Foreign Relations, September 2016.

Williams, P.D. *Global and Regional Peacekeepers*, Discussion Paper Series on Global and Regional Governance. New York: Council on Foreign Relations, September 2016.

World Trade Organisation. *World Trade Report 2011. The WTO and Preferential Trade Agreements: From co-existence to coherence*. Geneva: World Trade Organisation, 2011.

Zhang X. and Li X. "China's Regionalism in Asia". *The Asan Forum*, 23 May 2014.

Present at the Destruction? The Liberal Order in the Trump Era

John Peterson

ABSTRACT

The election of Donald Trump in 2016 sent shock waves across political classes globally and prompted debates about whether his 'America first' agenda threatened the liberal international order. During his first year in office, Trump seemed determined to undermine the hallmarks of the liberal international order: democracy, liberal economics and international cooperation. So, are we witnessing the emergence of a "post-liberal" and "post-American" era? Four sources of evidence help frame – if not answer – the question: history, the crisis of liberal democracy, Trump's world view, and the power of civil society (globally and nationally) to constrain any US President. They yield three main judgements. First, continuity often trumps change in US foreign policy. Second, the liberal international order may have been more fragile pre-Trump than was widely realised. Third, American power must be put at the service of its own democracy if the US is to become the example to the world it used to be.

Any investigation of the current role of the United States (US) in the liberal international order must begin by acknowledging the utter shock to which many Americans and political classes globally awoke on 9 November 2016, when Donald Trump's election as US President was confirmed. Not only did nearly all pollsters and political professionals consider Trump's possible path to victory so narrow – everything that went right for him in battleground states *had* to go right – that it was almost certain that Hillary Clinton would be elected.[1] The shock never really subsided during Trump's first year in office. Trump's 'America First' campaign rhetoric quickly took on tangible foreign policy consequences. Even before taking office, Trump announced that the US would pull out of the painstakingly negotiated Trans-Pacific Partnership (TPP). He repeatedly threatened to do the same with the North American Free Trade Agreement (NAFTA). One of his first acts as President was to try to impose a travel ban on nationals of seven mainly Muslim countries. Then came the bombshell of US withdrawal from the Paris agreement on climate change.

Reports in summer 2017 that North Korea had successfully miniaturised a nuclear warhead on top of multiple successful long-distance missile tests led to fears of real bombshells

---

[1] As of 30 October 2017, nearly a year after the 2016 US election, the highly influential *New York Times* website "The Upshot: Who Will be President?" was still listing its 8 November 2016 estimation that Clinton's chances of winning were 85%. See https://www.nytimes.com/interactive/2016/upshot/presidential-polls-forecast.html.

falling. Trump thundered that a US military response was "locked and loaded" and North Korean provocation would "be met with fire and fury like the world has never seen".[2] Soon afterwards, one (unabashedly liberal) commentator termed it an "inescapable fact" that "on November 9th, the United States elected a dishonest, inept, unbalanced, and immoral human being as its President and Commander-in Chief".[3] Trump's America appeared to have abandoned the traditional US role of bolstering and reinforcing the global liberal order of which the first postwar US Secretary of State claimed – with considerable pride and justification – he had been *Present at the Creation*.[4] In fact, Trump seemed bent on destroying it. Was that inescapable, too?

It obviously is risky to try to extrapolate from a sample size of one year to judge whether the present era marks the beginning of what Riccardo Alcaro terms a 'post-liberal' and 'post-American' age in his Introduction to this issue.[5] A more profitable exercise is to consider what evidence we have about factors determining how the tectonic plates of the international order may be shifting now and might shift in the future. One source of evidence is history, especially the relative weight of agency versus structure in the evolution of US foreign policy (see the first section below). Another is the rise of multipolarity as an indelible trend in recent history. Relatedly, we have had ample indication over time to judge whether and how the emergence of non- or quasi-democracies as rising powers constitutes "a wider crisis across the liberal democratic world"[6] (second section). Accordingly, we have to consider whether Trump is, according to the leading liberal IR scholar John Ikenberry, "less a cause than a consequence of the failings of liberal democracy". Judging whether he is right means interrogating how and why escalating nationalism, populism, inequality and protectionism have fused in Trump's worldview and with what consequences for the global order (considered in the third section). Finally, we can reflect on how state institutional or non-state actors – civil society, whether domestic (in the US) or global – might deploy their own considerable power to shape US foreign policy outcomes (the last section).

No one can yet know whether Alcaro's vision of a 'post-liberal, post-American' future is prescient or not. But he is hardly alone in thinking, along with the vastly experienced US diplomat and analyst Richard Haas, that "it is difficult not to take seriously the possibility that one historical era is ending and another beginning".[7] We can at least begin to get an analytical handle on how likely such prognostications might be right, and *to what extent* they might be right. In other words, how much less liberal and less American is the next historical era likely to be? We may well be living through a period of crisis in which the postwar liberal order faces unprecedented peril. Equally, connections that bind together the liberal order – arguably wider, deeper and denser by an order of magnitude than ever before in history – may mean it is more durable than it sometimes appears.

---

[2]Quoted in CNN, "Trump Warns North Korea: US Military 'Locked and Loaded', 11 August 2017, http://edition.cnn.com/2017/08/10/politics/trump-north-korea/index.html.

[3]Remnick, "The Divider", 28.

[4]Acheson, *Present at the Creation*.

[5]Alcaro, "Liberal Order and its Contestations", 7.

[6]Ikenberry, "Plot Against American Foreign Policy", 3 (same reference for the next sentence).

[7]Haas, *A World in Disarray*, xii. It should be noted that Haas advised Trump on foreign policy during the 2016 campaign and was even considered for an appointment in his administration, although Haas subsequently soundly criticised the administration for its unprofessional 'ad-hoc-ery' in making foreign policy. See Haberman, "Donald Trump Held Briefing with Haas", Appelbaum, "Trump's Foreign Policy 'Adhocracy'".

The liberal order and IR theory: Agency vs structure

There are few other subjects of study in the political world than international relations (IR) in which history becomes more of a testing ground for the relative explanatory power of *agency* – of individuals or states to influence their environment – as opposed to *structure*: environments that contain pressures that bear down so hard on states or statespersons that they effectively determine their behaviour. Structure is usually the winner in IR theory. Most IR theorists describe, explain and predict outcomes in international politics based on the distribution of power in the international system of states. Kenneth Waltz's neo-realism is perhaps the most widely-debated variant of 'structural realism' in that it assumes that states are unitary-rational actors competing for power in a state of international anarchy.[8] Since states are functionally similar in pursuing security in an insecure world, they may even be described (theoretically) as "billiard balls". What is inside them – democratic or authoritarian regimes, wise or foolish statespersons and so on – literally drops out of the theoretical explanation. Structure, determined by how power is distributed between states, is (nearly) all that matters.

Of course, theoretical assumptions are not descriptions of reality. Moreover, liberal and constructivist IR theorists challenge many (neo)realist assumptions about structure and agency. For them, the two not only shape but create each other. In other words, agents and structure are "mutually constitutive: states make the structures, and structure makes states".[9] So, by extension (in the classic constructivist view), "anarchy is what states make of it".[10]

For all of their differences, a leading (liberal) theorist insists that all IR theories are "systemic theories in a Waltzian sense".[11] That is, all theorise on the basis of the distribution of power between states, thus privileging structure over agency. Crucially, however, liberals (and constructivists) take a different view than realists about how structure constrains agents in modern IR. The liberal order created in the postwar period features a more or less robust international society. Recalling Vincent's memorable analogy, it acts as an egg carton that protects states (cast as fragile eggs) from smashing into each other and thus cracking and disintegrating.[12] International society is buttressed by advanced regional cooperation and international organisations and law that have steadily gained in strength, authority and legitimacy. The liberal international system of states limits the agency of potential change agents such as Trump because all states, including powerful ones like the US, benefit from its existence.

If we take 1945 as 'year zero' of the current international order and then trace its evolution from there, we could plausibly conclude that a progressively more forceful liberal structure emerged that increasingly constrained the choices of agents or statespersons. That was the case at least for one side in a bipolar Cold War, the alliance of (mostly) democratic states consisting of the West plus Australasian states including Japan. On the other side, after (first) the Warsaw Pact and (then) the Soviet Union collapsed in 1989-91, virtually all states sought to become members of the liberal order. After all, joining was voluntary and the promise of peace and prosperity incentivised states to accept its rules and norms of

[8]Waltz, *Theory of International Politics*.
[9]Buzan, "The Level of Analysis Problem", 214.
[10]Wendt, "Anarchy is what states make of it".
[11]Moravcsik, "Liberal international relations theory", 7.
[12]Vincent, *Human Rights and International Relations*, 123-5.

behaviour. From that point onwards, most statespersons embraced the three hallmarks of the liberal international order: democracy, liberal economics and international cooperation.

The result, significantly spurred by technological advance, became a movement for which the shorthand term is globalisation. Realists such as Waltz questioned how far globalisation really had advanced, as well as whether it was powerful or durable enough to qualify anarchy.[13] But he and other realists were swimming against a tide of claims that the liberal order had advanced to the point where its norms eclipsed and delegitimised the interstate conflict that was endemic to earlier eras of anarchy.

Of course, intensified *intrastate* conflict was an almost inevitable consequence of the end of the Cold War. States whose boundaries had been more or less randomly drawn in the past – Yugoslavia, Somalia, Rwanda and Iraq – descended into civil wars (in the case of Saddam Hussein's Iraq, forestalled only by brutal internal repression). For a time, US-led humanitarian intervention to try to limit the bloodshed of internecine conflicts appeared to become something like a norm of the liberal order. It even provided a (flimsy) measure of liberal political cover to the US-led invasion of Afghanistan after the terrorist atrocities in New York and Washington on 11 September 2001 (9/11). The George W. Bush administration extolled the overthrow of a Taliban government that repressed women and imposed a ruthless form of fundamentalist Islamist rule. In retrospect, however, the contemporary debate about the durability of the liberal order is rooted in an eventuality for which that order was entirely unequipped: a massive terrorist attack by a stateless network on what many considered the most asymmetrically powerful hegemon in modern history.

The list of liberal norms that were quickly jettisoned by the US was breath-taking. A US President declared a 'war on terror'; that is, on a tactic instead of an enemy. Other states were "with or against" the US in the prosecution of the war, regardless of how Washington chose to prosecute it. The Geneva Convention and other landmark human rights agreements were brazenly violated in the treatment of enemy combatants and resort to extreme surveillance methods. The 2002 US *National Security Strategy* (NSS), unveiled one year and one day after 9/11, arrogated to the US the right to pre-emptive military action against perceived threats purely on the basis of US intelligence and without obligation to consult other states.[14] American hegemony obviously entailed special privileges enjoyed only by the US. But the list of privileges never included the ability to act as an agent untethered by the globally accepted constraints of the liberal order without undermining its structural foundations.

One consequence was that after 9/11 competition between competing traditional doctrines of US foreign policy was turned upside down. Mead handily identifies four discrete visions of America's role in the world.[15] The first is Hamiltonianism, inspired by the first US Treasury Secretary, which prioritises America's international commercial interests, embraces a balance of power, and takes an essentially realist view of IR. The second is Wilsonianism, the brainchild of Woodrow Wilson, which seeks a global civil society and pursues international cooperation, democracy and human rights with almost missionary zeal. Third is Jeffersonianism, based on the third US President's conviction that foreign entanglements should never be allowed to damage precious US political institutions and traditions; put simply: "the object of foreign policy should be to defend [American] values at home rather

---

[13]Waltz, "Globalization and governance".
[14]Dannreuther and Peterson, *Security Strategy and Transatlantic Relations*.
[15]Mead, *Special Providence*.

than extend them abroad".[16] Fourth, Jacksonianism embraces the militaristic, hawkish, populist and honour-bound doctrine of the seventh US President, Andrew Jackson. Mead ascribes what he views as the success of the US as a global power to healthy debate and competition between these four schools. They ensure that US foreign policy is a "symphony... rather than a solo".[17]

However, post-9/11, the Bush administration appeared to embrace a sort of Wilsonianism on steroids: a unipolar vision in which American power would be used aggressively to combat tyranny, promote freedom and fight a war on terrorism. Its leading neoconservatives (Vice-President Richard Cheney, Defense Secretary Donald Rumsfeld, and Deputy Defense Secretary Paul Wolfowitz) blithely predicted that Iraqis would greet invading US troops with flowers. Freed of Saddam's tyranny, Iraq could quickly become a "beacon of democracy".[18] The demonstration effect would unleash a democratic "wave of change" in the Middle East.[19] One group of liberal IR thinkers, with considerable and palpable anger, poured scorn on Bush's foreign policy for tragically betraying Wilson's vision of a multilateral, cooperative, rules-based order.[20]

We now know that the chain of causation between 9/11 and Saddam's Iraq was made almost immediately by Bush's neoconservative foreign policy advisors.[21] The disastrous aftermath of the US-led 2003 invasion was mirrored by a surge in anti-Americanism globally that became a primary concern of IR scholars within a few years.[22] The election of Barack Obama as US President in 2008 – and again in 2012 – was in key respects a balm to America's wounded international reputation. Yet, given that his rise from obscurity to the White House occurred largely because of his self-identification as the anti-war candidate, it was always likely that he would leave office as the first post-hegemonic US President. Every attempt Obama made to reassert US global leadership can be matched with a case of retrenchment. Assertive US diplomacy on climate change sits next to Obama's diplomatic disengagement from Iraq – by one view "his only interest in Iraq was ending the war"[23] – thus creating the conditions for the rise of ISIS in 2013. Obama's (reluctant) commitment to NATO airstrikes on Libya in 2011 (with the US "leading from behind") contrasts with his undelivered commitment to attack Assad's Syria if it crossed his "red line" and used chemical weapons against its own people. Revealingly, those straining to identify an "Obama doctrine" by the end of his Presidency were left with little more than his own insistence "that the first task of an American President in the post-Bush international arena was 'don't do stupid sh_t'".[24]

Realists can claim analytical purchase on Obama's failure as a change agent in US foreign policy, as well as the fraying of the liberal international order. After all, international politics is a realm of "recurrence and repetition"[25] in which structure trumps agency and any notion that states can institutionalise cooperation in the pursuit of absolute gains is illusory. Meanwhile, liberals are almost desperately left to insist that "in terms of wealth creation, the provision of physical security and economic stability, and the promotion of

---

[16]*Ibid.*, 175.
[17]*Ibid.*, 54.
[18]George W. Bush quoted in Khalaf, "Iraq's difficult decade of democracy".
[19]UK Foreign Secretary Jack Straw quoted in BBC News, "Iraq helped 'Mid-East democracy'".
[20]Ikenberry *et al.*, *Crisis of American Foreign Policy*.
[21]Woodward, *Bush at War*, 42.
[22]See Farber, *What They Think of Us*; Katzenstein and Keohane, *Anti-Americanism in World Politics*.
[23]Sky, *The Unravelling*, 338.
[24]Goldberg, "The Obama doctrine".
[25]Wight, "Why is there no International Theory?", 123-5.

human rights and political protection, no other international order in history comes close" to the present one.[26] Still, Obama clearly presided over a period of declining US ownership of the international order, not least because of secular changes in the distribution of power amongst the components in an increasingly multipolar world.

Multipolarity: New winners, old losers?

In 2004, a leading (liberal) intellectual and historian, Timothy Garten Ash, published a prophetic work on the "crisis of the West" post-Iraq. He was ahead of the curve in foreseeing that "the old Atlantic-centred West, which has been shaping the world since about 1500, probably has no more than twenty years left in which it will still be the main world-shaper".[27] Most of that time has now passed. Meanwhile, the European Union (EU) is still reeling and presently fixated on 'Brexit': the shock vote of the United Kingdom (UK) to leave the EU in its June 2016 referendum. There is no sign that Trump's America will seek to renew the transatlantic alliance, or even its alliance with the UK, especially after slapping more than 200 percent tariffs on Bombardier, a Canadian airline manufacturer that employs 4000 workers in the UK's economic backwater of Northern Ireland.

Trump's refusal even to mention the US Article 5 Treaty commitment (an attack on one is attack on all) at the unveiling of a memorial to the victims of 9/11 at NATO's new head-quarters in Brussels – despite agreeing with his foreign policy team that it would feature in his speech[28] – marked a truly low moment in US-European relations. Soon afterwards, Germany's Chancellor Angela Merkel spoke for many in Europe in urging "we must fight for our future on our own, for our destiny as Europeans…. The times in which we could fully rely on others – they are pretty much over".[29] There were at least rumblings about a possible renewal of the EU post-Brexit and following the election of the strongly pro-EU Emmanuel Macron as French President in 2017. They were reflected (for instance) in the commitment in the EU's 2016 *Global Strategy* (its equivalent of the US NSS) to European "strategic autonomy". But whether or not Europe is on a long-term downward spiral in terms of its international power (as many think it is), the continent seems to be drifting towards more independence in IR because Trump's America First agenda effectively precludes close transatlantic ties.

If the West's collective decline signals a global power shift, then there's little debate about to where much of the power is shifting: Xi Jinping's China. By October 2017, *The Economist* was unqualified in deeming Xi "the world's most powerful man".[30] The five-yearly Communist Party Congress of that month consolidated Xi's power as no Chinese leader had achieved post-Mao by writing his name and dogma into China's constitution. In a nearly three and half hour speech to open the congress, Xi highlighted how China had "taken a driving seat in international cooperation on climate change". He also insisted that China did not seek hegemony, but equally vowed that "no one should expect China to swallow anything that undermines its interests".[31]

---

[26]Ikenberry, "Plot against American foreign policy", 3.
[27]Garton Ash, *Free World*, 192.
[28]Glasser, "Trump team blindsided by NATO speech".
[29]Quoted in Smale and Erlanger. "Merkel is looking past Trump".
[30]*The Economist*, "The world's most powerful man", 14 October 2017, 11.
[31]Quoted in Phillips, "Xi Jinping hails 'new era'".

Xi's assertiveness seemed carefully calibrated to the dawn of the Trump era. He had earlier endeared himself to global elites at the January 2016 Davos World Economic Forum by staking China's claim to be a champion of globalisation, free trade and the Paris climate change agreement. Meanwhile, China's Belt and Road Initiative promised huge investments in railways, ports, power stations and other infrastructure that would create jobs and growth across the Eurasian continent. It acted to reinforce the impression that the power shift towards China was mostly economic, involving a little additional 'soft power', or the ability to attract other states and convince them to want for themselves what China wanted for them.[32]

But China may now wield more soft power than might be assumed, especially given the emergence of Trump's America. At home, Xi has tightened controls over China's nascent civil society, presided over increased human rights abuses, and kept the Chinese economy firmly in control of state-run enterprises. The effect has been to reinforce the rise of a new competitor to liberal democracy as a political form that states can emulate: the 'Chinese model' combining authoritarianism, state-led capitalism and nationalism. After all, no other system in history has ever successfully pulled so many people out of poverty. Any soft power that Xi's China wields has flowed from that empirical fact.

For his part, Donald Trump seems to admire Xi's ability to impose his personal will on China, phoning to congratulate him on the results of the 2017 party congress ahead of his own visit to Beijing. If we are concerned with how the US under Trump is positioning itself relative to China, two things seem clear. One is that Trump's personal admiration for Xi creates scope for compromise, if not cooperation, between the world's two most powerful states. A second is that nothing about Xi's China suggests that multipolarity is not on the rise as a fundamental fact of international politics.

If China's rise signals a reversal of the postwar era's progressive strengthening of international society – and a consequent loss of predictability – then the case of Russia is much less ambiguous. Russian military adventurism in, first, Georgia, and then, Ukraine in the early 21st century signalled the dawn of what many termed a "new Cold War" in Europe.[33] Allegations of Russian interference in the 2016 US election, still under investigation at time of writing, are both astounding and unsurprising. Astounding because, if substantiated, the deployment of an authoritarian tactic entirely unthinkable in the modern liberal international order could mark a major escalation in a new Cold War.[34] Unsurprising because of the public statement of Vladimir Putin's choice for chief of the Russian army, Valery Gerasimov, in 2013 that stressed a "blurring of the differences between war and peace.... The emphasis in the methods of confrontation being employed is shifting toward widespread use of political, economic, information...and other non-military measures".[35]

From one perspective, Putin's "managed democracy" that mimics democratic parties, institutions and elections while the Kremlin tightly controls both politics and, perhaps more importantly, the economy has been necessitated by its declining, pre-modern economy and falling standards of living. With energy prices low and genuine Western solidarity producing economically painful sanctions after the annexation of Crimea in 2014, Putin is playing a game he will inevitably lose. He has had to distract Russians with patriotic adventurism abroad, including in Ukraine, on Russia's border with NATO and in Syria's

---

[32]Nye, *Soft Power*.
[33]One example amongst many is Osnos *et al.*, "Trump, Putin and New Cold War". See also Lucas, *The New Cold War*.
[34]Far less so, of course, during the Cold War international order when the US interfered in multiple democratic elections.
[35]Wright, *All Measures Short of War*, 765-72.

civil war. Russia is powerful enough to violate the norms of the liberal international order. But not with impunity and not for much longer. Short-term geopolitical muscle-flexing creates the appearance of Russian success in pushing towards a new multipolar order but shrouds a Russia that is fundamentally in decline.

From another perspective, Putin's methods have found admirers in EU countries such as Hungary, Slovakia and even – despite its profound suspicion of Russia – Poland. Governments in all three states have shifted towards "illiberal democracy", to use the term that Victor Orban, the autocratic Hungarian Prime Minister, openly avowed as his aspiration. Revealingly, Orban's most focused speech on the concept – the basis of which was ethnic nationalism – was delivered in 2014 in Romania to an audience of ethnic Hungarians. The speech excoriated liberal values for encouraging "corruption, sex and violence" and condemned non-governmental organisations as "paid political activists who are attempting to enforce foreign interests here in Hungary [sic]." Orban asserted that "the stars of the international analysts today are Singapore, China, India, Russia and Turkey".[36]

Two questions arise from such a claim and list, even if the latter forms an *ersatz* group (outright or quasi-dictatorships along with democratic India). First, is the liberal international order being undermined from within by its constituent states? Has Huntington's "third wave" of democratisation[37] now gone into reverse as more states emulate autocratic methods? Second, even if its main members do not match Orban's "stars", are the agents of multipolarity accelerating their rise via concerted action by the so-called BRICs: Brazil, Russia, India and China (sometimes including South Africa – BRICS)? And, as an ancillary question, are Trump's own autocratic inclinations likely to fuel both of these fires?

The first question must be taken seriously. According to Freedom House, the democracy watchdog that receives US government funding but claims independence, more states have restricted than increased democratic freedoms every year since 2008. By its count, at least 25 fewer truly free democracies existed in 2016 than at the turn of the century.[38] At China's October 2017 National Congress, Xi Jinping explicitly claimed that the Chinese model offered "a new option for other countries and nations who want to speed up their development while preserving their independence".[39] Independence seemed a code word for autonomy from Western, particularly American, influence. A 2017 Freedom House report on "modern authoritarianism", which mostly focused on China and Russia, starkly stated that "a basic assumption behind the report is that modern authoritarianism will be a lasting feature of geopolitics" and that, moreover, "[a]uthoritarian systems will seek not just to survive, but to weaken and defeat democracy around the world".[40] The stakes may be higher than ever before for the ability of US democracy to demonstrate its resilience to the world under Trump.

The second question – ostensibly, are the BRICs a true alliance? – is easier to answer. As early as 2012, a senior Morgan Stanley analyst put the commonly-shared and rapid rise of the BRIC states down to an unusual and fleeting set of economic circumstances in the preceding decade.[41] Of course, the convening of annual BRICS summits beginning in 2009, and the subsequent creation of the BRICS New Development Bank in 2013 (to rival the

---

[36]Quoted in Freedom House, *Breaking Down Democracy*, 35.
[37]Huntington, *The Third Wave*.
[38]Freedom House, *Freedom in the World 2017*.
[39]Quoted in Phillips, "Xi Jinping hails 'new era'".
[40]Freedom House, *Breaking Down Democracy*, 4.
[41]Sharma, *Broken BRICs*.

International Monetary Fund) encouraged the rest of the world to sit up and take notice. But the BRICS Development Bank soon had to compete for finance with the China-inspired Asian Infrastructure Investment Bank, after the latter was created in 2015. More generally, all of the BRICS countries face their own severe domestic political problems.[42] Put simply, their interests in IR sometimes overlap, but are by no means identical. As Alcaro puts it, "The BRICS format…is no check on Western power. It is a means to manage inter-BRICS relations – which entail a good deal of competition, particularly along the Russia-China and China-India borders".[43]

The ancillary question, what might be the knock-on effects of Trump's election and authoritarian sensibilities, is considerably more complicated. We need to reflect on both what his election means for the liberal international order as well as the robustness of American democracy to mitigate any tendency of his Presidency to undermine it. These two analytical tasks are tackled in the sections that follow.

Trump and the liberal democratic crisis

In a provocative analysis of the implications of Trump's election (of special interest to some readers of this journal), Clementi and colleagues argue that it marked the "Italianization" of American politics.[44] Rejecting any suggestion that Trump's rise could result in Mussolini-style authoritarianism, they instead find clear analogies between Trump and Italy's longest-serving contemporary prime minister: Silvio Berlusconi. Both embraced similar brands of populism, shared personality traits, personalised politics as rarely seen before, and leveraged to their advantage deep anti-establishment sentiment.

Whether we accept the analogy or not, there are clear parallels between Berlusconi and Trump in how their domestic political programmes inevitably had/have consequences for foreign policy. While Berlusconi actively supported the US-led invasion of Iraq, his brand of politics also involved cosying up to Putin's Russia and fomenting the rise in Euroscepticism in Italy. In Trump's case, his America First mantra cast doubt on the US commitment to its traditional alliances and caused severe tensions and declining trust within them. His claim to represent directly and work for the interests of ordinary Americans who suffered from the economic "carnage" over which his predecessor allegedly presided threatened to lead to the embrace of protectionism or even mercantilism in US trade policy. The effects of the Great Recession, rising inequality, and advancing automation on America's shrinking middle class, especially regionally concentrated in 'rust belt' states Trump had to (and did) win, created a perfect storm for turning attacks on free trade agreements such as NAFTA and TPP into tangible votes and strengthening Trump's base. After taking office, Trump's attacks on US manufacturers with planned investments in Mexico, his pledge to revive US coal mining, and blockage of appointments to the judicial apparatus of the World Trade Organisation had tangible effects on private sector planning within the US business community.[45]

---

[42]Peterson *et al.*, "Multipolarity, multilateralism and leadership", 52-4.
[43]Alcaro, "The paradoxes of liberal order", 210-1.
[44]Clementi *et al.*, "Making America grate again".
[45]The Trump administration continually blocked new appointments to the WTO dispute settlement body, its top arbiter of trade cases, in 2017 leading to concerns that the US was seeking a breakdown of the entire WTO system. The EU's Trade Commissioner, Cecilia Malmström, accused the Trump administration of "killing the WTO from the inside". See Brunsden and Beattie, "Trump risks killing WTO".

Whether moves even more damaging to the liberal international economic order were forthcoming was unclear at time of writing. Astonishingly, in the teeth of the crisis over North Korea's nuclear threats, reports circulated in autumn 2017 that Trump was considering abrogating the US bilateral free trade agreement with South Korea, a step that would have obviously negative strategic consequences.[46] US trade policy professionals were then shocked by a memo written by the top Trump trade advisor, Peter Navarro (previously co-author of polemical works such as *Death by China*[47]), that linked declining US manufacturing capability to increases in abortion, spousal abuse, divorce, infertility, child poverty, opioid use, and crime on the basis of no data or evidence.[48] Credible reports emerged that Canadian and Mexican trade officials were being told by their US counterparts that they should not expect the US to be bound by WTO rules if Washington pulled out of NAFTA since the Trump administration failed to accept its constraints, just one sign amongst many that it wished to blow up global trade rules in order to shrink America's trade deficit.[49]

Arguably, however, Trump's moves on the strategic side have threatened to do even more damage to the liberal international order. On NATO, North Korea, Iran and immigration, bedrock US commitments to international cooperation that have remained consistent over more than 60 years under administrations of both political parties risk being discarded if Trump thinks it would benefit him politically. The ideological consensus that has underpinned such US commitments is clearly fraying, with Democrats far more focused on domestic contestation of Trump's agenda than its foreign policy consequences. They, like Trump and the Republicans, could no doubt read polls that suggested 70 percent of voters in 2016 wanted the next President to focus on domestic, not foreign policy. No fewer than 62 percent thought "[s]ince the US is the most powerful nation in the world, we should go our own way in international matters, not worrying too much about whether other countries agree with us or not".[50] Trump's laser-like focus on America First as a slogan and agenda reflected not only his extraordinary raw political instincts. It also reflected how unprecedentedly fierce partisan contestation of Trump's domestic political agenda was feeding through to disintegration of the US postwar consensus on liberal internationalism and the belief that absolute gains were possible by being true to its principles. Thus far in the Trump-era US domestic political arena, there has been no one to defend liberal international principles.

The problem, of course, is not confined to Trump's America. Trump-like nationalist-populists made gains in 2016-17 in Germany, Austria, France, Norway, Greece, Finland, the Philippines and Turkey. That is not even to mention the consolidation of power of such forces in the non-liberal democratic worlds of Hungary, Russia, China and elsewhere. It remains difficult to judge whether the trend is inexorable and unstoppable, with clearly damaging implications for the liberal international order. It could be just the product of a fleeting time when the Great Recession provoked massive discontent in liberal democracies and flattered the models offered by non-democratic states. What is undeniable is that 2016 showed that – for now and possibly the foreseeable future – liberal internationalism simply does not pay domestically in US democratic politics.

---

[46]Thrush and Harris, "Trump mulls exit from South Korea".
[47]Navarro and Autry, *Death by China*.
[48]Paletta, "Internal White House documents allege".
[49]Porter, "Trump's endgame could end global rules".
[50]"US policy and politics. America's global role, superpower status", Pew Research Center, 4 May 2016, http://www.people-press.org/2016/05/05/1-americas-global-role-u-s-superpower-status/1_4/.

Institutions and civil society: Checks on Trump's agenda?

The aforementioned work on the "Italianization" of American politics is clear on what divides Italy from the US: "if Italy could have weathered the long Berlusconi era without too much lasting damage being inflicted upon the vitality of its democracy, then America, with its much more hearty network of institutional constraints upon executive power, will prove itself highly capable of accommodating its own version with much less difficulty".[51] In short, the US model of democracy with its system of checks and balances is likely to limit the eccentricities of a rogue President. One source of constraint arises from the nature of the foreign policy team that any elected President must appoint and then rely upon.

Trump ran as a Republican Party outsider for the 2016 presidential nomination. His total lack of foreign policy experience meant he had to rely, at first, on amateurs for foreign policy advice. As late as August 2016, when Trump had the nomination locked up, no fewer than 50 senior GOP foreign policy professionals signed a public letter saying they would not serve in his administration because he would "put at risk our country's national security and well-being".[52] One result was that one of Trump's top foreign policy advisors, Michael Flynn – former head of the US Defense Intelligence Agency, forced to resign by Obama because of his strange statements about Islamist terrorism – became Trump's National Security Advisor (NSA). Flynn was forced to resign again, this time as NSA, after 24 days for lying about his paid work for Turkey and contacts with Russian agents. Trump, the candidate, was also advised on foreign policy by George Papadopoulos, a 28-year old Greek-American who was swept up, as was Flynn, in the federal investigation of Russian interference in the 2016 US election, pleading guilty to lying to federal agents about his own contacts with Russia.

Trump then had little choice but to turn to foreign policy professionals who agreed to serve in his administration. The result was a so-called "axis of adults" who, together, acted to moderate his eccentric statements on foreign policy: James Mattis, a former military general, as Defense Secretary; Herbert McMaster, another respected former general as National Security Advisor; and Rex Tillerson – former CEO of Exxon/Mobile – as Secretary of State.[53] Trump clashed with Tillerson over North Korea and other issues, especially after Tillerson reportedly referred to Trump as a "moron" in private meetings, leading Trump to challenge Tillerson to an IQ test that Trump was sure he could win. Still, Tillerson brushed off the drama and doggedly insisted that he would pursue a diplomatic solution on North Korea up until "the first bombs drop". Similarly, Mattis reassured US Asian allies that diplomacy remained "our preferred course of action" and that the US commitment to deterrence and defending its allies was "ironclad". After the May 2017 NATO summit debacle, McMaster co-authored a *Wall Street Journal* article that was widely condemned by US foreign policy professionals for claiming (wrongly) that Trump had "reconfirm[ed] America's commitment to NATO and Article 5" at the Brussels summit and baldly denying the existence of a "global community". Trump's vision of IR instead consisted of "nations, nongovernmental actors and businesses [that] engage and compete for advantage". Still, the piece took as its title "America first doesn't mean America alone" and declared that "strong alliances and economically thriving partners" were a "vital American interest".[54]

---

[51]Clementi *et al.*, "Making America grate again", 515.
[52]Sanger and Haberman, "50 GOP officials warn Donald Trump".
[53]Mann, "The adults in the room". As a caveat, by the end of 2017, it was widely reported that Trump was on the verge of firing Tillerson and replacing him with CIA chief Michael Pompeo.
[54]McMaster and Cohn, "America first doesn't mean America alone".

Trump's America First agenda has also had its roughest edges at least moderated on trade policy. Navarro's peculiarities, as well as those of trade sceptic Robert Lighthizer, in charge of the renegotiation of NAFTA as US Trade Representative, were reined in by more moderate voices. They included Gary Cohn, head of the National Economic Council, Treasury Secretary Steven Mnuchin, Trump's chief of staff, John Kelly (another former military general), and even McMaster as NSA. Cohn managed to block multiple mooted moves to abrogate NAFTA unilaterally and impose steep tariffs on US imports of steel. Kelly folded the newly-created Office of Trade and Manufacturing Policy headed by Navarro into the National Economic Council, thus requiring Navarro to report to Cohn. At a certain point, whatever their political agenda, any US President must come to grips with how promises made during an electoral campaign clash with the hard graft of actually governing, and turn to foreign policy professionals for workable compromises. The professional US foreign policy community is generally conservative with few sharp differences of view between Republican and Democratic operatives. Consequently, far more continuity than change in policy occurs even when partisan control of the White House changes, and even when a severely partisan figure like Trump comes to office.

Moreover, other even more institutionalised and powerful constraints on presidential prerogative exist in US government, even in foreign policy where that prerogative is often most pronounced. The power of the US courts was on full display when Trump rolled out Executive Order 13769: the travel ban on seven predominantly Muslim countries. The ban was repeatedly blocked by federal courts over the course of more than a year despite multiple revisions by the Trump administration, before finally being put in place. Trump's ban on transgender service in the US military met much the same fate. A federal judge blocked its main provisions and additionally blasted the President for announcing the policy on Twitter "without any of the formality or deliberative processes that generally accompany the development and announcement of major policy changes that will gravely affect the lives of many Americans".[55] After multiple court judgments, the Pentagon chose to low-ball the ban by subjecting it to a "policy review", before it announced that transgender people would be free to join the US military from 2018, whatever Trump wanted or had said.

On Iran, Trump's refusal to certify the Joint Comprehensive Plan of Action (JCPOA), the multilateral nuclear deal, was no more than a Presidential notification to Congress with no legal effect. It was then left up to Congress to decide whether to exit the JCPOA and reimpose sanctions on Iran, with little sign on Capitol Hill of much appetite to do so. One reason was strong support for the Iran deal in a statement to Congress by more than 90 top US nuclear scientists including a designer of the hydrogen bomb and all three winners of the 2017 Nobel prize in physics. Stressing that Congress bore "momentous responsibilities", the proclamation dismissed Trump's call for renegotiation of the JCPOA an "unrealistic objective".[56] The scientists were joined in lobbying Congress by European parties to the agreement, with the UK, including its Foreign Secretary, Boris Johnson, French, German and also EU diplomats working Capitol Hill hard and impressing upon dozens of Senators Europe's united and firm support for the JCPOA.

Judging the impact on policy of civil society more broadly speaking – especially in a continent-sized, pluralistic country such as the US – is obviously difficult in the best of

---

[55]Quoted in de Vogue. "Judge blocks Trump's transgender military ban".
[56]Quoted in Gladstone, "Nuclear scientists urge Congress".

times. Still, we can reasonably conclude that US businesses with investments or supply chains in Mexico or Canada or reliance on imported steel were acting as allies of Cohn or Mnuchin in the Trump administration's internal trade policy debates. Meanwhile, even Republicans in Congress were backstops to the Trump agenda, with John McCain casting the deciding vote on Trump's failed attempt to repeal Obamacare (the US federal health insurance scheme) and Bob Corker, the chair of the Senate Foreign Relations Committee, breaking with Trump on a range of foreign policy questions.

Meanwhile, there have been signs that the Democratic party is emerging from its post-Hillary malaise. The Indivisible movement, a grassroots progressive mobilisation movement conceived by former Democratic Congressional staff, claimed nearly 6000 local chapters by late 2017, including in reliably 'red', Republican-dominated states such as Idaho and Wyoming.[57] The Democratic Congressional Campaign Committee reported that candidate recruitment ahead of the 2018 mid-term US elections was far ahead of where it was at a similar stage of the electoral cycle prior to the 2016 election.

In short, the ideological basis on which the US supported and bolstered the postwar liberal order is now contested, probably as never before since the end of the Second World War. The Trump administration in many respects seems to have mimicked the George W. Bush administration by upsetting the balance of debates between different US foreign policy doctrines and embracing both ultra-aggressive Jacksonianism and (on trade) a highly isolationist form of Jeffersonianism. Regardless of how lasting Trump's impact will be, the bipartisanship on foreign policy that led to the Marshall Plan, the creation of the UN and NATO, and the progressive strengthening of international law on trade and human rights clearly will not reappear anytime soon, if ever. But where America positions itself in the liberal international order is not and will never be where Donald Trump would like to position it.

Conclusion

Whatever Alcaro might have right or wrong, he is on strong ground in claiming that the liberal order is based on "a paradox: US power is what has enabled the liberal international order and at the same time the ultimate obstacle to its most complete realisation".[58] The paradox directs us towards three points by way of conclusion. The first is that Trump's Presidency in many, perhaps surprising, ways illustrates how continuity often trumps change in US foreign policy. Exceptions prove the rule, which brings to mind the enormously powerful shock to the liberal system that occurred on 11 September 2011. The response of the George W. Bush administration did much to undermine the idea that IR should be rules-based and seek both peace and justice in equal measure.

Its utter disregard for established rules – especially conventions on human rights and the treatment of foreign prisoners – clearly changed at least at the level of rhetoric and public diplomacy under Obama, who himself could be considered a foreign policy change agent. But Obama proved unable, say, to close Guantanamo Bay. Leaving aside the Iranian nuclear deal, there is little to cite when sifting through Obama's eight years in power to support the argument he extended or strengthened multilateralism. He and his administration

---

[57]Tomasky, "The resistance so far", 42.
[58]Alcaro, "Liberal order and its contestations", 7.

repeatedly made clear their discontent with the EU and NATO. Obama did little or nothing to invest in his own Democratic Party as an institutional defender of the liberal order and, in retrospect, facilitated the groundswell of populism that propelled Trump to the White House by neglecting the plight of Americans who were "left behind" by globalisation. Obama cannot be held responsible for the rise of Trump. It is far easier to find causation in 9/11 and all that came after it. But neither did Obama's Presidency accomplish much in terms of making the liberal international order less vulnerable to attack by a populist demagogue who could ride dissatisfaction with its effects as part of a successful US presidential campaign.

Second, the liberal international order may always have been more fragile than it appeared in the first decades of the 21st century. One result was dangerous assumptions about its resilience that led, for example, to Chinese adventurism in the South China Sea or Russia's brazen assertion of its interests in Crimea and Syria. In all of these cases, pushing at the boundaries set by a liberal international order may have seemed not to involve unbearable costs. By this reading, Trump's America is an almost logical consequence of a general US aversion post-9/11 to try to legitimise the liberal international order and mitigate the domestic political costs of defending it. IR theorists who privilege structure over agency in their explanations need obviously to re-examine their assumptions. Equally, liberals and constructivists might usefully question their own views about how much international society constrains states that violate its norms.

Third and finally, the embrace of illiberal nationalism now offers a viable political strategy for political leaders for whom the repression of dissent and abandonment of the rule of law is seductive. Others have shown that the strategy does not preclude societal gains, especially in terms of economic advancement. Arguably, the liberal international order relies fundamentally on the health of liberal democracies, in which politics involves compromise, open debate and respect for rules. After all, it was liberal democratic states – with the US in the lead – that built the order in the first place. But illiberal states – including China (witness Xi's defence of globalisation at Davos) and even Russia (given Europe's energy dependence on the free flow of Russian energy) – are still, perhaps unlikely, natural defenders of the liberal international order from which they benefit.

Ikenberry is surely right to argue that "Trump is less a cause than a consequence of the failings of liberal democracy".[59] We are now light years – in political terms – away from an era in which liberal democracy could be termed (by Francis Fukuyama) "the final form of human government".[60] It matters that "from a Western perspective, the 2008 meltdown was first and foremost an economic event. The rest of the world, however, regarded 2008 and its aftermath through a much wider aperture...the so-called global recession was primarily an Atlantic one".[61] All politics is local, and charity begins at home. The threat to the liberal order posed by the US under the Trump administration may be fleeting and temporary (four or fewer years). But it will not disappear until American power is put at the service of its own democracy, which must be renewed to become the example to the world that it used to be. What is perhaps most surprising about the rise of Donald Trump is how close that moment, when it happens, might well be.

---

[59]Ikenberry, "Plot against American foreign policy", 3.
[60]Fukuyama, *The End of History*.
[61]Luce, *The Retreat of Western Liberalism*, 974.

References

Acheson, D. *Present at the Creation: My Years in the State Department*. London and New York: Norton, 1987.

Alcaro, R. "The liberal order and its contestations. A conceptual framework". *The International Spectator* 53, no. 1 (2018).

Alcaro, R. "The paradoxes of the liberal order: transatlantic relations and security governance". In *The West and the Global Power Shift: Transatlantic Relations and Global Governance*, edited by R. Alcaro, J. Peterson, and E. Greco. London: Palgrave Macmillan, 2016.

Appelbaum, Y. "Trump's foreign policy adhocracy". *The Atlantic*, 27 June 2017. https://www.theatlantic.com/international/archive/2017/06/trumps-foreign-policy-adhocracy/531732/.

Brunsden, J., and A. Beattie. "Trump risks killing WTO from inside, warns EU's top trade official". *Financial Times*, 17 October 2017.

Buzan, B. "The level of analysis problem in international relations reconsidered". In *International Relations Theory Today*, edited by K. Booth and S. Smith. Oxford: Polity, 1995.

Clementi, M., D.G. Haglund and A. Locatelli. "Making America grate again: the 'Italianization' of American politics and the future of transatlantic relations during the era of Donald J. Trump". *Political Science Quarterly* 132, no. 3 (Fall 2017): 494–525.

Dannreuther, R., and J. Peterson, eds. *Security Strategy and Transatlantic Relations*. London and New York: Routledge, 2006.

de Vogue. A. "Judge blocks enforcement of Trump's transgender military ban". *CNN Politics*, 30 October 2017. http://edition.cnn.com/2017/10/30/politics/judge-blocks-trump-transgender-military-ban/index.html.

Farber, D., ed. *What They Think of Us: International Perceptions of the United States since 9/11*. Princeton NJ: Princeton University Press, 2007.

Freedom House. *Breaking Down Democracy: Goals, Strategies and Methods of Modern Authoritarians*. Washington DC, June 2017. https://freedomhouse.org/sites/default/files/June2017_FH_Report_Breaking_Down_Democracy.pdf.

Freedom House. *Freedom in the World 2017*. Washington DC, 2017. https://freedomhouse.org/report/freedom-world/freedom-world-2017.

Fukuyama, F. *The End of History and the Last Man*. New York: Penguin, 1993.

Garton Ash, T. *Free World: America, Europe and the Surprising Future of the West*. New York and London: Vintage, 2005.

Gladstone, R. "Nuclear scientists urge Congress to protect Iran deal". *New York Times*, 30 October 2017. https://www.nytimes.com/2017/10/30/world/middleeast/iran-nuclear-deal-scientists.html.

Glasser, S.B. "Trump national security team blindsided by NATO speech". *Politico*, 5 June 2017. https://www.politico.com/magazine/story/2017/06/05/trump-nato-speech-national-security-team-215227.

Goldberg, J. "The Obama doctrine". *The Atlantic*, April 2016. https://www.theatlantic.com/magazine/archive/2016/04/the-obama-doctrine/471525/.

Haas, R.N. *A World in Disarray. American Foreign Policy and the Crisis of the Old Order*. London: Penguin, 2017.

Haberman, M. "Donald Trump held briefing with Richard Haas, Head of Council on Foreign Relations". *New York Times* (First Draft), 3 March 2016. https://www.nytimes.com/politics/first-draft/2016/03/03/donald-trump-held-briefing-with-richard-haass-head-of-council-on-foreign-relations/?_r=0.

Huntington, S.P. *The Third Wave: Democratization in the Late 20th Century*. Norman: University of Oklahoma Press, 1991.

Ikenberry, G.J. "The plot against American foreign policy. Can the liberal order survive?". *Foreign Affairs* 96, no. 3 (May/June 2017): 2–9.

Ikenberry, G.J., T.J. Knock, A.-M. Slaughter and T. Smith. *The Crisis of American Foreign Policy: Wilsonianism in the Twenty-First Century*. Princeton NJ and Oxford: Princeton University Press, 2008.

Katzenstein, P.J., and R.O. Keohane, eds. *Anti-Americanisms in World Politics*. New Haven and London: Cornell University Press, 2007.

Khalaf, R. "Iraq's difficult decade of democracy". *Financial Times*, 4 March 2013. https://www.ft.com/content/e729b3e0-84c4-11e2-aaf1-00144feabdc0.

Luce, E. *The Retreat of Western Liberalism*. London and New York: Little Brown, 2017 (Kindle edition).

Lucas, E. *The New Cold War: Putin's Threat to Russia and the West*. London: Bloomsbury, 2012.

McMaster, H.R., and G.D. Cohn. "America first doesn't mean America alone". *Wall Street Journal*, 30 May 2017. https://www.wsj.com/articles/america-first-doesnt-mean-america-alone-1496187426.

Mann, J. "The adults in the room". *New York Review of Books*, 26 October 2017. http://www.nybooks.com/articles/2017/10/26/trump-adult-supervision/.

Mead, W.R. *Special Providence: American Foreign Policy and How it Changed the World*. New York and London: Routledge, 2002.

Moravcsik, A. "Liberal international relations theory: a scientific assessment" in *Progress in International Relations Theory: Appraising the Field*, edited by C. Elman and M. Fendius Elman. Cambridge MA: MIT Press, 2003.

Navarro, P., and G. Autry. *Death by China*. Upper Saddle River NJ: Prentice Hall, 2011.

Nye Jr, J. *Soft Power: the Means to Success in World Politics*. New York: Public Affairs, 2004.

Osnos, E., D. Remnick and J. Yaffa. "Trump, Putin and the New Cold War". *The New Yorker*, 6 March 2017. https://www.newyorker.com/magazine/2017/03/06/trump-putin-and-the-new-cold-war.

Paletta, D. "Internal White House documents allege manufacturing decline increases abortions, infertility and spousal abuse". *Washington Post*, 17 October 2017. https://www.washingtonpost.com/news/business/wp/2017/10/17/internal-white-house-documents-allege-manufacturing-decline-increases-abortions-infertility-and-spousal-abuse/?utm_term=.da0d40523cdb.

Peterson, J., R. Alcaro and N. Tocci. "Multipolarity, Multilateralism and Leadership: the Retreat of the West?" In *The West and the Global Power Shift: Transatlantic Relations and Global Governance*, edited by R. Alcaro, J. Peterson and E. Greco. London: Palgrave Macmillan, 2016.

Phillips, T. "Xi Jinping hails 'new era' of Chinese power at Communist party congress". *The Guardian*, 18 October 2017.

Porter, E. "Trump's endgame could be the undoing of global trade rules". *New York Times*, 31 October 2017. https://www.nytimes.com/2017/10/31/business/economy/trump-trade.html.

Remnick, D. "The Divider". *The New Yorker*, 28 August 2017: 27–8.

Sanger, D.E., and M. Haberman. "50 GOP officials warn Donald Trump would put nation's security at 'risk'". *New York Times*, 8 August 2016. https://www.nytimes.com/2016/08/09/us/politics/national-security-gop-donald-trump.html.

Sky, E. *The Unravelling: High Hopes and Missed Opportunities in Iraq*. London: Atlantic Books, 2015.

Sharma, R. "Broken BRICs: why the rest stopped rising". *Foreign Affairs* 91, no.6 (November/December 2012): 2–7.

Smale, A., and S. Erlanger. "Merkel, after discordant G-7 meeting, is looking past Trump". *The New York Times*, 28 May 2017. https://www.nytimes.com/2017/05/28/world/europe/angela-merkel-trump-alliances-g7-leaders.html?smid=nytcore-ipad-share&smprod=nytcore-ipad&_r=0.

Straw, J. "Iraq helped 'Mid-East democracy'". *BBC News*, 10 March 2005. http://news.bbc.co.uk/1/hi/uk_politics/4335629.stm.

Tomasky, M. "The resistance so far". *New York Review of Books*, 9 November 2017: 42–3.

Thrush, G., and G. Harris. "Amid nuclear tensions, Trump mulls exit from South Korea trade deal". *New York Times*, 2 September 2017. https://www.nytimes.com/2017/09/02/world/asia/us-south-korea-trade.html.

Vincent, R.J. *Human Rights and International Relations*. Cambridge: Cambridge University Press, 1986.

Waltz, K.N. "Globalization and governance". *PS. Political Science and Politics* 32, no. 4 (December 1999): 693–700.

Waltz, K.N. *Theory of International Politics*. Reading: Addison-Wesley, 1979.

Wendt, A. "Anarchy is what states make of it". *International Organization* 46, no. 2 (1992): 391–425.

Wight, M. "Why is there no International Theory?" In *Diplomatic Investigations*, edited by H. Butterfield, and M. Wight. London: Allen and Unwin, 1966.

Woodward, B. *Bush at War*. New York: Simon and Schuster, 2002.

Wright, T.J. *All Measures Short of War: the Contest for the 21st Century and the Future of American Power*. New Haven and London: Yale University Press, 2017 (Kindle edition).

The EU and the Global Order: Contingent Liberalism

Michael H. Smith and Richard Youngs

ABSTRACT

Politicians, diplomats and analysts commonly assume that commitment to multilateralism and liberal norms is part of the EU's very DNA. Increasingly, however, the EU's commitment to the liberal global order is more selective. We demonstrate the shift to a more contingent liberalism by examining the EU's recent record in relation to four different challenges: international trade; US leadership; Russian actions in the eastern neighbourhood; and security in the Middle East. We speculate on what this may portend for the EU's self-identity, European interests and the integrity of the prevailing global order.

The European Union has gained a reputation for being the strongest proponent and defender of the liberal global order. It is widely presumed that the EU defends liberal order almost reflexively, as part of its core identity and beyond rationalised cost-benefit calculation. This ostensibly involves firm support for multilateral institutions and norms; open markets and trade liberalisation; cooperative approaches to security; and human rights and democratic values.

With the United States and other actors increasingly ambivalent towards the liberal global order, the EU's commitment to these norms is of unprecedented importance. In some areas of policy, however, the EU's record in defending the liberal order looks increasingly mixed. Compared to the other actors covered in this issue, the EU's trade, foreign and security policies are indeed relatively strongly imbued with liberal principles. Yet, in recent years the EU's own approaches to global order and international challenges have adopted a more *selective* or *contingent liberalism*.

The 2016 EU Global Strategy (EUGS[1]) contains standard commitments to "rules-based order" but also gestures towards a more flexible or "principled pragmatism" in foreign policy. The strategy does not specify what this might mean in practice, although it does not talk of an especially thick form of liberal order. Instead of trying to second guess the meaning of the Global Strategy's still largely unimplemented text, we look at actual EU policy changes and assess how 'liberal' these are in the way they approach concrete order-related challenges.

---

[1]European Union, *Shared Vision, Common Action.*

Trade and the liberal economic order

Centred initially around the establishment of a common commercial policy, the European Economic Community was from its beginnings committed to the promotion of an open liberal trading order. However, trade has become increasingly politicised. The Union has a major stake in the continuation of liberal practices within the global political economy, but has also become a centre of frictions, with tensions seen in the EU's relations with major economic partners and in the rocky interaction between the Union's regional and more global roles.

One illustration of these tensions lies in the EU's commitment to both the idea and the institutions of multilateralism. The Union has been one of the cheerleaders for multilateral approaches to global governance and regulation. Yet its record in practice has become increasingly open to challenge. One reason for this is the clash between the Union's commitment to multilateral rules and order, on the one hand, and its own needs as an economic and political system, on the other. In recent, crisis-hit years, the tensions have grown between the EU's internal needs for economic recovery and the rules of the multilateral system.

Within the Union, there has always been a tension between the generally free-trading 'north' and the more instinctively protectionist 'south'. This broadly reflects a divide between those member states that see government as an enabler and those that see it as director of economic activity. The 'north-south divide' is visible in trade and broader commercial policies, and in the practices of economic and monetary integration. The divide has widened in the context of the financial and sovereign debt crises since 2008. The loss of economic momentum between 2008 and 2015 and the rise of new centres of economic power have combined to challenge the EU's investment in and continuing commitment to the over arching liberal order.

The result has been a series of shifts in the balance between cooperation and competition at the centre of the EU's engagement with the liberal economic order. The EU has moved in a number of areas away from 'cooperative interdependence' – the notion that interdependence stimulates renewed investment in institutions and rules – towards 'competitive interdependence'. The latter centres on the contest for economic 'territory' and the use of institutions in support of regional or sub-regional initiatives.[2] As a result, the EU has become actively engaged in the promotion of 'competitiveness' in commercial policies, and also in a series of initiatives to enhance its position in interregional and bilateral relationships.

This engagement with a 'post-multilateral' order is visible in a number of areas of EU global activity. One example is the pursuit of free trade agreements on either a bilateral or an interregional basis. These agreements can of course be sold as a move to strengthen the multilateral system through the implementation of 'WTO plus' and similar provisions, but they can also constitute a net loss of legitimacy and efficacy for the multilateral system in general; the EU did not offer any significant concessions to avert the apparent demise of the WTO trade talks in 2016. Alongside this process has gone the growth of 'twenty-first century trade politics',[3] with its focus more on the domestic impact of trade policies. The move has been from an essentially technocratic form of commercial policymaking to a much more politically-sensitive commercial policy agenda. From many quarters within the EU, resistance has grown to neoliberal trade liberalisation.

---

[2]Sbragia, "The EU, US and Trade Policy".
[3]Young and Peterson, *Parochial Global Europe*.

While the EU's commitment to liberal economic order remains stronger than that shown by other international powers, it has begun to exhibit a more notable degree of what might be labelled as 'soft mercantilism'. Since the Eurozone crisis began, nearly all member state governments have developed strategies of commercial diplomacy that often rub against the principles of liberal order.[4] Commission President Jean-Claude Juncker indicates that the EU will "not be naïve" in the face of rising protectionism around the world, including US President Donald Trump's 'America First' policy.[5] The Commission's 2015 *Trade for All* policy document promises that the Union will move against unchecked trade liberalisation and more strictly deploy regulatory norms to protect consumers from many types of imports.[6] The obstacles raised in trade talks with both the US and Canada illustrated a tide of changing opinion over trade policy from member states and some EU policymakers, not just protestors. The EU insisted on multiple safeguards, sectoral exclusions and other limits to liberalisation in both the CETA and EU-Japan agreements in 2017.[7]

In summer 2017, the Commission – backed by the European Parliament – moved to widen its use of anti-dumping penalties against markets with significant government intervention.[8] EU Trade Commissioner Cecilia Malmström warns that Europe "will not hesitate to use the tools at hand when countries don't play by the rules".[9] French President Emmanuel Macron has pushed hard for a range of new trade defence mechanisms and for an EU 'trade prosecutor' to ensure that Europe's commercial partners open their markets in reciprocal fashion to the Union's market-opening moves. Several member states are increasing protection against Chinese investment in so-called 'strategic sectors'. Striking the kind of balance that captures the notion of contingent liberalism, the Commission has begun pushing for new trade deals around the world, while also preparing a tough new EU-level mechanism for screening inward foreign investment.

In sum, as mercantile geo-economics has become more salient, the EU has begun to be more conditional in its defence of the multilateral system. The net result is a series of sharpened tensions, and a set of challenges for EU policymakers that have been linked to and exacerbated by the problems of internal economic performance. The EU has moved from being a compulsive multilateralist to being a selective one, at least in some areas. Its narrative is one of 'fair' and balanced trade, allied with a more directly instrumental defence of European commercial interests. There is a fluctuating but generally growing gap between the EU's rhetoric and its practices in relation to the global political economy and the liberal economic order.

Relating to US hegemony

Fundamental to the EU's engagement with the liberal order has been the nature of its relationship with the United States. The US broadly supported the European integration project as one part of the overarching post-1945 liberal order. As US power has waned, so the EU

---

[4]Youngs, *The Uncertain Legacy of Crisis*, Chapter 5.
[5]http://trade.ec.europa.eu/doclib/press/index.cfm?id=1564&title=Commission-urges-Member-States-to-support-propos-als-to-strengthen-European-defences-against-unfair-trade
[6]http://trade.ec.europa.eu/doclib/docs/2015/october/tradoc_153846.pdf
[7]http://trade.ec.europa.eu/doclib/docs/2017/july/tradoc_155701.pdf
[8]http://www.eubusiness.com/news-eu/anti-dumping.57vt/
[9]http://www.eubusiness.com/news-eu/trade-barriers.26gg/

has been forced to rethink its own understanding of and commitment to liberal order. While this has opened up spaces in which the EU can assert itself as a distinctive advocate of liberal order, it has also raised the stakes and increased the risks associated with the development of a distinctive and autonomous European foreign policy. Meanwhile, the rise of new powers has had a sometimes contrasting impact on US and EU perceptions of security issues. This has bred much uncertainty about the EU's global role in the political-security order, and a shift in the Union's relationship with the US.

European concerns have been growing for some years over the US' reluctant investment in global governance.[10] Whilst there are ambiguities in the EU's view of global governance, these are minor compared to those that can be witnessed in US policy. Even under the Obama administration there was a clear difference in the approaches of Washington and Brussels. Yet, it is well known that differences between the EU and US have sharpened dramatically since Donald Trump became president in January 2017. The first major clash took place on climate change and the US withdrawal from the Paris Accords.[11]

Against this background, the key question for this article relates to the EU's ability to influence the US' current tendency to downplay the liberal order. There is much evidence that the EU has experienced a secular decline in its capacity to persuade the US of the benefits of a continuing adherence to the rules and institutions of the liberal world order. Under the Obama administration, the EU found it difficult to meet the US' pleas for support in its role as global police force – or to shape the way that the US played that role.

The challenge posed by the Trump administration is of a different order.[12] Where its predecessors at least paid lip-service to the idea of transatlantic order and to the notion of the EU being a key pillar of the liberal world order, the current administration initially had a severely transactional view of the world. It categorised the EU as a consistently under-performing ally and pressed it to deliver in practice the European support habitually promised in rhetoric.

The EU's response has so far been hesitant, partly as a reflection of internal economic problems, partly as a result of Brexit, and partly as a result of the continuing differences within the Union about the feasibility and desirability of developing a stronger and genuinely more independent foreign policy. While there has been much talk of Germany now being the primary upholder of the liberal world order, German foreign policy commitments suggest this is a long way from being the case in reality. The EU collectively and member states individually have tried to confront the US on some issues but maintain a core framework of cooperation, even if this sits uneasily with commitment to the liberal order.

There are very specific issues on which the EU is beginning to react against the US' move away from liberal order norms. Yet, in all these cases, a balance is evident between the EU countering the US, on the one hand, and maintaining coordination, on the other hand. On China, the EU has joined the US' efforts to get China to respect more reciprocal trade rules, but has been wary about cooperating with Trump too extensively on China-related challenges.[13] The EU as a whole cannot quite decide if it can work with China on upholding elements of the liberal order, or not. For example, EU member states are split on how to react to the One Belt, One Road Initiative – that is, on whether this is a dangerous

---

[10]Smith, "European Union, United States and Global Governance".
[11]Milman and Carrington, "Anger as Trump rejects climate accord".
[12]Quinn, "The World According to Trump", 14-5.
[13]Donnan, "US tries to enlist EU and Japan".

circumvention of liberal order or a way of bringing Chinese funding into deepening economic interdependence. This has militated against any clear EU line on the Trump administration's position towards China.

Probably the clearest example of European states trying to work round the US is in relation to Iran, as the EU seeks to uphold the nuclear agreement with Tehran while President Trump threatens to withdraw – a clear divide over the value of liberal cooperative security frameworks. In another example, the EU has begun to confront the US on its unwillingness to press Israel to cease illegal settlement construction in the Occupied Palestinian Territories. Yet here too the EU's willingness to confront the US is still highly circumscribed, and its general role in the Israeli-Palestinian conflict of a lower profile now than some years ago. Another example of European uncertainty is the North Korean nuclear threat. President Macron has expressed some sympathy with the US' hardline towards counter-proliferation, while German Chancellor Angela Merkel has advocated more multilateral engagement to counterbalance Trump's promise of "fire and fury" against Pyongyang.[14]

Moreover, where transatlantic differences have appeared, it has not always been the EU focusing on order-related questions more than the US. Initially there was much talk of Trump's new engagement with Russian President Vladimir Putin and of Angela Merkel now being the only leader standing up to the Russian president. But when the US imposed sanctions on Russia to penalise it for election meddling, the EU refused to support the US in this more punitive approach, rather prioritising its own economic and energy ties with Russia. Germany's support for the Nordstream II energy pipeline from Russia continues to cause consternation within the European Commission and several other member states, as well as the United States.

A broader manifestation of the continuing dilemmas faced by the EU in relation to Trump's United States is a renewed debate about the Atlantic Alliance. By implication this is an unfolding debate about the extent to which the Europeans can still trust the Americans. Concern over this has been articulated explicitly by Angela Merkel, and has extended into a new discussion about whether or not Europe can develop a stronger defence capability.[15] The Trump phenomenon has certainly been one factor behind the EU's raft of new commitments to deepen defence cooperation. The EU has set up a new defence fund and a 'permanent structured cooperation' (or Pesco) initiative to spur common military capacity-building and missions. The EU's move towards a security and defence union is not necessarily antithetical to the global liberal order. But it does shift the focus, with the EU now prioritising its own defence imperatives rather than working with the US on order-related security rules.

In sum, the impact of the Trump administration cuts in opposing directions. On the one hand, it prompts the EU to move up a gear in its own commitment to the global liberal order. On the other hand, to the extent that EU support for liberal order has been inseparable from robust Atlanticism, the current conceptual distance between Europe and the US represents yet another menace to liberal order. The erratic nature of US foreign policy under Trump means that more than ever the US is a challenge to – rather than amplifier of – EU support for the liberal world order. The question of whether the EU can or should become a 'contestant' of the US in terms of the changing world order now has greater weight than previously.

---

[14]Godement, "North Korea showdown".
[15]Chazan and Sevastopulo, "Trump shakes Germany's faith".

Of course, this set of transatlantic debates is taking place in a changed world, where new economic and political powers share neither the European nor the American view of desirable world order.[16] For the Europeans, this raises new questions of geostrategy. Even if Europeans fundamentally disagree with Trump, is 'soft balancing' against the US practicably possible in this changed world? Or conversely, as other potential strategic partners emerge, has the concept of bandwagoning in relation to the US lost its absolute primacy? Amidst all the sound and fury of current reactions to the mercurial Trump, the EU has still not clarified how the US' present strategic behaviour changes the core European approach towards the global liberal order.

Political-security liberalism: Russia, Ukraine and the East

In parallel to the concern over US policies, the EU has for some years been trying to manage Russia's more explicit threat to the liberal order. Reflecting perhaps the most profound challenge to Europe's regional liberal order, EU leaders have felt alarm at Russia's revanchist geopolitics, its annexation of Crimea and the subsequent conflict that has blighted eastern Ukraine since early 2014. The series of challenges facing the EU's eastern neighbours – stemming from Russia's actions not only in Ukraine but also states such as Armenia, Belarus, Georgia and Moldova – have had a profound impact on EU foreign policy and the way European powers conceive liberal order-based security.

In a core conceptual sense, Russia's actions have led many in the EU to reconsider the relationship between liberal order and European strategic interests. Some of the same ambiguities and tensions evident in EU international economic policies and the EU-US relationship now infuse the Union's foreign policy challenges in the east. These eastern crises have pushed the EU towards a new kind of geopolitical strategy that mixes liberal and *realpolitik* strategic principles. This involves an upgraded EU diplomacy mixing assertive and defensive tactics, with the Union using its distinctive tools aimed at deepening cooperation, interdependence and political transformation in the east both more instrumentally and more variably to further immediate-term security interests. The EU has begun to deploy its central liberal-cooperative practices in ways that are more selective and calibrated than in previous European policies, and superimposed with a layer of geostrategic diplomacy.

A key debate since the Ukraine conflict erupted in 2014 has been over how far the EU is willing to extend the liberal inclusiveness of its own norm-based order into the region of the Eastern Partnership (EaP, which includes Armenia, Azerbaijan, Belarus, Georgia, Moldova and Ukraine). While the EU has certainly offered some elements of stronger strategic backing to EaP states, it has also sought to keep the region as a 'middle-land' between it and a more abrasive Russia. Elements of EU responses to the post-2014 crisis suggest at least some implicit acceptance of Russia's view that the region should be geostrategically managed/juggled in an east-west balance, sometimes not sitting easily with what citizens in EaP states might prefer. In effect, the EU has provided some additional support to EaP states in order to shore up the wider European security order, but has not tried formally or institutionally to extend its own liberal 'security community' into the eastern region.

The EU has offered stronger support for the six EaP partners, but there has been no effort to gain strategic control over the EaP space. While the EU has not undertaken the

---

[16]Alcaro *et al.*, *The West and Global Power Shift*.

kind of geopolitical 'tactical retreat' that 'defensive realists' advocate, neither has it moved far in the other direction of seeking to assert greater tutelage over the region as the best way of bolstering norms of the liberal-based order. The EU's geopolitical response to Russian actions and the Ukraine conflict has been as much about strategic balancing and diplomatic trade-offs as any principled commitment to the norms of liberal order *per se*.

Russia's presence within contested zones in Moldova, Georgia and Ukraine has dissuaded many EU member states from any dramatically upgraded commitments to these countries. The EU has declined to offer EaP states full protection or assume responsibility for their security and territorial integrity. It has offered neither the prospect of EU accession, nor major new benefits short of membership. Overall European financial support to EaP partners has increased since 2014, but not dramatically. If the EU has not fully retreated from the region, neither have it efforts sufficed to gain significantly more strategic influence over EaP states.

Rather, the EU has increasingly balanced its strategic responses between EaP states and Russian demands. European approaches are today more strongly conditioned than previously by a triangular relationship between the EU, Russia and EaP partners. European governments have adopted some new elements of geostrategic policy in response to Russian actions and developments in the EaP states, while eschewing the Russian understanding of geopolitics. The fraught politics and conflicts of the EaP region have in recent years dragged the EU towards a delicately balanced combination of liberal and non-liberal approaches to geopolitics.

The EU's response to Russia itself has shifted from a logic of inclusion to one of partial exclusion. Although the EU has used restrictive measures elsewhere in the world, this is the most notable case of sanctions being used as a central pillar of European statecraft. Sanctions have been off-set by selective accommodation and a very modest form of strategic balancing. In parallel to restrictive measures, some European governments have focused on more classical forms of diplomacy that seek trade-offs with Russia outside the scope of EU institutional instruments. EU policies to the east now build in 'the Russia factor' in a way that the EaP had conspicuously not previously done.

The EU has not allowed its Russia policy entirely to dictate its EaP policy, but neither has its EaP policy entirely taken precedence over its Russia policy. Many in the EU and member states have veered toward the logic of joint negotiation with Russia over core issues in the region. The EU's new preference is for *bounded containment*. This mixes elements that unwind interdependence with those that actually solidify the logic of inclusion in terms of talking with Russia on Ukraine's trade arrangements, internal political arrangements and conflict mediation issues.

One apparently liberal evolution since 2014 is the EU's insistence that its geopolitical advantage lies in its focus on democratic reforms in EaP partners. Yet in practice, the EU's commitment to liberal democratic norms has become more varied between EaP states in accordance with geopolitical calculation and less rigid in the tactics through which it pursues democracy support. Funds related to democratic reform have increased in Ukraine, Moldova and to some extent Georgia, along with selective points of diplomatic pressure. In contrast, the EU's focus on political change has weakened in Armenia, Belarus and Azerbaijan. The reform-oriented dimension of EU policies is now framed and calibrated more instrumentally as a tool of purposive power – sometimes enhanced for this use, other times set aside where this is judged not to be geopolitically optimal.

In terms of direct involvement in the ongoing Donbas conflict, member states have been extremely wary and the EU as a whole appears willing to accept a degree of implicit 'defeat' in eastern Ukraine and allow Russia to take practical control not only of Crimea but also limited parts of the Donbas region. This is judged to be an outcome less damaging to European interests than open conflict with Russia. The geopolitical script is one of indirect conflict containment rather than direct measures of conflict transformation – an approach that involves more *ad hoc* expediency than suggested by the EU's rhetorical commitments to so-called liberal peace-building. In autumn 2017, the EU supported the notion of a UN peacekeeping force in Donbas – an initiative very much in tune with multilateral norms, but one viewed by the Ukrainian government as legitimising Russia's *de facto* hold over parts of its territory.

Overall, the Russia-Ukraine crisis has contributed to making the EU a different kind of foreign policy actor. The EU has shifted towards a more *consequentialist-utilitarian* foreign policy – that is, more concerned with immediate outcomes and less uniquely driven by the Union's institutionally embedded liberal norms and identity. In this consequentialist balancing of different policy options' geopolitical impact, liberal security and political norms are sometimes judged useful, but sometimes judged expendable. Certain member states have also become more predominant actors relative to the EU institutions. Most member states express deep unease with the German and French lead and positions in the Minsk peace process. Yet the other member states have themselves ceded power to Germany and France to limit their own exposure and commitment to the crisis. Today, the overall EU presence in the east includes a heavy dose of realpolitik national diplomacy alongside the liberal instruments of the EU institutions.

In sum, while the EU has upgraded some elements of its commitment to liberal order, the Russia-Ukraine conflict has not prompted the Union to accord unequivocal, make-or-break importance to order-related norms in the east. Most assessments of the mixed EU responses to the conflict have been highly critical. Criticisms have come from diametrically opposed directions. While many analysts admonish the EU and its member states for having been overly weak and insipid, others accuse European governments of intruding clumsily in the EaP region without thinking through Russia's likely reaction or interests.[17] Yet it is perhaps best to describe the EU's response as half-effective. The EU has not been able to resolve the crisis nor prevent tragic loss of life, but at best uneasily to contain instability and conflict from spiralling more seriously out of control. Its own power stands attenuated; but the crisis has equally revealed the limits to Russian power.

Political-security liberalism: the Middle East

Meanwhile, security concerns emanating from the Middle East and North Africa (MENA) have also become more acute and paramount within EU foreign policies in recent years. The EU has been hit by dozens of terrorist attacks and has struggled to manage an unprecedented influx of refugees and migrants either from MENA states or passing through these from sub-Saharan African states. EU policymakers argue routinely that these security threats

---

[17]Nitoiu, *Avoiding a new 'Cold War'.*

now menace the very liberal order upon which the EU itself rests – a prominent line of reasoning made in the EU Global Strategy.[18]

Many of the most notable recent developments in EU foreign and security policies towards the MENA region have not been especially liberal. Indeed, EU policies towards the Middle East appear more clearly to undercut some fundamentals of liberal order than do EU policies towards Russia and the EaP. These MENA policies reflect a strategic script of defensive exclusion more than inclusive-cooperative security or strong support for human rights and democratic norms. Many policy responses denote a concern that the demarcation lines need to be far stronger between the European project and what lies beyond it – quite the inverse of liberal notions of shared, cooperative security norms. Aimed at strengthening a *protective perimeter* around the European Union, they revolve around efforts to make EU borders more robust and keep refugees and migrants in their own country or region.

In 2016, the EU extended Frontex's mandate and transformed this border-control initiative into a fully-fledged European Border and Coast Guard Agency. This will have a yearly budget of over 300 million euros by 2020 to control refugee inflows. From mid-2016, the EU released several tranches of emergency aid to southeastern member states, the bulk of which was spent on strengthening border fences.[19] One of the priority focuses of the Global Strategy is the commitment to strengthen surveillance capacities. Operations Sophia and Triton in the Mediterranean have been progressively beefed up to provide more extensive patrols. Germany has proposed intercepting migrants and refugees at sea and returning them to North Africa to apply for asylum there; to speed readmissions, it has also opened a migration centre in Tunis.[20]

An apparently liberal element to EU policy includes a raft of new commitments to deepen cooperation with MENA and African states to invest more in development and better security governance. The EU launched an Emergency Trust Fund of 2.5 billion euros for Africa and the Middle East. EU member states promised an extra 200 million euros for multilateral agencies like the World Food Program and the UN refugee agency to care for refugees in the Middle East. The EU's 1 billion euro Madad Trust Fund was set up to provide support for Syrians. The EU also introduced a European Investment Plan in November 2016, covering African and Mediterranean states, with the Commission providing 3.35 billion euros for guarantees designed to leverage private investment. Germany also launched its own development-oriented 'Marshall Plan for Africa'.[21]

However, there are serious question marks over how far these new funds represent liberal approaches to security – and whether they are really about shoring up the principles of liberal order. The Emergency Trust Fund is not nearly big enough to make a meaningful impact on economic or political conditions over the 23 eligible recipient countries and is at best a small top-up to existing spending on development. Moreover, much of the new funding is being directed towards border controls and migration management in the recipient countries rather than 'root causes' development-related work.[22] In early 2016, a group of EU donors pushed the OECD to change its definition of 'aid' to include some military spending and funds for refugee camps. In a similar move, governments have sought to

---

[18]European Union, *Shared Vision, Common Action.*
[19]"EU funds for Bulgaria target border security", EUObserver.com, 28 September 2016.
[20]"German ministry wants migrants stopped at sea", EUObserver.com, 8 November 2016.
[21]Alghoul, "Merkel Under Fire For 'Uncritical Engagement'".
[22]Castillejo, *European Union Trust Fund for Africa.*

change the rules governing the Commission's financial instruments to allow development funds to be used for border controls and other measures to restrict migrant flows. None of this represents a particularly liberal use of development aid, even as the EU adheres to the norms of the multilateral Social Development Goals.

The EU has begun to tie external cooperation more tightly to readmission, partner countries receiving aid only if they agree to take back migrants from Europe. Under a first round of 'migration compacts' with Jordan, Lebanon, Niger, Nigeria, Senegal, Mali, Ethiopia, Tunisia and Libya, EU aid is being used explicitly to dissuade refugees and migrants from travelling to Europe. In February 2017, European leaders agreed on a new 200 million euro initiative to train and equip the Libyan coastguard to intercept and turn back migrants embarked for Europe. In the MENA, the EU is in effect outsourcing security to poorer and authoritarian states – in some ways the very antithesis of liberal-cooperative security.

The EU and member states have eschewed any significant commitment to supporting democratic reforms in the MENA.[23] Most EU states have spent far more on beefing up domestic capabilities in surveillance, policing, border controls and intelligence than defending liberal political norms in MENA states. The increase in European funding for internal counter-terrorism within the EU itself has exceeded many times over these investments in liberal political reforms in the MENA region. The EU's Internal Security Fund has been increased to 3.8 billion euros for 2014-20.[24] National governments have followed suit. The UK's counter-terrorism spending, for example, is now over 2 billion pounds a year.[25] In contrast, the overall European involvement in operations against the Islamic State in Iraq and Syria have been limited, more indirect than direct.

European enhanced security engagement with regimes does not denote an especially liberal perspective on the MENA regional order. Member states' arms sales have increased to states like Egypt, Algeria, Saudi Arabia and Jordan, which are all tightening repression. In Bahrain, the UK has started to build its first permanent naval base in the region in forty years, even as the Bahraini regime intensifies repression against opposition forces. The EU is now providing aid to Sudanese security bodies to control migration, despite having tried to take President Omar al-Bashir to the International Criminal Court for many years. France's Serval mission in Mali and other military operations across the Sahel had mandates tightly drawn to steer clear of internal political issues in the region. In 2016 the EU introduced a new strategy to strengthen its cooperation with security forces in fragile contexts.[26]

Policy towards Turkey demonstrates the mixed or contingent nature of EU commitment to liberal-order norms. The EU provided Turkey with 3 billion euros to help provide refugees with better humanitarian conditions. While this indubitably provided help, the very realpolitik strategic-political aim was to keep refugees from leaving for Europe. Moreover, European leaders did little to try to limit Turkish President Recep Tayyip Erdogan's centralisation of power and assault on opposition leaders after the attempted coup against him in July 2016. Indeed, France and Germany still pressed for more security cooperation with Turkey after the April 2017 referendum that opened the way for Erdogan to assume even more unchecked, authoritarian power. In autumn 2017, however, several member states

---

[23]For updated aid figures, see www.oecd/dac.stats
[24]European Political Strategy Centre, *Towards a Security Union*.
[25]Black *et al., Defence and Security after Brexit*.
[26]European Commission and High Representative for Foreign Affairs and Security Policy, "Elements for EU-wide strategic framework".

were beginning to reduce cooperation and ratchet up pressure on Turkey as the country's illiberal regression reached alarming levels.

Conclusion

In principle, the EU has in recent years doubled down on its commitment to liberal approaches to trade, defence and external security. Many EU policy statements insist that the EU can only address current challenges by stepping up its defence of liberal order. In practice, the EU's approach to the economic, political and security components of the liberal order has become more mixed and eclectic. There is increasingly a combination of stronger EU commitment to liberal order, on the one hand, and an EU move away from liberalism, on the other hand. Crucially, this mix differs between policy sectors – this article has shown the variation across trade policies, relations with the US and security strategies towards the east and the south. EU positions towards liberal order are increasingly contingent upon instrumental calculations of European strategic and economic interests. Revealingly, when President Macron talks of 'refounding global order' he links this tightly to the revival of French strategic independence, power and prestige.

The contingency in the EU's commitment is not simply a pragmatic dilution of principles. Contingent liberalism is not quite the principled pragmatism promised in the EU Global Strategy; it is a different kind of geopolitical logic from the standard trade-off between interests and values. The EU and its key member states will now often devise policies that broadly defend liberal order but through tactics that are more eclectic, opportunistic and flexible than was previously the case. Many diplomats and observers insist this is a welcome and overdue change;[27] yet it certainly brings the EU close to some serious inconsistencies between its liberal rhetoric and its actual policies. To some extent, EU contingent liberalism produces a geopolitically-oriented balance of different strategic logics, but it also generates polices that sit uneasily with each other.

The impact of economic recession and relative decline makes EU states need international markets and open trading relations to an even greater extent. Yet it also propels them towards moderately more mercantile economic strategies that prioritise immediate commercial gain over the diffuse benefits of global rules. It enourages them to seek ways to safeguard domestic vulnerabilities and use the EU market more expressly as a negotiating tool. In the realm of security, threats to liberal order are both driving EU member states together and placing new strains on their cooperation. On the one hand, the turbulent strategic context reinforces the case for liberal, cooperative security principles. On the other hand, it encourages European governments to see core liberal notions of cross-border openness and cooperation as an obstacle to security. Internal and external challenges are likely to continue pulling the EU towards a more carefully rationalised, contingent support for the international liberal order.

Crucially, other powers may not see the EU's changed understanding of 'liberal order' as particularly liberal. While the EU wants to change the functioning of the liberal order to deliver more selective and tangible benefits, having more control over specific policy agendas, this sets the Union very much against the rising powers: when they talk about a reformed liberal order they envisage an increase in their own control over that order.

---

[27] Biscop, *Geopolitics with European Characteristics.*

Europeans often criticse rising powers for a selective adherence to liberal multilateral norms, but the EU and its member states are in fact moving in a similar direction.

References

Alcaro, R., J. Peterson, and E. Greco, eds. *The West and the Global Power Shift: Transatlantic Relations and Global Governance*. Basingstoke: Palgrave Macmillan, 2016.

Alghoul, D. "Merkel Under Fire For 'Uncritical Engagement' With Egypt During Visit". *Middle East Eye*, 2 March 2017.

Biscop, S. *Geopolitics with European Characteristics: An Essay on Pragmatic Idealism, Equality, and Strategy*, Egmont Paper 82. Brussels: Egmont Institute, March 2016.

Black, J., A. Hall, K. Cox, M. Kepe and E. Silfversten. *Defence and Security after Brexit, Understanding the possible implications of the UK's decision to leave the EU*, Overview Report. Cambridge and Brussels: Rand Europe, 5 March 2017.

Castillejo, C. *The European Union Trust Fund for Africa: A Glimpse of the Future for EU Development Cooperation*, Discussion Paper 22/2016. Bonn: German Development Institute, 2016.

Chazan, G., and D. Sevastopulo. "Trump shakes Germany's faith in US support for transatlantic alliance". *Financial Times*, 2 June 2017.

Donnan, S. "US tries to enlist EU and Japan in China tech fight". *Financial Times*, 21 September 2017.

European Commission and High Representative for Foreign Affairs and Security Policy. "Elements for an EU-wide strategic framework to support security sector reform". Joint Communication, 5 July 2016.

European Political Strategy Centre. *Towards a Security Union: Bolstering the EU's counter-terrorism response*, Issue 12. Brussels: European Political Strategy Centre, 2016.

European Union. *Shared Vision, Common Action: A Stronger Europe. A Global Strategy for the European Union's Foreign and Security Policy*. Brussels, June 2016.

Godement, F. "North Korea showdown: Europe can only watch". *CEIP Eurasia Review*, 16 August 2017.

Milman, O., and D. Carrington. "Anger at US as Trump rejects climate accord". *The Guardian*, 2 June 2017.

Nitoiu, C., ed. *Avoiding a new 'Cold War': The future of EU-Russia relations in the context of the Ukraine crisis*, LSE Ideas Report. London: London School of Economics, 2016.

Quinn, A. "The World According to Trump". *The World Today*, December 2016-January 2017.

Sbragia, A. "The EU, the US and Trade Policy: Competitive Interdependence in the Management of Globalization". *Journal of European Public Policy* 17, no. 3 (2010): 368–82.

Smith, M. "The European Union, the United States and Global Governance". In *The European Union and Global Governance: A Handbook*, edited by J.-U. Wunderlich and D. Bailey. London: Routledge, 2011.

Young, A., and J. Peterson. *Parochial Global Europe: Twenty-First Century Trade Politics*. Oxford: Oxford University Press, 2014.

Youngs, R. *The Uncertain Legacy of Crisis, European Foreign Policy Faces the Future*. Washington, DC: Carnegie Endowment for International Peace, 2014.

Global Reordering and China's Rise: Adoption, Adaptation and Reform

Shaun Breslin

ABSTRACT

While much of the debate over the implications of China's rise tends to dichotomise around either status quo or revisionist predictions, the reality seems to lie somewhere in between. In broad terms, China has embraced multilateral forms of cooperation and governance. This does not mean, however, that it is satisfied with the distribution of power in many international institutions, or some of the norms and principles that underpin them. This has resulted in a reformist position, with China increasingly willing to offer its own supplementary alternatives. China's rise has also provided an important economic alternative to dealing with the West, and considerably undermined the ability of others to establish their preferences and world views. China's lack of commitment to democracy and the external promotion of human rights remains a key reason why some analysts remain unconvinced about the long-term ambitions of an illiberal actor in a global liberal order.

It is now a quarter of a century since William Overholt predicted that an emerging China would become a threat to the existing order, and Denny Roy identified a "hegemon on the horizon" that would likely undermine regional stability and security.[1] In the intervening years, the concept of a China challenge to the way the world is organised and governed has become an oft repeated and important meme in the debates over the nature of the global order. To be sure, what an alternative non-liberal Chinese world order might look like (rather than China simply having more power within the existing global order) is difficult to pin down, and is often left undefined; the focus is typically on the challenge itself, rather than its consequences.[2] Nevertheless, Martin Jacques is not alone in thinking that it is not a case of *if*, but *when* China will rule the world and reshape it to reflect its own values and interests.[3]

There are very good reasons for expecting China to challenge the liberal order – in fact, in some areas and in some respects, it already has. After all, China's interests did not inform the creation of the existing institutions of global economic governance, where voting rights in some ways still reflect the geopolitical realities of 1944 rather than the distribution of

---

[1]Overholt, *The Rise of China*, and Roy, "Hegemon on the Horizon".
[2]Christensen, *The China Challenge*, 56.
[3]Jacques, *When China Rules the World*.

global power today.[4] China's leaders have openly and repeatedly expressed their dissatisfaction, actively sought to bring about change in these institutions, and shown that they have both the desire and the capacity to introduce new institutions where such change is slow in coming or does not go far enough (or both). Not only have the supposed universal nature of some liberal norms and their consequent policy prescriptions been challenged, but new Chinese norms are being proposed as the basis for governance discussions and regulation in some issue areas. And while economic neoliberalism may have done much to discredit itself and its own efficacy and legitimacy, the continued growth of the Chinese economy has reinvigorated proponents of the developmental benefits of following strong state forms of capitalism.

So for those that assume that power transitions are inherently destabilising and dangerous,[5] or who focus on the specific ambitions of a non-Western country led by an illiberal Communist Party,[6] there is at least some evidence to justify their predictions and/or suspicions. And yet, while China clearly does not meet the democracy and human rights component of Riccardo Alcaro's definition of "the liberal order" outlined in the Introduction to this collection, in the other dimensions we have seen significant movement towards the liberal status quo.[7] China has moved from fearing Asian regionalism to embracing and promoting it,[8] become an active participant in many multilateral institutions, and recognised the need for international collaboration to deal with non-traditional security challenges. Dealing with the environment has become an urgent policy goal and, not least because of a reversal of policy in the United States, some have even identified China as the future "global climate leader".[9] Moreover as China has been a – perhaps *the* – main national beneficiary of the globalisation of production and the liberal economic order in the post-Cold War era, it is difficult to see why it would want to change it radically. Indeed, at Davos in 2017, Xi Jinping argued that it was China that was the defender of "global free trade and investment" in the face of a protectionist turn elsewhere.[10]

How do we reconcile these conflicting views of what China has done to date and, more important, what it wants to do in the future? Is the creation of the Asian Infrastructure Investment Bank (AIIB) a first sign of a new sinocentric economic order, or rather a reflection of China's commitment to multilateralism and the provision of Chinese global public goods – albeit with some minor revisions to existing rules?[11] Or is it a result of Washington's reluctance to accommodate Chinese interests even though Beijing has gone a long way to integrate itself into existing Western-dominated governance forms?[12]

The suggestion here is that the China challenge to the liberal order is likely to be partial and selective, rather than holistic and systemic. Emboldened by a perception of a significant

---

[4]China, in the form of the Republic of China, was an original charter member of the United Nations, and participated in the Bretton Woods conference. Communist Party members were part of the process, including the future first governor of the People's Bank of China after 1949. Nevertheless, it is fair to say that the interests and goals of the Chinese Communist Party were not exactly central to the forms of governance that emerged in the post-WWII era. For details, see Jin, *The Chinese Delegation*.

[5]For example, Mearsheimer, "China's Unpeaceful Rise", and Allison, *Destined for War*.

[6]For an overview of the emergence of such responses to China's rise and an assessment of them, see Broomfield, "Perceptions of Danger".

[7]Alcaro, "Liberal Order and its Contestations".

[8]Breslin, "Understanding China's Regional Rise".

[9]Hilton, "China Emerges as Global Climate Leader".

[10]Xi, "President Xi's Speech to Davos".

[11]Renard, *The Asian Infrastructure Investment Bank*.

[12]Etzioni, "The Asian Infrastructure Investment Bank".

rise in Chinese power, but moderated by an understanding that the US is likely to remain the dominant global power for some time to come, there has been a push in Beijing to bring about changes that best suit Chinese objectives and interests. This entails being rather supportive of the status quo in some issue areas, while being quite forceful in pushing Chinese ideas and initiatives in other policy domains. In addition to specific attempts to reform (or not, as the case may be) the existing order, the nature of China's economic rise has also provided an important challenge to the dominance of neoliberal ideas and practices. By becoming an important economic partner for other developing economies, China creates a space for elites in the developing world to make choices, diminishing their dependence on traditional economic partners, and thus undermining the ability of more established global actors to impose their liberal ideational and policy preferences. The result might not be a Chinese-led world order, but one in which there are significant, specific and deliberate Chinese challenges to the status quo in some policy domains, and significant consequences of China's rise that might undermine the force of liberal arguments and preferences in other issue areas.

Studying China's future(s)

Students of all countries have an eye to how events might unfold and how the country is going to evolve; but it is probably fair to say that few countries have been the subject of as much futurology and prediction as China. This stems from a fundamental uncertainty over China's commitment to the existing international order. China might not be widely considered to be communist in any meaningful way anymore, but it is equally widely perceived to be "different"; "an illiberal, non-Western state in a western-centric, liberal order".[13]

Not surprisingly, there are considerable differences in opinion, ranging from Jacques' prediction of a sinocentric world, on the one hand,[14] to Minxin Pei's and Gordon Chang's predictions of economic and political crises and collapse, on the other.[15] Space precludes an in-depth analysis here of the various predictions and how likely they are to come true. But it is worth briefly noting three collective consequences of these studies that provide an important context to thinking about China and the (future) liberal order.

First, while not all predictions take China's continued rise for granted, there does seem to be an implicit assumption in some that things will continue to go well for China. This seems to be particularly the case when there is a theoretical inclination to separate the study of domestic dynamics out from the study of international relations. Whilst there is no prediction of an imminent crash in this article, it acknowledges that an inward turn to deal with, for example, domestic financial problems, could slow and/or alter the nature of China's rise. Long-term lower growth with less of an emphasis on investment and infrastructure would also reduce the importance of the Chinese market for some exporters (and in some cases, already has). And, as we saw in 2017, increased regulations to prevent capital flight can have a very quick impact on overseas Chinese mergers and acquisitions,[16] and also perceptions of China's long-term goals and ambitions. At the very least, it is worth reminding ourselves that the inevitability of Japan's rise to dominance that was still being identified as recently as the start of the 1990s ultimately proved not to be inevitable at all.

---

[13] Muller, "China an Illiberal, Non-Western State".
[14] Jacques, *When China Rules the World*.
[15] Pei, *China's Trapped Transition*, and Chang, *The Coming Collapse of China*.
[16] See Huang and Tang, "Why China is Curbing Outbound Direct Investment".

Second, the idea that pre-existing understandings and theoretical preferences tend to shape the way that events are understood and interpreted is well established across the social sciences. This helps explain why different people have very different understandings of the question about the significance of the AIIB. In the case of China's rise, an added dimension is the way that past and current behaviour is often discounted as a guide to future actions and objectives. As Pan Chengxin argues, any good paradigm has effectively to deal with anomalies that might suggest an alternative explanation or prediction of the future.[17] So what China did when it was relatively weak, so the argument goes, will not be the same as what it will do when it has even more power in the future.[18]

Third, and perhaps most significant here, in his extensive analysis of different studies of China's futures, Roger Irvine identified a "strong tendency to polarise" around extreme and opposing potential outcomes.[19] Of course, there are also more nuanced positions. But the temptation to simplify potential outcomes down to two competing alternatives remains, and can still be seen and heard in debates over China's future(s). We have already noted one such cleavage in the assumptions of China's continued rise to global power (and even dominance) versus the conviction that China (or Communist Party leadership at least) will collapse. Another dichotomisation is the theoretically driven (neo)realist prediction of an "unpeaceful rise"[20] and liberal expectations of an integrated and socialised risen China as a stakeholder in the existing global order.

The idea that China is, can, or wants to be either a wholly status quo or a wholly revisionist power seems somewhat problematic. There are parts of the liberal order that do not sit at all comfortably with Chinese preferences; for example, norms relating to sovereignty and intervention. There are other areas where the desire is to push for change in existing institutions and practices and to assume more power *within* existing frameworks. The nature of global economic governance could be a good example here. We might argue that the overall goal is to revise the way the liberal order works, but to different extents and in different ways in different policy domains. But as the word *revise* suggests a revisionist agenda, and the word *revisionist* seems to have lost its original meaning and become equated with fundamental and revolutionary change (when it comes to debating China), then the idea of a selective reformist agenda is perhaps more appropriate.

Actors and objectives

It is not surprising that there tends to be a focus on China's top leaders when it comes to assessing Chinese objectives and goals; they really are very powerful individuals. That said, it is a mistake to think of China as having one single view and voice. In China's more isolationist days, international interactions were very much dominated by the business of diplomacy, overseen and undertaken by a small number of senior leaders. As China engaged the capitalist global economy and became involved with a range of functional transnational multilateral regulation and governance mechanisms, the number of Chinese international actors increased significantly; actors who operate with differing degrees of autonomy to pursue their own specific goals and objectives.

---

[17]Pan, *Knowledge, Desire and Power*, 26.
[18]Kang, "Getting Asia Wrong".
[19]Irvine, *Forecasting China's Future*, 1.
[20]Mearsheimer, "China's Unpeaceful Rise".

As a result, the Ministry of Foreign Affairs has lost considerable power within the central decision-making hierarchy, with a range of economic ministries and specialist agencies (for example, the Ministry of Environmental Protection) playing increasingly important roles.[21] At the higher levels of the authoritarian state bureaucracy, there can be considerable disagreement over specific policy areas. The conflict between the Ministry of Commerce and the People's Bank of China over currency reform and renminbi internationalisation seems a particularly pertinent example here given their significance to the global liberal economic order.[22] The commercial objectives of major enterprises are important too,[23] and many local governments pursue their own agendas, particularly when it comes to facilitating and regulating cross border flows.[24] As a result, in 2012, the International Crisis Group described an almost anarchic situation in the South China Seas with a range of different Chinese actors pursuing different policy objectives, making the task of identifying "what China wants" rather difficult.[25]

There are also a range of opinions on the nature of the liberal order and what China can (in terms of capacities) and should (in terms of ambitions) do to change it. In the 1990s, the idea that China should "say no" and turn its back on the West gained considerable popular support,[26] and this highly critical and rejectionist position is still extremely easy to find on various Chinese internet platforms today. The *Global Times* newspaper also tends to take a more nationalist position on many issues than other official media outlets, and was openly criticised by Chinese diplomat Wu Jianmin for potentially harming relations with Japan in 2016.[27] This diversity allows outside observers to go "opinion shopping" to find the Chinese view that reinforces pre-existing understandings of what China is and what it wants.

Xu Jin argues that the mainstream position within Chinese academia is somewhat less assertive and more cautious (about the real extent of Chinese global power) than the position that Xi Jinping is projecting. But Xu also notes the key role of the paramount leader in establishing the "theme of the time" that creates the overarching framework within which these debates can take place; for example, the nature of the global order, Chinese interests and objectives, and the fundamental principles that should inform Chinese thinking and action.[28] So notwithstanding the diversity noted above, it seems reasonable to focus here on how what we might call 'official China' articulates its views of the liberal order, and how China can and should act within it.

China's as global power

When it comes to considerations of the fundamental nature of the liberal order, Chinese positions have been relatively consistent. Where things have changed – and changed quite considerably in recent years – is when it comes to thinking about the relative power of

[21]Lai and Kang, "Domestic Bureaucratic Politics".
[22]Freeman and Yuan, *China's Exchange Rate Politics.*
[23]Zhao, "The myth of China's overseas energy investment".
[24]Li and Lee, "Local Liberalism".
[25]Though there have been attempts to consolidate the number of actors and coordinate activities since then. International Crisis Group, *Stirring up the South China Sea*, I.
[26]Des Forges and Xu, "China as a Non-Hegemonic Superpower?"
[27]Wu was widely considered to be China's most influential foreign policy 'dove', and his death in a car crash prompted a (not always very respectful) debate over the nature of the world order and China's place within it, spanning the full range of Chinese perceptions and positions. Hornby, "Wu Jianmin".
[28]Xu, "Debates in IR".

China and other actors within this order, and what China might be able to do to bring about change. Facing widespread opprobrium and the possibility of international isolation in the post-Tiananmen period, China's international strategy came to be dominated for the best part of two decades by the *taoguang yanghui* concept associated with Deng Xiaoping. Directly translating as "hide brightness and foster obscurity" it was part of a wider exhortation to effectively "keep a low profile" while China was still relatively weak and the dominant (liberal) global powers unprepared to accommodate its interests. In the 1990s, the same basic understanding was manifest in the *China threat thesis* – the idea that those hostile to China would look for any evidence to show that China was mounting a challenge to the Western-led order. Thus, even as China's relative global power increased, the logic of maintaining a low profile remained firm.[29]

Perceived changes in the nature of the global order in the new millennium, and China's position within it, began to generate a rethink. The US-led intervention in the Middle East was seen as exacerbating dissatisfaction with US hegemony in the rest of the liberal world, starting a gradual shift away from unipolarity, and creating a "period of strategic opportunity" [*zhanlue jiyuqi*] for China.[30] Nevertheless, acutely aware that how others viewed China could do a lot to either help or hinder China's rise, it was deemed prudent to accompany attempts to exploit this period of opportunity with a concerted, orchestrated and oft repeated articulation of the peaceful nature and consequences of China's rise. The length of this period of opportunity was subsequently extended as other changes presaged important global power shifts that also played into China's hands. Chief among these was the global financial crisis – a crisis that was perceived in China to be of a form specific to deregulated Western neoliberal capitalism (albeit one with global consequences) that fundamentally undermined the legitimacy and authority of the Western liberal way.[31]

While Chinese policymakers and analysts might disagree over many things, they seem to agree that at some point in and around the global financial crisis, a significant power shift occurred. The US might be destined to remain the world's predominant actor for some time to come, but China has emerged as the most important of the rising powers, and "second amongst global equals" behind the US.[32] While Michael Yahuda noted a new emphasis on "striving for achievements" [*fenfa youwei*] from 2009,[33] Yan Xuetong argues that the 18th Party Congress and Xi Jinping's ascension to the apex of the Chinese power structure in 2012 marked a new era in China's global proactivity.[34] Quite simply, Xi was prepared to express openly what many people had been thinking for some time. Not only had China's self-confidence increased,[35] but its "comprehensive national power" had also risen to the extent that the Chinese people and the government no longer thought of China as a developing country, but instead as developed, a great power and maybe even a superpower.[36]

---

[29]Chen and Wang, "Lying Low No More?".

[30]Feng, "Rethinking China's Grand Strategy".

[31]Xu, "Rethinking China's Period of Strategic Opportunity".

[32]Zhang, "China and Liberal Hierarchies".

[33]Yahuda, "China's New Assertiveness".

[34]Yan, "From Keeping a Low Profile".

[35]Referred to in China as the "Three Self-confidences" [*sange zixin*]; Path or Road self-confidence [*lu zixin*], theory self-confidence [*lilun zixin*] and system self-confidence [*zhidu zixin*]. See Yuan, "China's Grand Strategy in the New Era" ["*Xin shiqi zhongguo de da zhanlüe*"].

[36]Yang, "Strategic Adjustment" ["*Zhan zai xin qidian*"].

To be sure, the commitment to rising peacefully in a way that does not fundamentally undermine the current order remains. China's leaders have also been explicit in arguing that China has "neither the ability nor the intent to challenge the United States".[37] Even so, it is hard to argue against the suggestion that since this change in perceptions (and leadership), there has been an increasing Chinese preparedness to articulate and defend its 'core interests' [*hexin liyi*], to push for change in some liberal governance institutions, and to challenge the supposed universal nature and applicability of many liberal norms.

Power and influence in multilateral institutions

The starting point for any assessment of China's views of the liberal order is a long-standing dissatisfaction with the distribution of power within the major institutions of global governance; particularly (but not only) of global economic governance. This generates two of the now relatively often repeated goals of Chinese diplomacy: "improving global economic governance, and promoting the democratization of international relations".[38] We should note here that democratisation in this Chinese context does not mean the participation of civil society groups and non-state actors in global governance as proposed by some cosmopolitan thinkers. Rather, it is a statist agenda, and refers to increasing the participation and power of those states that have been sidelined and/or underrepresented in international institutions, and reforming voting structures to reflect the new realities of the global distribution of power. In this respect, China's preferences can perhaps ironically be interpreted as more liberal than the uneven and unequal forms of representation that characterise many governance structures today.

Notwithstanding the considerable reform that has taken place in China to ensure membership and active participation in a whole range of governance institutions (including those that originated in Bretton Woods), there is a clear preference for the structure of some over others. The G20, for example, is seen in China as providing a platform for a new form of multilateralism – one that it can influence and one that is certainly more representative than the G7/8 (of which China is not a member). It is notable that China used its power as host of the 2016 Summit to invite more representatives from developing states than ever before. This "host diplomacy" was an articulation of the idea of China striving for globally inclusive multilateralism (where the interests of the developing world are heard and promoted) in contrast to the Western liberal states' commitment to maintaining their privileges in existing unrepresentative institutions; most notably the G7, but also the IMF and the World Bank.[39]

However, it is the United Nations that is considered to be "the most universal and representative intergovernmental organization in the world"[40] and has become what Rosemary Foot calls "China's venue of choice".[41] China's leaders have used the UN as a key venue to articulate China's preferred global order, and a preferred image of what type of great power China will be in that order. But this commitment to the UN is not just rhetorical. In recent years, China has become a major funder of UN activities through direct contributions

---

[37]Chen, "Relax".
[38]This example is taken from Lan, "Chinese President Proposes".
[39]Kirton, *China's G20 Leadership*.
[40]In the words of China's Permanent Representative, Liu Jieyi, on the official China pages of the UN website, http://www.china-un.org/eng/dbtxx/ambliu/
[41]Foot, "Doing Some Things".

(third behind the US and Japan) and via the China-UN Peace and Development Fund. It has also provided more peacekeeping troops than any of the other permanent members of the Security Council (SC).[42]

China is formally committed to supporting reform of the SC that brings about greater representation of developing countries, smaller states, and to provide a more even geographical spread of membership (particularly to include African membership).[43] Where this leaves the membership ambitions of larger or already developed Asian states like India and Japan (that do not always share Chinese ambitions) is another question, and it is fair to say that from India, for example, China looks more like a "principle opposition" to democratising UN reform than a proponent of it.[44] And it is also fair to say that China has been able to use the current unrepresentative nature of the SC to support its interests over the years.

Nevertheless, China has used its veto power less than any other SC permanent member.[45] But when it has been used, China, along with Russia, has been identified as a key obstacle to the emergence of the Responsibility to Protect (R2P) as a *functioning* principle underpinning the global (liberal) order. In truth, the Chinese position on intervention is not quite so absolute as it is sometimes depicted. But it is also true that China really has acted to block or moderate UN sanctions against countries like North Korea and Syria, and to try to prevent military and other forms of intervention that breach territorial integrity and sovereignty.[46]

So within this Chinese commitment to multilateralism, we see a key difference between China and the liberal West over what multilateralism should be for. Even though there is broad agreement that one goal should be to bring about peace, there is a rather fundamental disagreement on the limits that the principle of sovereignty should place on how that peace could and should be brought about. This is compounded by a suspicion that intervention is sometimes (at the very least) about securing other material and geopolitical aims and objectives of major Western powers.

Universalism and global (liberal) norms

This suspicion is also compounded by a belief that what is often proposed as universal norms are in fact the norms of a few. These norms – and also many of the theories of politics and international relations that are used to study them – are the result of the histories, experiences and cultures of a globally small number of now developed and relatively wealthy Western liberal societies. Whereas this might once have resulted in a Chinese rejection of these liberal norms as simply not applicable to China and other non-Western developing states, the emphasis now is on moderating or redefining them in light of China's experiences.

For example, Sarah Teitt shows how China's acceptance of a form of R2P (having initially rejected and condemned it) results from a significant redefinition of what R2P means (or should mean); one that rejects the use of force, and has to have not only both full UN

---

[42]Breslin and Ren, "China and Global Governance".

[43]Xue, *China as Permanent Member*.

[44]Bagchi, "China emerges as principal opposition".

[45]Though this does not tell the full story of China's influence, as the threat of a veto can lead to proposals either not being formally tabled, or modified and 'diluted' to get Chinese approval. There are also times when China does not have to use the veto because a Russian veto is enough to block the proposal. See Wuthnow, *Chinese Diplomacy*.

[46]This understanding is formalised in the Five Principles of Peaceful Coexistence first designed to find a solution to tensions in Sino-Indian relations. They are mutual respect for each other's territorial integrity and sovereignty, mutual non-aggression, mutual non-interference in each other's internal affairs, equality and mutual benefit, and peaceful co-existence.

agreement and supervision but also 'local' support.[47] Similarly, we have seen a redefinition of what constitutes 'human security' (in and for China) built on the specifics of the Chinese case. Chinese analysts note that when human security first came on the international agenda, there was considerable disagreement between countries like Canada and Norway that wanted to emphasise the importance of freedom from fear, and Japanese preferences for the dominance of freedom from need and crime.[48] Given that understandings of human security differ between even developed liberal countries, then clearly (so the argument goes) there will be even greater differences between developed and developing countries, and each country should develop their own national definitions. In the Chinese case, this not only results in the primacy of ensuring socioeconomic security rather than political freedoms, but also places the state front and centre in defining what China's human security challenges actually are, prioritising the most important of them, and developing strategies to effectively combat them.[49]

This process of the 'nationalisation' of norms has a defensive component. It helps explain Chinese differences from the dominant Western political tradition and why China *will not* become like Western liberal states. These newly 'sinified' norms should also provide the basis for judging and assessing China, rather than 'inappropriate' Western benchmarks of what constitutes a good and effective human rights regime, democracy, legal system and so on. This explains why the suffix "with Chinese characteristics" – which is in fact a prefix in Chinese [*you zhongguo tese de*] - has become so ubiquitous and added to, amongst others, concepts and terms such as legal system, democracy, human rights, justice, military modernisation, democracy and free market. The *China Daily* has even identified a unique and specific "sexual revolution with Chinese characteristics".[50]

Four important conclusions follow from this way of thinking. First, no matter how far China might move towards liberal principles on the international arena, this is not accompanied by any move towards liberalism at home. The "political system established by the constitution" has been established as one of China's "core interests";[51] an area of "bottom line thinking" [*dixian siwei*], that China is simply not prepared to compromise on or negotiate with others.[52] Under Xi Jinping, the room for debating alternatives to the current system has been considerably reduced, with even the relatively limited calls (in liberal terms) of Chinese constitutionalists to create a "law-based political order and institutionalization of fundamental relationships between the Party, the state and citizens" being silenced.[53] In short, the commitment to democracy outlined as a key component of the liberal order in the introduction to this special issue is lacking in China, with no signs that this will change any time soon.

Second, using the same term to refer to very different ideas can lead to considerable confusion about shared goals and ambitions. China can say that it believes in human rights and human security, but if what China means by these terms differs considerably from

---

[47]Teitt, "The Responsibility to Protect".
[48]Hu, "Human Security Concept" ["Ren de Anquan Gainian"] .
[49]For details, see Breslin, "Debating Human Security".
[50]http://www.chinadaily.com.cn/china/2013-05/14/content_16498056.htm
[51]State Council, *White Paper: China's Peaceful Development*.
[52]Yang, "Strategic Adjustment". The other core interests defined by the White Paper are "state sovereignty, national security, territorial integrity and national reunification, …. social stability, and the basic safeguards for ensuring sustainable economic and social development". State Council, *White Paper: China's Peaceful Development*.
[53]Creemers, "China's Constitutionalism Debate", 91.

other definitions, then the Chinese search for it might go in very different directions to what others want and do.

Third, if norms need to be nationally defined, this implies that sovereignty is the fundamental basis and starting point for locating norms (and arguably that it is the state that is responsible for interpreting them). In the State Council's *White Paper on Building Political Democracy in China,* this argument is more than implied, and sovereignty and independence emerge as the most basic and fundamental of all rights.[54] So if other (liberal) states try to impose their specific view of what they argue are universal norms, they are abrogating a more fundamental norm in the form of the sovereign right of others to develop their own nationalised definitions, priorities and policies.

Fourth, the logical conclusion of this way of thinking is that if China should develop its own distinctive (national) understanding, then so should everybody else. If this were followed through, then it would not lead to the replacement of Western norms (disguised as universal ones) with Chinese ones and the creation of a sinocentric normative world. Rather, it would lead to a form of normative and/or ideational anarchy and the rejection of universalism *per se.* What this might mean for China's abilities to externalise its preferences and interests is not wholly clear. But what is clear is that it would make it much harder for others to impose their preferences and interests as well – including Western proponents of a global liberal order. As Pan Wei put it in discussing China's challenge to dominant (neo)liberal economic norms: "The Chinese System does not boast itself as an alternative to the Western System. However, it weakens the argument for the exclusive legitimacy of the Western System."[55]

From norm reviser to norm maker?

While the claim not to be presenting a clear Chinese alternative might have been valid in the past, this position has now changed. There is now an official exhortation for China to increase its "institutional voice" [*zhiduxing huayuquan*] and promote China's "norms, protocols and definitions" as the basis for international interactions.[56] Chief among what Chinese diplomat Fu Ying calls "an array of newly developed diplomatic policies and guidelines put forward by China" is the idea of a "community of common destiny" [*minyun gongtong ti*] first enunciated by Xi in 2012.[57] At first sight, the emphasis on "cooperative security, common development, and political inclusiveness" does not sound particularly radical. Indeed, the promotion of the concept seems more about establishing a set of non-threatening and thus widely acceptable general goals and ambitions than articulating a clearly defined new set of (alternative) Chinese norms and principles. In this respect, its main utility is in establishing the idea that Xi and China are ready for a form of responsible global leadership, which might be seen as an updated version of "China's peaceful rise".

However, as Andrea Worden shows, it can have more specific uses as well. China has long been trying to establish its understanding and definitions as the basis for discussion at the UN Human Rights Council – if not for all, then at least for states that have some sort

---

[54]State Council, *White Paper: Building of Political Democracy.*
[55]Pan, "Western System".
[56]Kelly, "The CCP's Acceptance of Market Principles", 49.
[57]Fu, "China's Vision for the World". Fu uses the alternative translation of a 'Community of Shared Future' which is also in wide usage.

of shared suspicion of Western political and individualist preferences. In 2017, Worden argued that this process increased in intensity, with Chinese officials using the promotion of the "community of common destiny" as a way of trying to elevate the importance of developmental rights over political and civil (individual) rights (and also of the primacy of sovereignty over human rights concerns). This included issuing a statement on behalf of 140 countries on poverty reduction and human rights, and managing to insert the concept of "building a community of shared future" into two Council resolutions.[58]

Sonja Sceats, who has also investigated the promotion of Chinese alternative definitions of human rights, identifies attempts to establish a preferred Chinese understanding of "internet sovereignty" as a basis for emerging cyber security agreements as another area of Chinese proactivity. This is built on the understanding that maintaining social order and stability and state security is more important than guaranteeing freedom of speech and expression.[59] More tentatively, we might suggest that through the AIIB and the cumulative impact of its various overseas investment projects and financing/loan initiatives, China might be slowly emerging as a (if not the) leader in international development; not just through the provision of finance, but also in promoting a specific conception of what development is, or should be, that is stripped of 'good governance' democratising and liberalising elements. Finally, although still very much a minority endeavour, some Chinese intellectuals are also promoting the idea that a Chinese conception of how to build a harmonious world order (derived from China's past) might provide the basis for solving some of the more serious and apparently intractable conflicts between states in the future.[60]

The "China model" and the (neo)liberal economic order

It is in the economic realm, however, that a China challenge to global liberalism is most commonly identified. In some respects, this seems quite ironic, as the sources of this challenge are often initiatives that on the face of it seem to represent China's further integration into the existing order – perhaps even an embrace of liberal principles. For example, China has become an enthusiastic member and proponent of regional forms of governance to deal with transnational issues; one of the core components of the global liberal system defined by Alcaro.[61] Yet this first acceptance and subsequent promotion of multilateral cooperation and the extension of trade and aid relationships in Asia have been taken by some not as a move towards the status quo but instead as part of a Chinese strategy to replace the US as the dominant power (or even to eject it from the region).[62]

Similarly, as we have already noted, China's decision to take some form of multilateral leadership in the shape of the AIIB has been described as the first sign of a new Chinese challenge to the existing financial and broader economic order.[63] Yet, even if it does utilise some different criteria than existing financial institutions, the AIIB is still overwhelmingly a system-conforming institution that adds to and complements existing funders, rather than a revolutionary one that replaces them; and indeed it has actively sought to co-finance projects with the World Bank and the Asian Development Bank. As the US has not joined

---

[58] Worden, "China Pushes Human Rights".
[59] Sceats, "China's Cyber Diplomacy".
[60] For a review of debates over IR theory in China, see Noesselt, "Revisiting the Debate".
[61] Alcaro, "Liberal Order and its Contestations".
[62] Windybank, "The China Syndrome".
[63] Koike, "The AIIB".

this China-led project (unlike most other major Western economies), this has created a situation in which the AIIB is a challenge to the "US-led international structure" and at the same time "firmly situated within the existing international financial order".[64] Whilst this might sound contradictory, it is in fact an excellent example of the lack of clarity about what it is that China is actually thought to be challenging; the liberal order *per se*, or US leadership *within* that global order? If, as it seems, it is the latter, then we might see the AIIB as an example of China not so much challenging the West as beating the West by "playing by the rules that Westerners themselves have formulated".[65]

The creation of new institutions is just one of the challenges that China has been said to present to the existing liberal economic order. Another is the extent to which China's 'model' of strong state capitalism might lure others away from more liberal paths and programmes; particularly given the perceived failure of neoliberal models and forms during and after the global financial crisis. Identifying what exactly the China model of development is, and why it has been successful, is a far from easy task. But even John Williamson, who is often identified as the architect of the free market 'Washington Consensus', has reflected on how the Chinese experience has revalidated the efficacy of the strong state and interventionist form of capitalism as a model for other developing countries to follow, vis-à-vis the neoliberal alternative that he previously championed.[66] Even if other developing countries might not simply be able to copy all that China has done themselves, China's success in generating economic growth stands as an example of what can be done if you follow your own path rather than follow neoliberal economic prescriptions.

We might also add to this list the idea that China is free riding on liberal global economy as US President Barack Obama stated in 2014.[67] This in part refers to the way that the Chinese state supports Chinese economic actors' overseas activities while not allowing the same access to the Chinese economy that others grant to China. As a result, the nature of the liberal order is in some ways diluted by the toleration of a major illiberal (in economic terms here) actor within it. Hence the reluctance in the US and parts of Europe to grant China the full market economy status in the WTO that China's leaders assumed it would be given in December 2016, 15 years after entry. It also refers to China's condemnation of US security activity overseas, even when China gains economically from this action, as Obama claimed had been the case in Iraq.

Chinese financial power

The final addition to this list of challenges is the consequences of the spread of Chinese financial and other economic flows. While this might sound like repeating concerns about the development of the AIIB (and the BRICS New Development Bank), here the focus is a much broader one, and relates to the totality of Chinese loans, investment projects and other financial interactions funded by the Chinese state, or undertaken by Chinese commercial actors.[68] We can further break this area of concern into three (interrelated) areas.

The first is the way that this reinforces the position of illiberal Chinese state enterprises as key actors in the global economy, and potentially also reinforces the attraction of less

---

[64]Wan, *The Asian Infrastructure Investment Bank*, 58.
[65]Hu, "A Competitive Edge", 27.
[66]Williamson, "The Impact of the Financial Crisis".
[67]See Feng, "Obama's Free Rider Comments".

than neoliberal forms of capitalism. The second is the potential for a reorientation of current economic geographies and a recentring towards China, based on Chinese investment and trade priorities. The argument is that this might not just have economic consequences (for example, in terms of the distribution of key resources), but because of increased reliance on China, make other countries less likely to challenge China on other issue areas as well (for example, on Chinese territorial claims). The way in which the Rodrigo Duterte publically announced the Philippines' realignment away from the US and towards China in October 2016 seems to provide a very pertinent example of such a process.[69] Whether similar changes will come about as China moves to implement its One Belt, One Road initiative remains to be seen.

Third, we noted above the ideational alternative that China presents for other developing countries. More important, it provides a hard material economic alternative as well. For countries like North Korea and Zimbabwe, this might take the form of an alternative to isolation. For others, it means an alternative to either the existing international financial organisations, or the existing major Western economies. It is not quite the case that international economic contacts with China, including development projects, come with no political or economic conditions attached. Not recognising Taiwan remains a very significant condition and, increasingly, Chinese funders seem to want at least some sort of guarantee that their money simply will not just disappear. Nevertheless, what China is not (the West) and what it does not do (in terms of imposing conditionalities) can make it an attractive economic partner for some – particularly in a post global crisis economy that is not exactly awash with investment capital from the traditional heartlands of the global liberal economy. One consequence is that attempts to punish or undermine 'rogue states' and to try to lever others into adopting liberalising and/or democratising agendas becomes considerably more difficult.

The global and the regional

The example of the consequences of Chinese investment shows that any challenge might emerge from the bottom up, rather than (just) from changes to governance forms and norms at the global level (from the top down). And it is important to note that China's leaders have deliberately developed a differential set of strategies for dealing with different types of international actors in different parts of the world.

Most often, a distinction is made between big powers as the key [*guanjian*], the periphery (the neighbourhood) as the priority [*shouyao*], and developing countries as the foundation [*jichu*].[70] As Yuan Peng points out, one of the strategic problems that China faces is that the US is a major actor in both of the first two categories – it is both the most important big power and also a key actor in China's neighbourhood.[71] And while China might not have the power or the desire to challenge the US or the liberal order at the global level, the same is not true in China's backyard. Power and politics in southeast Asia are dealt with in detail in this special issue by Richard Stubbs,[72] but it is still worth noting here China's

---

[68]Often with support from the state in the form of financial backing, diplomatic initiatives to secure a political foundation for economic interactions, and so on. See Babic *et al.*, 'States vs Corporations', Figure 5.

[69]"Duterte: Philippines is Separating from US and Realigning with China", *The Guardian*, 20 October 2016, https://www.theguardian.com/world/2016/oct/20/china-philippines-resume-dialogue-south-china-sea-dispute.

[70]And sometimes also "multilateralism as the stage [*wutai*], and public diplomacy as the complement [*buchong*]".

commitment to defending its 'core interests' in the South China Sea, the above noted plan to establish strategic economic interactions along the Belt and Road, and China's promotion of the Regional Comprehensive Economic Partnership plan in direct opposition to the Trans Pacific Partnership at one time favoured by the US.

China has 'bottom up' influence in other regions as well. Yu Zhengliang distinguishes between different international environments (and therefore the need for different strategies), in four mega zones; to China's north, south, east and west.[73] One of the crucial determinants of what China can (and already is) doing in each is the extent of Western (and in particular American) influence and commitment. In the North, this suggests the importance of forging a deeper alliance with Russia to pursue common interests. In the East (very broadly defined), the decline of US power in Latin America has created an opportunity for China to increase its economic influence, while New Zealand and Australia are somewhat caught between Chinese (economic) and US (security) initiatives. In the West:

> China's strategic expansion of the West is the establishment of strategic fulcrums in the East African continent (Kenya, Tanzania and Mozambique) and the Seychelles, connecting the Indian Ocean and the whole of Africa, especially in sub-Saharan Africa. At present [2012], the United States and Europe are in crisis, weakening their influence on Africa, and China-Africa cooperation is outstanding and the foundation is solid. China is in a very favourable strategic opportunity in Africa.[74]

Conclusions

Yu's analysis of China's opportunities in Africa reminds us that power transitions are not just about the choices, actions and preferences of those that are rising; what happens in and to the existing (or declining) predominant powers is important too. The consequences of regime change in Iraq and Libya have not exactly enhanced arguments for liberal interventionism, the global financial crisis has undermined the logic of (neo)liberal prescriptions for economic progress,[75] and new security challenges have highlighted tensions between the provision and guarantee of personal freedoms, on the one hand, and protecting and defending (both individuals or states), on the other. And after the election of President Donald Trump, there seems to be a vacancy for a new global leader in at least some issue areas (like the environment).

As a result, we might expect there to be relatively fertile ground for the promotion of an alternative set of norms and policy initiatives that challenge existing dominant paradigms; and to some extent that has been the case. This is especially true for those looking for an economic alternative (or perhaps more often, supplement) to dealing with Europe, North America, and the existing international financial institutions. It is also true for those who want to be left to organise their own political systems as they see fit, free from outside influence and interference.

---

[71]Yuan, "Reflections on the Great Epoch" ["*Guanyu da shidai yu da zhanlüe*"], 14.
[72]Stubbs, "Order and Contestation in the Asia-Pacific Region".
[73]Yu, "Reflections on China's Grand Strategy" ["*Guanyu zhongguo da zhanlüe de sikao*"] .
[74]*Ibid.*, 100.
[75]Here, it is important to make a distinction between neoliberalism as one specific form of capitalism (that China's rise has indeed challenged), and capitalism in general (which, it can be argued, China's rise actually reinforces by legitimising its strong state incarnation).

In some areas, China is prepared to provide that alternative and leadership. Having emerged from the era of keeping a low profile, Chinese actors have made it clear that they want a greater voice in the international order, and also greater respect for what China has done. Under Xi Jinping, the country has gained greater self-confidence in itself, and a greater preparedness to articulate Chinese preferences and concepts as the basis for some governance discussions and forms. As Xi put it at the 19th Party Congress in October 2017, the country was entering a new era that would see it "moving closer to the centre of global politics" with China now prepared and able to make "greater contributions to mankind".[76] While the specifics of what a community of common destiny might actually entail are not always clear, it is increasingly being touted in China as the foundation of a new Chinese "agenda setting" strategy that opposes "injustice, inequality, hegemonism, power politics and neo-interventionism".[77]

The rejection of democracy and liberal political structures as relevant to China is an example of this internal self-confidence; and no matter what China has done so far, the nature of the domestic political order remains the key reason why some will simply never be convinced about what it will do in the future. China's conviction that respecting sovereignty is more important than R2P (as defined and understood in the liberal world) and that economic development is a more important human right than political and civil individual rights are both examples of a Chinese normative contribution to global politics; and both also point to key cleavages between a rising China and the supporters of a more liberal order that is unlikely to shrink in the future.

In other policy domains, the China challenge has been much less clear, with instead China seeking to "play a responsible role (fostered by multilateralism) on the world stage"; partly because being a more status quo actor supports Chinese interests in some areas, and also partly as a means of "gaining legitimacy and appearing trustworthy" as a putative global leader.[78] What this suggests is a rather patchy set of different types of Chinese relationships with the liberal global order in different policy areas depending on the extent of Chinese satisfaction with the status quo, the identification of a clear Chinese policy (or normative) alternative, and the likelihood of Chinese preferences gaining "followership" from others.

This patchiness is in itself a reflection of the partial and ongoing nature of the power transition from unipolarity to something else, and uncertainty over what that something else might be. We have yet to see the sort of "ordering moment" that Kupchan reminds us are typically established through "postwar settlements"[79] – and hopefully we will not have one. Nor hopefully will we see the sort of victory by one side (and set of beliefs) over the other that marked the end of the Cold War and the bipolar global order.

What this suggests is an immediate future at least where China is an important – but far from the only – actor in the formation of fluid issue-specific sets of alliances and coalitions. One where China might ally with European powers to establish new parallel and largely system-conforming financial institutions like the AIIB, but at the same time be on the opposite side of the debate with a different set of allies when it comes to establishing basic conceptions of human rights. Or where China and India might come together to

---

[76]Xi, "Secure a Decisive Victory".

[77]Neo-interventionism refers to the arguments that are put forward to justify intervention rather than just the act of intervention itself. Hua, "China takes strides" ["Zhongguo Dabu Zouxiang"].

[78]Caffarena, "Diversity Management", 9 and 10.

[79]Kupchan, Nobody's World, 182.

express a common dissatisfaction with the distribution of power in global institutions, but hold very different positions when it comes to the composition of security relations and alliances in Asia; or even for that matter when it comes to the question of whether institutional reform should see India gain a seat as a permanent member of the UN SC. The still rather common polarisation of thinking of China as being either a status quo power or a revisionist one misses the point; it misses the point about what China's leaders want and their (differential) ability to get it. And it also misses the point about the nature of the post-unipolar global order itself.

Acknowledgement

This article emerges from research funded by a Leverhulme Major Research Fellowship on "China risen? What is global power (and in what ways does China have it)?" and the author gratefully acknowledges the support of the Leverhulme Trust.

References

Alcaro, R. "The Liberal Order and Its Contestations. A Conceptual Framework". *The International Spectator* 53, no. 1 (2018): https://doi.org/10.1080/03932729.2018.1397878
Allison, G. *Destined for War: Can America and China Escape Thucydides's Trap?* New York: Houghton Mifflin, 2017.
Babic, M., J. Fichtner and E. M. Heemskerk. "States versus Corporations: Rethinking the Power of Business in International Politics". *The International Spectator* 52, no. 4 (2017).
Bagchi, I. "China emerges as principal opposition to UNSC reforms". *Times of India*, 1 August 2015. http://timesofindia.indiatimes.com/india/China-emerges-as-principal-opposition-to-UNSC-reforms/articleshow/48303032.cms.
Breslin, S. "Understanding China's Regional Rise: Interpretations, Identities and Implications". *International Affairs* 85, no. 4 (2009): 779–813.
Breslin, S. "Debating Human Security in China: Towards Discursive Power?" *Journal of Contemporary Asia* 45, no. 2 (2015): 243–65.
Breslin, S., and Ren Xiao. "China and Global Governance". In *International Organization and Global Governance*, edited by T. Weiss and R. Wilkinson. Abingdon: Routledge, forthcoming 2018.
Broomfield, E. "Perceptions of Danger: The China Threat Theory". *Journal of Contemporary China* 12, no. 35 (2003): 265–84.
Caffarena, A. "Diversity Management in World Politics: Reformist China and the Future of the (Liberal) Order". *The International Spectator* 52, no. 3: 1-17.
Chang, G. *The Coming Collapse of China*. New York: Random House, 2001.
Chen, D. "Relax, China Won't Challenge US Hegemony". *The Diplomat*, 14 January 2015. http://thediplomat.com/2015/01/relax-china-wont-challenge-us-hegemony.
Chen, D., and J. Wang. "Lying Low No More? China's New Thinking on the Tao Guang Yang Hui Strategy". *China: An International Journal* 9, no. 2 (2011): 195–216.
Christensen, T. *The China Challenge: Shaping the Choices of a Rising China*. New York: Norton, 2015.
Creemers, R. "China's Constitutionalism Debate: Content, Context and Implications". *The China Journal*, 74 (2015): 91–109.
Des Forges, R., and X. Luo. "China as a Non-Hegemonic Superpower? The Uses of History among the 'China Can Say No' Writers and their Critics". *Critical Asian Studies* 33, no. 4 (2001): 483–507.

Etzioni, A. "The Asian Infrastructure Investment Bank: A Case Study of Multifaceted Containment". *Asian Perspective* 40, no. 2 (2016): 173–96.

Feng, B. "Obama's Free Rider Comment Draws Chinese Criticism". *New York Times*, 13 August 2014, https://sinosphere.blogs.nytimes.com/2014/08/13/obamas-free-rider-comment-draws-chinese-criticism/?partner=rss&emc=rss&smid=tw-nytimesworld.

Feng, Z. "Rethinking China's Grand Strategy: Beijing's Evolving National Interests and Strategic Ideas in the Reform Era". *International Politics* 49, no. 3 (2012): 18–345.

Foot, R. "'Doing some things' in the Xi Jinping Era: The United Nations as China's Venue of Choice". *International Affairs* 50, no. 9 (2014): 1085–100.

Freeman, C., and Yuan W. *China's Exchange Rate Politics: Decoding the Cleavage between the Chinese Ministry of Commerce and the People's Bank of China*. Washington DC: Centre for Strategic and International Studies, 2011. https://csis-prod.s3.amazonaws.com/s3fs-public/legacy_files/files/publication/110615_Freeman_ChinaExchangeRatePolitics_Web.pdf.

Fu Y. "China's Vision for the World: A Community of Shared Future". *The Diplomat*, 22 June 2017. https://thediplomat.com/2017/06/chinas-vision-for-the-world-a-community-of-shared-future/

Hilton, I. "China Emerges as Global Climate Leader in the Wake of Trump's Triumph". *The Guardian*, 22 November 2016.

Hornby, L. "Wu Jianmin: China's most influential 'dove' dies in car crash". *Financial Times*, 18 June 2016.

Hu, X. "A Competitive Edge". *Chinese Security* 4, no. 3 (2008): 26–7.

Hu Y. "Human Security Concept, Controversy and Practice" ["Ren de Anquan Gainian, Zhengyi ji Shijian"]. *Human Rights [Renquan]* no. 2 (2011): 17–9.

Hu Y. "China Takes Strides towards the World's Centre Stage" ["Zhongguo Dabu Zouxiang Shijie Wutai Zhongyang"]. *People's Daily Overseas Edition*, 5 January 2017. http://cpc.people.com.cn/pinglun/n1/2017/0105/c78779-29000064.html

Huang Z., and Tang H. "Why China is Curbing Outbound Direct Investment". *Peterson Institute China Economic Watch*, 22 August 2017. https://piie.com/blogs/china-economic-watch/why-china-curbing-outbound-direct-investment

International Crisis Group. *Stirring up the South China Sea (I)*, Asia Report no. 223. Brussels: International Crisis Group, 23 April 2012. http://www.crisisgroup.org/~/media/Files/asia/north-east-asia/223-stirring-up-the-south-china-sea-i.pdf

Irvine, R. *Forecasting China's Future: Dominance Or Collapse?*. London: Routledge, 2016.

Jacques, M. *When China Rules the World*. London: Penguin, 2009.

Jin, Z. *The Chinese Delegation at the 1944 Bretton Woods Conference: Reflections for 2015*. London: Official Monetary and Financial Institutions Forum, 2015. https://www.omfif.org/media/1067515/chinese-reflections-on-bretton-woods-by-jin-zhongxia.pdf.

Kang, D. "Getting Asia Wrong: The Need For New Analytical Frameworks". *International Security* 27, no. 4 (2003): 57–85.

Kelly, D. "The CCP's Acceptance of Market Principles". In *State and Market in Contemporary China: Toward the 13th Five Year Plan*, edited by S. Kennedy: 48–50. Lanham: Roman and Littlefield, 2016.

Kirton, J. *China's G20 Leadership*. London: Routledge, 2016.

Koike, Y. "The AIIB key to Beijing's new economic order". *The Japan Times*, 1 June 2015. http://www.japantimes.co.jp/opinion/2015/06/01/commentary/japan-commentary/the-aiib-key-to-beijings-new-economic-order/#.V8XznvkrLIV.

Kupchan, C. *No One's World: The West, the Rising Rest, and the Coming Global Turn*. New York: Oxford University Press, 2012.

Lai, H., and Kang S. "Domestic Bureaucratic Politics and Chinese Foreign Policy". *Journal of Contemporary China* 23, no. 86 (2014): 294–313.

Li, M., and Lee D. "Local Liberalism: China's Provincial Approaches to Relations with Southeast Asia". *Journal of Contemporary China* 23, no. 86 (2014): 275–93.

Mearsheimer, J. "China's Unpeaceful Rise". *Current History* 105, no. 690 (2006): 160–2.

Muller, W. "China: An Illiberal, Non-Western State in a Western-Centric, Liberal Order?" *Baltic Yearbook of International Law* 15, no. 1 (2016): 216–37.

Noesselt, N. "Revisiting the Debate on Constructing a Theory of International Relations with Chinese Characteristics". *The China Quarterly*, no. 222 (2015): 430–48.

Overholt, W. *The Rise Of China: How Economic Reform Is Creating A New Superpower*. New York: W.W. Norton, 1993.

Pan, C. *Knowledge, Desire and Power in Global Politics: Western Representations of China's Rise*. Cheltenham: Edward Elgar, 2012.

Pan W. *Western System Versus Chinese System*, China Policy Institute Briefing Series no. 61. Nottingham: University of Nottingham, 2010. http://www.nottingham.ac.uk/cpi/documents/ briefings/briefing-61-chinese-western-system.pdf.

Pei, M. *China's Trapped Transition: The Limits of Developmental Autocracy*. Cambridge MA: Harvard University Press, 2006.

Renard, T. *The Asian Infrastructure Investment Bank (AIIB): China's new multilateralism and the erosion of the West*, Egmont Security Policy Brief No. 63. Brussels: Egmont Royal Institute for International Relations, 2015. http://aei.pitt.edu/64789/1/SPB63-Renard.pdf.

Roy, D. "Hegemon on the Horizon: China's Threat to East Asian Security". *International Security* 19, no. 1 (1994): 149–68.

Sceats, S. "China's Cyber Diplomacy: a Taste of Law to Come". *The Diplomat*, 14 January 2015. http:// thediplomat.com/2015/01/chinas-cyber-diplomacy-a-taste-of-law-to-come.

State Council. *White Paper: China's Peaceful Development*. Beijing: Information Office of the State Council, 2011.

State Council. *White Paper: Building of Political Democracy in China*. Beijing: Information Office of the State Council, 2005.

Stubbs, R. Order and Contestation in the Asia-Pacific Region: Liberal vs Developmental/ Non-interventionist Approaches. *The International Spectator* 53, no. 1 (2018) doi: 10.1080/03932729. 2018.1402581.

Teitt, S. "The Responsibility to Protect and China's Peacekeeping Policy". *International Peacekeeping* 18, no. 3 (2011): 298–312.

Wan, M. *The Asian Infrastructure Investment Bank: The Construction of Power and the Struggle for the East Asian International Order*. Basingstoke: Palgrave, 2016.

Williamson, J. "The impact of the financial crisis on development thinking". Max Fry Annual Lecture, University of Birmingham, 13 October 2011. http://www.iie.com/publications/papers/ williamson20101013.pdf

Windybank, S. "The China syndrome". *Policy* 21, no. 2 (2008): 28–33.

Worden, A. "China Pushes 'Human Rights With Chinese Characteristics' at the UN". *China Change*, 9 October 2017. https://chinachange.org/2017/10/09/china-pushes-human-rights-with-chinese-characteristics-at-the-un

Wuthnow, J. *Chinese Diplomacy and the UN Security Council: Beyond the Veto*. London: Routledge, 2013.

Xi J. "Secure a Decisive Victory in Building a Moderately Prosperous Society in All Respects and Strive for the Great Success of Socialism with Chinese Characteristics for a New Era". Speech to the 19th National Congress of the Communist Party of China, 18 October 2017. http://news.xinhuanet. com/english/special/2017-11/03/c_136725942.htm

Xi J. "President Xi's Speech to Davos in Full". World Economic Forum, 17 January 2017. https://www. weforum.org/agenda/2017/01/full-text-of-xi-jinping-keynote-at-the-world-economic-forum.

Xinhua. "Chinese President Proposes Closer, more solid BRICS Partnership". *Global Times*, 16 July 2014. http://www.globaltimes.cn/content/870869.shtml.

Xu Jian. "Rethinking China's Period of Strategic Opportunity". *China International Studies*, March/ April 2014: 51-70. http://www.ciis.org.cn/english/2014-05/28/content_6942258.htm

Xu Jin. "Debates in IR Academia and China's Policy Adjustments". *Chinese Journal of International Politics* 9, no. 4 (2016): 459–85.

Xue, L. *China as Permanent Member of the United Nations Security Council*, International Policy Analysis. Bonn: Friedrich Ebert Stiftung, April 2014. http://library.fes.de/pdf-files/iez/10740.pdf.

Yahuda, M. "China's New Assertiveness in the South China Sea". *Journal of Contemporary China* 22, no. 81 (2013): 446–59.

Yan, X. "From Keeping a Low Profile to Striving for Achievement". *The Chinese Journal of International Politics* 7, no. 2 (2014): 153–84.

Yang J. "Strategic Adjustment of China's Diplomacy at a New Starting Point ["Zhan zai xin qidian de zhongguo waijiao zhanlue tiaozheng"]. *Global Review* [*Guoji Zhanwang*] no. 1 (2014): 1-13.

Yu Z. "Reflections on China's Grand Strategy" ["Guanyu zhongguo da zhanlüe de sikao"]. *Research on Mao Zedong Deng Xiaoping Theory* [Mao Zedong Deng Xiaoping Lilun Yanjiu] no. 5 (2012): 95-101.

Yuan P. "Reflections on the Great Epoch and Grand Strategy: The Ten Pairs of Relationships that China Needs to Deal with in the New Period ["Guanyu da shidai yu da zhanlüe de sikao - jian lun xin shiqi zhongguo waijiao xuyao chuli de shi da guanxi"]. *Socialism and the Contemporary World* [*Dangdai Shijie yu Shehuizhuyi*] no. 4 (2012): 11-5.

Yuan P. "China's Grand Strategy in the New Era: A Strategic Interpretation of the Report to the 18th Party Congress [Xin shiqi zhongguo de da zhanlüe: Duì "shiba da" baogao de zhanlüa jiada"]. *Contemporary International Relations* [*Xiandai Guoji Guanxi*], no. 5 (2013): 1-9.

Zhang, Y. "China and Liberal Hierarchies in Global International Society: Power and Negotiation for Normative Change". *International Affairs* 92, no. 4 (2016): 795–816.

Zhao H. "The Myth of China's Overseas Energy Investment". *East Asia Forum*, 4 March 2015. http://www.eastasiaforum.org/2015/03/04/the-myth-of-chinas-overseas-energy-investment.

Russia's Neorevisionist Challenge to the Liberal International Order

Tatiana Romanova

ABSTRACT

A conventional opinion is that Russia is trying to destroy the liberal international order. Russia indeed defies it, but also justifies its foreign policy with the liberal order's normative frameworks and reproaches the West for not standing up to these norms. Moreover, Moscow does not present any alternative vision. Russia complains about the internal contradictions of the liberal order: sovereignty vs. intervention, pluralism vs. universality, US hegemony vs. equality and democracy, although it also exploits these contradictions. In fact Russia demands an adjustment of the liberal order rather than its eradication and should, therefore, be classified as a neorevisionist power. Two elements underlie Russia's at times aggressive foreign policy conduct. The first one, its feeling of being ill-accommodated in the present order, predefines the direction of the policy. The second, the prioritisation of foreign policy over domestic reforms, explains the intensity of Russian discontent and its occasional aggressive manifestations. Russia's domestic consensus regarding its foreign policy, including views on the liberal international order, facilitates this aggressiveness. Three policy conclusions can be drawn: acknowledging that Russia uses the inherent contradictions of the liberal international order opens up possibilities for dialogue and an eventual overcoming of the crisis; the survival and strengthening of the *liberal* order depends on its embrace of all major players, including Russia, and hence, the need for some adjustments to the order itself; and finally such adjustments presuppose Russia's readiness to shoulder responsibility for the (reformed) liberal international order.

Accounts of the current state and future developments of the liberal international order are contradictory. Some argue that despite current difficulties it will survive and thrive;[1] others insist that challenges are insurmountable.[2] What is 'international' and 'liberal' is also frequently challenged.[3] The definitions of the liberal international order and its components

---

[1] Ikenberry, "Future of Liberal World Order: Internationalism" and "Future of Liberal World Order"; Kortunov, *Neizbezhnost strannogo mira* [*Inevitability of a Strange World*]; Sorensen, *Liberal world order in crisis*.
[2] See, for example, the interview with Henry Kissinger in Goldberg, "World Chaos and World Order".
[3] Kundnani, *What is Liberal International Order*; Dunne and Flockhart, *Liberal World Orders*.

provided in the Introduction by Riccardo Alcaro are used in this article to discuss the case of Russia.[4]

Recently, Russia has mostly been seen as a challenger of the international order, as an actor that "wants to do away with many of [its] basic concepts" and return to *Realpolitik*.[5] Russia's blusterous foreign policy (especially in Ukraine but also Syria) provides evidence for these claims. As a result, Russia has turned into "a symbol of an anti-liberal trend"[6] whereas the "Russian threat" is used as an "instrument of identification and a means to fight against any dissent" in the West.[7] Talks about a new Cold War are illustrative of this established belief. Many Russian practitioners and analysts argue that the liberal order has already been dismantled as a result of the rise of new powers and global processes, which make the "Western-patterned world" irrelevant,[8] but also as a result of challenges in the West itself (economic problems, immigration, terrorist threats).[9]

A closer look reveals that Russia is intent on exposing three well documented contradictions of the liberal order.[10] The first is the collision between sovereignty (particularly non-intervention in internal affairs) and the responsibility to protect (R2P), which posits human rights as supreme. The R2P concept emerged after the end of the Cold War.[11] Since then, some have argued for 'conditional sovereignty' because sovereignty is conceived of not only as a given right of a state but also as an obligation of that state to ensure protection of the basic human rights of its population.[12] Others have insisted on neoliberal pluralism or discussed resilience as a way of getting around the interventionist zeal implicit in the R2P norm while promoting domestic change via other means.[13] The second contradiction is linked to the first; it is between plurality, national specificity, including various concepts of democracy,[14] on the one hand, and universality and the eventual 'end of history',[15] on the other. The final contradiction juxtaposes American hegemony, which made the liberal international order viable, with the equality of all states and democracy in international relations,[16] meaning taking views of the majority into account when working out an international solution. In fact, the hegemon itself contradicts the very core of the *liberal* ideology. Moreover, to cite John Ikenberry, "the struggle today is about ... who sits at the table and over how to reorganize the platforms of authority".[17] These three contradictions are the crux of the difference between "liberalism of imposition" and "liberalism of restraint";[18] they provide the first theoretical reference point for this article.

The second theoretical reference point is the concept of neorevisionism. While revisionism would describe Russian efforts to revise key rules and norms of the international system,

---

[4]Alcaro, "Liberal Order and its Contestations".
[5]Liik, *What does Russia want?* See also Kagan, *Twilight of liberal world order*.
[6]Miller and Lukyanov, *Sderzhannost vmesto naporistosti* [*Restraint instead of Assertiveness*], 5.
[7]*Ibid.*, 7.
[8]Lavrov, *Vystuplenie na Primakov Reading Forum* [*Speech at the Primakov Reading Forum*]; Russian Federation, *Concept of Foreign Policy*; see also Karaganov, "Buduschii miroporyadok" ["The Future World Order"].
[9]Miller and Lukyanov, *Sderzhannost vmesto naporistosti* [*Restraint instead of Assertiveness*]; Gromyko, "Speech at 'Studying EU-Russian Relations'" conference.
[10]See Sorensen, *Liberal world order in crisis*; Ikenberry, "Future of Liberal World Order: Internationalism".
[11]International Commission on Intervention and State Sovereignty, *The Responsibility to Protect.*
[12]Haass, "World Order: What Can be Done?".
[13]For debates, see Chandler, "International State-building"; and Joseph, "Resilience as embedded neoliberalism".
[14]Well known in the West, but now forgotten in Russian official discourse, the concept of 'sovereign democracy' (developed by Vladislav Surkov) falls into this category.
[15]Fukuyama, *The End of History.*
[16]Alcaro, "Liberal Order and its Contestations".
[17]Ikenberry, "Future of Liberal World Order", 452.
[18]Sorensen, *Liberal world order in crisis.*

neorevisionism suggests that Russia "does not repudiate the present balance in international order, but seeks to create what it considers to be a more comprehensive and equal system"[19] in order to upgrade Moscow's status in it. This thesis is developed by demonstrating that Russia seeks to transform the global order so that it accommodates its views and concerns better, but does not attempt to replace it with a completely new set of rules.

Discourse analysis of the 2016 Russian Foreign Policy Concept[20] and official speeches of President Vladimir Putin and Minister of Foreign Affairs Sergei Lavrov reveal that Russia exploits the internal contradictions of the liberal order. Moscow does not voice any alternative, however. Rather it justifies its actions with the order's normative frameworks, reproaches the West for non-consistency in observing the letter of international law and seeks to secure for itself a position among those that have the right to interpret these norms on a par with the US / the West.

Finally, the article opens the black box of Russia to illustrate the sources of this Russian attitude, drawing on some provisions of neoclassical realism.[21] The latter informs us that the foreign policy of an actor depends on its interests, but that these interests result from elite perceptions and a particular constellation of various domestic groups. The established perception in Russia that the current order is disadvantageous for the country determines its challenge to it. The vehement critique of the current functioning of the global order and confrontation with the West also serves as an excuse for postponing domestic reforms and for the rise of a new – patriotic – contract between the state and its citizens. Russia's choice of an active foreign policy rather than domestic reforms increases the intensity of its criticism of the global order. The article also reveals a broad consensus on current foreign policy in Russia, documented with various opinion polls and statistical data.

In the following, first the discourse of Russia on the 'normative frameworks' of the liberal international order and on US hegemony (as described in the Introduction[22]) is reviewed through the prism of the three aforementioned contradictions and neorevisionism. The international and domestic sources of Russia's neorevisionist attitude towards the liberal order are then addressed and related domestic debates examined. The conclusion is policy-oriented. First, understanding Russia's critique through the prism of the three contradictions and neorevisionism opens up space for negotiations and eventual concessions. Second, for the international order to remain liberal, it has to integrate Russia (and other major players) into it, so that it provides a context for their internal reforms. Third, Moscow has to reciprocate with a more responsible attitude toward the liberal order. The sequence of the last two steps remains a point for further discussion and research.

Russia and the components of the liberal international order

The Introduction to this special issue identifies five normative frameworks in the liberal international order: internationalism; institutionalism; regionalism; interdependence and democracy. It also identifies American hegemony as an essential component of the order.

---

[19]Sakwa, "'International' in Russian identity formation", 449. See, by the same author, "Russia and Europe: Whose Society?" and "Dualism at Home and Abroad".

[20]Russian Federation, *Concept of the Foreign Policy*. This article does not examine the evolution of Russian foreign policy concepts closely as views have been mostly stable since 2000 (Frear and Mazepus, *New Turn or More of Same?*). For changes and fine-tuning of Russian foreign policy concepts since 1992, see Romanova, "Russia: Change or Continuity?".

[21]Lobell *et al., Neoclassical Realism, and Foreign Policy*.

[22]Alcaro, "Liberal Order and its Contestations".

Russia's current Foreign Policy Concept (FPC) as well as official speeches demonstrate that these notions are present in the official Russian discourse, but are affected by the three contradictions mentioned above.

Internationalism presupposes that states preserve their sovereignty and at the same time recognise that they are members of the international society. Hence, they are required to acquiesce in the possibility of intervening to defend human rights and other values.[23] Russia's position on the issue of sovereignty is clear and uncompromising. The FPC's first priority is ensuring "national sovereignty". It recognises the need to cooperate to mitigate economic and environmental problems, counter threats of terrorism, cyber attacks and other challenges, and to ensure non-proliferation. International rule of law is interpreted as serving to maintain "intended peaceful and fruitful cooperation among States". Yet the need to respect sovereignty is emphasised. A close reading reveals that Russia does not recognise any responsibility to protect, and interprets it as a "pretext" to challenge "sovereign equality" unless the intervention is approved by the United Nations Security Council as the only international body with legitimate authority on the matter.[24] This provision is much stronger in this FPC than in earlier concepts. However, there is a very important exception to this rule: the rights of "compatriots", that is ethnic Russian and Russian-speaking people, whose rights Russia promises to protect. The argument about protection of their rights was used to intervene on the side of the breakaway republics of South Ossetia and Abkhazia in 2008 and when recognising the results of the referendum on session in Crimea in 2014. Hence both the first and the third contradictions of the liberal order can be identified here.

Institutionalism is defined in this special issue as being about rules and norms. Here again, the FPC demonstrates that Russia supports multilateral cooperation in various fields. It argues for "collective approaches to international economic governance and regulation" and climate change mitigation. But most ardently Russia traditionally promotes the use of international organisations with a particular emphasis on the UN, where Moscow holds veto power in the Security Council. The UN, according to the FPC, "should maintain its central role in regulating international relations and coordinating world politics in the 21 century, as it has proven to have no alternative and possesses international legitimacy". Institutionalism for Russia is, therefore, a way to challenge US hegemony in the global order and provides venues in which to exert a similar influence (frequently also veto power). On security, Russia demands "solid and equal security for each and every member of the global community". It reveals Russia's deep insecurity *vis-à-vis* the unilateral actions of Western countries, interventions or crisis management operations without an explicit consent of non-Western players. It also demonstrates a deeper Russian insecurity with regard to arrangements in Europe / the West that exclude Russia. It is for this reason that in 2008 Dmitry Medvedev suggested a new security treaty in Europe, based on "equal and indivisible security" for all states.[25]

The FPC embraces *regionalism* as an established norm. Examination of geographic priorities for Russian foreign policy starts with a long discussion of the Commonwealth of Independent States (CIS) and the Eurasian Economic Union (EAEU), which have consistently been Russian priorities. Russia also asserts the need to develop cooperation with the European Union as well as other regions and their institutions. Yet, Russia has consistently

---

[23]*Ibid.*
[24]Russian Federation, *Concept of Foreign Policy.*
[25]Medvedev, *Berlin Speech.*

proclaimed that "[w]hile respecting the right of its partners within the CIS to establish relations with other international actors, Russia expects the CIS member States to fully implement their obligations within integration structures that include Russia". This provision is a standard norm for any organisation; the EU would also remind its members of the duty to cooperate and of the supremacy of EU law. However, Russia has not shied away from pressuring its CIS partners into cooperation, not via judicial remedies (like the EU), but rather with oil and gas prices, political pressure and support for opposition leaders in their territories. Ukraine is the most vivid example of this trend. Regionalism is also seen as a way to increase Russia's relative weight in the international arena. It is a source of multipolarity (or "policentricity", to cite the term used in the FPC) and, hence, challenges US hegemony. At the same time Russia has tested the EU's unity (especially on sanctions) through contacts with some of its members (trying to encourage their more pro-Russian behaviour). Moreover, Minister Sergey Lavrov has lambasted "an aggressive minority [of EU states] that is trying to take advantage of the so-called solidarity principle based on anti-Russian sentiment",[26] thus criticising the EU's unity on Russia as an expression of strong regionalism.

The FPC recognises *interdependence* and a tight web of transnational relations, both economic and non-economic, as key characteristics of today's world. The document stresses the global nature of economic relations, environmental challenges, and the dangers of proliferation, terrorism and cyber threats. Russia stresses both the advantages and potential dangers in the economic sphere. Moscow promoted Russia's gradual integration into the world economy before 2014. After the sanctions imposed by the EU and US as a result of its policy in Ukraine, however, it has modified this strategy. On the one hand, the Russian government has criticised sanctions as a protectionist measure, threatening to challenge them in the World Trade Organisation (WTO). It also regularly reminds the West of the need to cooperate to counter various global challenges (ranging from hard security through terrorism and cyber threats to environmental challenges). On the other hand, Russia has adopted its own protectionist measures and introduced an import-substitution policy.[27] The Russian attitude toward civil society contacts is even more complex. It is in favour of abolishing visas (notably with the EU) to simplify cross-border movements. Yet, Russian law on non-governmental organisations limits the possibilities of foreign finance for the latter, and the EU-promoted Civil Society Dialogue with Russia is mostly ignored by Russia's official bodies.

The FPC is ambiguous on the fifth normative framework, *democracy and the convergence of values*. Russian discourse on it clearly illustrates the contradictions between democracy and US hegemony and between plurality and universality. Democracy in the context of the international liberal order is first and foremost about the internal political regime.[28] The FPC, however, does not discuss internal features – Russia is simply defined as a democratic country. However, the international dimension of democracy becomes central for the FPC. It defines a "democratic international system" as one addressing "international issues on the basis of collective decision-making, the rule of international law ... as well as equal, partnership relations among States, with the central and coordinating role played by the

---

[26]Lavrov, *Statement and answers*.
[27]Import substitution policy is based on the idea of decreasing the share of imported goods and substituting them with domestic production. While the arguments for such a policy range from security to economic development, the policy also limits international trade and consequently interdependence with other states.
[28]Sorensen, *Liberal world order in crisis*.

United Nations". This is where the contradiction between democracy and hegemony is most evident in Russia's documents. American hegemony provokes strong Russian opposition. Russia criticises the "attempts made by Western powers to maintain their positions in the world, including by imposing their point of view on global processes and … contain[ing] alternative centres of power". The FPC suggests instead "collective leadership from the major States that should be representative in geographic and civilizational terms and fully respect the central and coordinating role of the UN".[29]

Russia is even more ambiguous on values. On the one hand, the FPC argues that "attempts to impose values on others can stoke xenophobia, intolerance and conflict in international affairs".[30] On the other hand, it admits that a "genuine consolidation of efforts of the international community requires a set of common values as a foundation for joint action, based on the common moral force of the major world religions, as well as principles and concepts such as aspiration to peace and justice, dignity, freedom and responsibility, honesty, compassion and hard work". This inconsistency in the text reflects a deep contradiction between universality and plurality in the liberal order itself. Russia proclaims its adherence to the human rights concept and its willingness to promote it, and at the same time is against "attempts to use human rights theories to exert political pressure and interfere in internal affairs of States", despite its claims to defend the rights of Russian nationals and compatriots abroad. This provision was also used to justify Russian activities in Georgia's breakaway provinces of South Ossetia and Abkhazia, recognition of the referendum in Crimea on secession from Ukraine and support for separatists in Eastern Ukraine. In Russia's view, there is no contradiction. The US ignores international rules that do not fit its calculations (be it the International Criminal Court, military strikes in the absence of a UN resolution or International Maritime conventions); Russia reserves the same right for itself.

The discourse on US hegemony naturally reinforces the demand for international democracy. The question of 'what kind of rules' becomes less important for Russia than the question of 'who provides these rules'. The key message is that Russia has the right to act like the West (hence the challenge to US hegemony).

In sum, Russia rhetorically supports most elements of the liberal international order and justifies its moves accordingly. Moreover, it condemns the West (in particular, the US) for inconsistency in the application of the letter of international law and liberal normative frameworks. However, Russia exploits the three internal contradictions of the liberal order (sovereignty vs. liberal intervention / R2P, plurality vs. universality, and American hegemony vs. equality / democracy). They are mutually reinforcing: pluralism goes hand-in-hand with non-intervention and international democracy, whereas universalism relies more on intervention and US hegemony.

Russia seeks to provide alternative definitions to values and democracy, and to find a balance between the promotion of values and their use to intervene and challenge sovereignty. But most importantly, Russia tries to change its status vis-à-vis the US, to become part of the governance structure with the same right to interpret the norms. Of the three contradictions, the one between hegemony and democracy is by far the most important for Moscow. As a result, Russia behaves in a neorevisionist way, seeking not so much to challenge the liberal international order as to upgrade its status within it.

---

[29]*Ibid.*
[30]Russian Federation, *Concept of Foreign Policy.*

Sources of the Russian position in the international liberal order

Russia's very first Foreign Policy Concept from 1993 stressed that foreign policy was to create essential conditions for Russian democratisation and economic transformation. It also emphasised the commonality of values and interest (but also limits of cooperation).[31] However, discourses on the need for international democracy (vs. US hegemony), on the respect for sovereignty as the supreme norm in international relations (vs. R2P), as well as on diversity of cultures and civilisations (vs. universality) emerged in the 2000 Foreign Policy Concept.[32] The 2000 FPC already called for a multipolar and democratic world order (meaning equal participation of all players), based on international law. It also stressed respect for human rights without, however, "belittl[ing] the role of a sovereign state" and classified "[a]ttempts to introduce … such concepts as 'humanitarian intervention' and 'limited sovereignty' in order to justify unilateral power actions bypassing the U.N." as unacceptable.[33] At the same time, the overall tone of the Foreign Policy Concept remained cooperative.

The exploitation of the three contradictions of the liberal order has been consistently strengthened since 2000. The 2008 FPC became more critical of unilateral actions and stated that Russia would be prepared to act unilaterally, should such a need arise. It further developed the notion of a democratic world order, and called for a "democratic system of regional collective security" in Europe (meaning inclusion of all players into a comprehensive system as opposed to selective NATO membership) and for multilateral interaction with the full use of UN bodies and instruments.[34] The 2008 FPC was also critical of attempts to challenge sovereignty. The specificity of the 2008 FPC lies in the introduction of the notion of civilisation competition; the document classified democracy and market economy as universal principles, which can be implemented in different and competing "value systems and development models".[35] The 2008 FPC, therefore, for the first time openly challenged the universality of these values.

Finally, the 2013 FPC further intensified the criticism of intervention, of concepts, "aimed at overthrowing legitimate authorities in sovereign states", as well as of the "risk of destructive and unlawful use of 'soft power' and human rights concepts to exert political pressure on sovereign states, interfere in their internal affairs".[36] On the other hand, it emphasized sovereign equality, international democracy and the policentricity of international relations (challenging US hegemony and the perception of a unilateral world). It also further developed the points about civilisational pluralism, defending the specificity of various states, challenging universality but also presenting Russia as experienced in fostering inter-civilisational dialogue. In sum, Russia has exploited the three internal contradictions of the liberal order since 2000; moreover this exposure of the contradictions has been increasingly developed and become more sophisticated.

Two factors determine Russia's position in the liberal international order. The first is external, it determines the direction, the neorevisionist challenge; it explains why Russia has consistently exploited the in-built contradictions of the liberal international order. It

---

[31]Russian Federation, "Conceptsiya vneshnei politiki" ["Concept of Foreign Policy"], 3.
[32]Russian Federation, *Foreign Policy Concept* 2000. See also Romanova, "Russia: Change or Continuity?".
[33]Russian Federation, *Ibid*.
[34]Russian Federation, *Foreign Policy Concept* 2008.
[35]*Ibid*.
[36]Russian Federation, *Foreign Policy Concept* 2013.

is Russia's dissatisfaction with the post-Cold War settlement, and in particular Moscow's belief that it does not have the place it deserves in today's global order. Russia's deeply rooted conviction is that it ended the Cold War together with the West,[37] had too much trust in the West[38] and was not recognised as a winner, but rather treated like a defeated power. It is also noteworthy that when replying to the question on what mistakes Russia made recently, Vladimir Putin at the meeting of the Valdai Club in 2017 stressed that Russia's "most serious mistake in relations with the West is that we trusted you too much. And [the West's] mistake is that [it] took that trust as weakness and abused it".[39] These words explain both the tone of the 1993 Foreign Policy Concept (when Russia had high expectations regarding cooperation with the West) and the gradual change since the late 1990s, manifested already in the 2000 FPC. It is because of this that the major Russian foreign policy texts start with the end of the Cold War and with the argument that Russia did its part of the work, but was not reciprocated in terms of being accepted into the circle of those who take key decisions in the world[40] and provide the governance of the international order.

This belief is exacerbated by the worldview of the current Russian political elite. As Dmitry Trenin rightly argues, at present the "Russian security community plays the key role in helping Putin conceive, shape, and execute foreign policy decisions. The group's worldview presents international relations in terms of a never-ending struggle for dominance and influence among a few powerful countries."[41] The liberal group is rather marginalised, mostly due to the Russian-Western alienation, disillusionment in cooperation, but also mutual sanctions and the decrease in economic interdependence. During his presidency (2008-12), Dmitry Medvedev tried to promote a new concept of global security based on the principle of equal security for all and on global institutions unlike those, such as NATO, which include only a narrow group of countries, but it was mostly ignored in the West. That reinforced the positions of the security community in Russia at the expense of the more liberal part of the elite.

The enlargement of NATO, which the current Russian leadership still perceives as an anti-Russia alliance, further strengthened suspicions as to whether credible and stable cooperation between Russia and the West is possible. It also explains the acuteness of geopolitical competition in Russia's immediate neighbourhood, particularly in Eastern Europe. Russian leadership perceives the post-Soviet region as the one of its immediate interests, but also as directly affecting its security (borders in some cases are still symbolic). This feeling of insecurity because of the NATO enlargement and geopolitical competition in Eastern Europe is further exacerbated by the gradual erosion of talks on arms limitation, and the freezing or postponement of relevant US obligations. In some cases, Russia is continuing to implement its obligations (for example, on the decommissioning of nuclear weapon) while, in others, NATO enlargement and the freezing or modification of US obligations have served to justify Russia's symmetrical freezing or non-implementation.

Finally, the fact that Russia is currently blamed for all the wrongs in the West (be it the rise of populists or the far right, migration, US elections, cyber attacks, Brexit or the vote for

[37] Morozov, "Europe".
[38] See, for example, Putin, *Meeting of Valdai International Discussion Club.*
[39] *Ibid.*
[40] See Lavrov, *Vystuplenie na Primakov [Primakov Reading Forum]* for a recent example.
[41] Trenin, *Five-Year Outlook.*

independence in Catalonia),[42] although perceived ironically in Russia, nurtures this feeling of being an outcast, a challenge for the West to contain rather than to engage.

The intensity and severity of Russia's neorevisionist challenge to the liberal order is shaped by the second factor, which is the interplay between domestic and foreign policy. The intensity of Russia's exploitation of the internal contradiction of the liberal order has grown in parallel to the increase in Russia's affluence, internal economic stabilisation, restoration of the 'power vertical' and the authority of state institutions. Internal stability and prosperity have led to greater demand for a role in the international arena. At the beginning of his third presidency (2012-18), Vladimir Putin faced the choice between internal reforms (further economic readjustments, improvement of the legal climate, fight against corruption, review of the division of competences between central and regional authorities) and external activism. He chose the latter because the risks involved in upsetting the internal balance among various interests groups were perceived to be higher. It, in turn, strengthened the intensity of Russia's exposure of the internal contradictions of the liberal order.

In other words, aggressive and bold foreign policy allowed President Putin to neglect domestic reforms. "By annexing Crimea, Putin capitalized on the foremost symbol of Russian imperial nostalgia and might"[43] and his popularity skyrocketed. Russia's national glory in the world became the basis for a new partnership between the state and the people of Russia. It replaced the consensus that had sustained earlier Putin presidencies (2000-08), which was about stability, personal security and increased welfare in exchange for loyalty to the state and its elite. Foreign policy, therefore, has become a substitute for domestic policy. It distracts attention from the needed internal reforms. It consolidates support for the government. It also provides an explanation and justification for economic problems and the absence of internal reforms. The turning into national heroes and TV stars of the Minister of Foreign Affairs, his spokesman or ambassadors provides a very good illustration of the interplay between foreign and domestic policy.

At the same time, the internal basis for responsible participation in the global liberal order has been degraded. As Sorensen legitimately argues, a liberal order "is based on domestic as well as on international change in a liberal direction",[44] a strong civil society, respect for human rights and a market economy. Yet Russia made the choice for a "mobilization model of 'a fortress under siege'" rather than "liberal economic and political reforms".[45] The interplay between domestic and foreign policy, hence, has both reinforced the intensity of Russia's critique of the liberal international order and given more leeway to the political elite in conducting foreign policy.

In a nutshell, Russia's feeling of not being integrated in the liberal global order has defined the direction of its policy (exposure of the contradictions of the order and demand for its

---

[42]See, for example, Paterson, "Russian President wooing populist parties"; Higginsmay, "Far-Right Fever"; Klapsis, *An Unholy Alliance*; Polyakova, "Putin and Europe's Far Right"; "Migrant crisis: Russia and Syria 'weaponising' migration", *BBC*, 2 March 201,. http://www.bbc.com/news/world-europe-35706238; "Is Russia 'Weaponizing Refugees' To Advance Its Geopolitical Goals?", *RFERL*, 19 February 2016, https://www.rferl.org/a/russia-weaponizing-syrian-refugees-geopolitical-goals/27562604.html; Riley and Robertson, "Russian Cyber Hacks U.S. Electoral System"; Committee to Investigate Russia, *Russian Cyber Attacks*; Meister, "Russia Blends Cyber Attacks"; Cadwalladr, "Brexit: how Russia pulls strings"; Castle, "Suspecting Russian Meddling"; Lucas, "Truth about Russia and Brexit"; "Catalonia held a referendum. Russia won", *The Washington Post*, 2 October 2017, https://www.washingtonpost.com/opinions/global-opinions/catalonia-held-a-referendum-russia-won/2017/10/02/f618cd7c-a798-11e7-92d1-58c702d2d975_story.html?utm_term=.a794405ea2ed; Scott and Torres, "Catalan referendum fears Russian influence".
[43]Kolesnikov and Makarenko, "Another Rubber Stamp Duma?". See also Suslov, "'Crimea Is Ours!'".
[44]Sorensen, *Liberal world order in crisis*, 4.
[45]Petrov, "Rossiya v 2014-m" ["Russia in 2014"], 58.

reform) since 2000, whereas the interplay between domestic and foreign policy and the eventual choice of foreign policy over (and as a replacement for) domestic reforms has determined the intensity of this criticism. These two sources explain continuity in Foreign Policy Concepts but also their evolution with respect to the liberal order's contradictions.

National consensus on the liberal international order?

Five internal forces contribute to shaping Russia's foreign policy. These are state institutions, political parties, the business world, civil society and epistemic communities. Do they significantly challenge the Russian view of the liberal international order described above?

The Russian system is built around an individual (the president, in this case Putin, and his 'court',[46] or Politburo,[47] both conceived as relatively closed elite circles) rather than institutions. This system does not exclude competition among government bodies. For example, there is rivalry between the Ministry of Foreign Affairs, on the one hand, and the Ministry of Economic Development (MED), on the other hand. The latter has always advanced modernisation partnerships and was the key force behind Russia's accession to the WTO. However, Russia's choice to pursue international confrontation has significantly decreased the influence of this actor in Russia. Moreover, a struggle in the political elite led to the former Minister of Economic Development, Alexey Ulukaev, being removed from his position in late 2016 on corruption allegations and substituted with a younger and less powerful figure. Finally, sanctions have cut the amount of foreign economic relations and priority has been given to import substitution (with the Ministry of Industry and Trade moving to the forefront as a result). Hence, there is no institutional challenge to the current Russian position on the liberal international order.

Although Russia has numerous political parties (73 were registered in June 2017),[48] just six are represented in the State Duma (lower chamber of the Russian parliament) with only four having political groups. The biggest one, *Edinaya Rossiya* [United Russia] led by Prime Minister Medvedev, controls 343 out of 450 seats. That gives the party effective control over all decisions of parliament. The other parties that have political groups in the State Duma form the so-called 'systemic opposition' and mostly support the Kremlin's policy line (including in the world arena). Liberal parties, which form a non-systemic opposition, are weak and fragmented. Some would support the current foreign policy, others argue for a more liberal position, which is a precondition for internal political reform. Some leaders of the non-systemic opposition would support universality of such values as human rights and democracy and might criticise Russian policy towards Ukraine, but no initiative has been put forward. In the current context opposition leaders advancing an alternative to the official foreign policy position are stigmatised as unpatriotic, which effectively emasculates their message. Moreover, the non-systemic opposition prioritises the domestic agenda (the need for economic reforms, strengthening the rule of law, fighting corruption, adjusting state finances) as being of more immediate interest to the people and hence increasing their chances of participation in political life.

---

[46]Haaze, "Kak Putin upravlyaet Rossiei" ["How Putin governs Russia"].
[47]For regular reviews of who is a member of the Politburo, see Minchenko, http://www.minchenko.ru/press/.
[48]Ministry of Justice, *Spisok zaregestrirovannyh politicheskih partii* [*List of registered political parties*].
[49]See Bremmer, *End of the Free Market.*

The Russian economic system can be characterised as state capitalism.[49] The state provides about 70 percent of the GNP (against 35 percent in 2005).[50] This is the result of the gradual deprivatisation since the beginning of the century, which has empowered the state at the expense of the business sector. The 2008 economic crisis increased the state's 'grip' on the economy.[51] Western sanctions have limited the access of Russian businessmen to international credit and made them rely on state-controlled finance, further strengthening the dependence of business on state authorities. Restrictive measures have increased the positions of oil and gas companies, military industries and sectors dealing with import substitution. Forty-eight percent of companies feel that they are treated like a 'purse', a source of money only, rather than a considerable domestic or foreign policy asset.[52] Small and medium businesses have come out as the biggest losers, negatively impacting the relative importance of the middle class, essential for the rule of law and democracy. Many of them are not happy with sanctions and would like them to be removed, but are not ready to fight to change the course of Russian foreign policy and prefer to concentrate on their own survival.[53]

Russian civil society remains relatively weak. Although it is developing in some fields (the social, environmental, local), its activities are limited in the political domain (not least as a result of the law on NGOs that constrains foreign finance, but also due to social bullying of alternative political activities). In 2008, Maria Ordzhonikidze cited an opinion poll that showed that 43 percent of Russians believed liberalism to be a negative thing (representing "demagoguery of people" and "wild capitalism") against 42 percent who believed it to be positive.[54] If anything, this perception has worsened recently due to the rhetoric of the political elite and mass media with the epithet 'liberal' becoming a humiliation if not an offence.

Sanctions and political choices since 2014 have led to a decline in the standard of living, which means that the population concentrates on survival rather than on any demand for change.[55] According to a recent poll, about 61 percent prefer to rely only on themselves, without any contact with the state.[56] An overwhelming majority, 76 percent of the population, believe that large protests in Russia are unlikely.[57] Moreover, decreased income has impacted on people's ability to travel, meaning less exposure to foreign countries and cultures. Sanctions have predictably produced a 'rally around the flag' effect. The attitude towards the US and the EU has slightly improved since 2014, but most Russians still perceive them as negative (61 percent and 55 percent, respectively).[58] Sanctions are understood as a sign that the West treats Russia as a rival (43 percent), does not like Russia (35 percent), does not understand life in Russia but wants to teach Russians a lesson (21 percent) or applies double standards, criticising Russia for what Western politicians themselves do (25 percent).[59] In sum, public opinion mostly supports Russia's official foreign policy and its critique of the current practice of the liberal order.

---

[50]Mereminskaya, "Gosudarstvo i goskompanii" ["State and state companies"].
[51]On different stages of the relations between the state and business in Russia, see Bounine and Makarkine, *Russia: Business and State*.
[52]Mereminskaya, "Gosudarstvo i goskompanii" ["State and state companies"].
[53]See also Trenin, *Five-Year Outlook*.
[54]Ordzhonikidze, "Russians' Perceptions of Western Values", 50.
[55]See, for example, Kolesnikov, 'Troinoi udar' ['Triple strike'].
[56]Levada, *Nepoliticheskaya natsiya* [*A non-political nation*].
[57]Levada, *Protestnyi potentsial* [*Protest potential*].
[58]Levada, *Mezhdunarodnye sanktsii* [*International sanctions*].
[59]Levada, *Kritika i sanktsii* [*Criticism and sanctions*].

Finally, epistemic communities have a relatively limited impact on Russian foreign policy. Two competing tendencies can be identified here. On the one hand, a large majority of experts support Russia's foreign policy. The Valdai Club, which regularly organises meetings between President Putin and foreign experts has extensively discussed the 'chaotisation' of today's world; the destruction and creation of a new order (with no clarity as to what a new order might be),[60] as well as contradictions between universality and specificity.[61] Some journals engage in self-censorship while others tend to encourage softer and ambiguous wording in line with the official foreign policy discourse. Certain experts either herald the chaotisation of international relations and world order with *Realpolitik* being the only strategy,[62] or take it as inevitable and advocate Russian restraint.[63]

On the other hand, some insist on a more cooperative type of foreign relations. Andrey Kortunov, director of the Russian International Affairs Council (RIAC), for example, argues that the liberal global order is here to stay and that, therefore, Russia has to balance its security concerns and its development needs (which warrant integration into the liberal economic order).[64] A comprehensive set of foreign policy recommendations was recently prepared by the Centre for Strategic Studies (an analytical think tank directed by liberal Alexey Kudrin, former Minister of Finance) and RIAC. This text advances the need for "a comfortable, democratic, controllable and safe international environment" for Russia's internal reforms.[65] Arguing against betting on the chaotisation of global affairs, the text cautiously urges Russia to "find an optimal formula for gaining benefits from globalization … while retaining room for broad foreign political manoeuvre".[66] It implicitly recognises that Russia is not properly integrated in the liberal international order, but argues for restraint in its criticism of the order (and not its radical reversal). This text has not had much public impact, however, remaining limited to epistemic communities.

In sum, Russia's social, economic and political actors are relatively concordant as concerns views of the global liberal order. Attempts to present an alternative view remain timid and are limited to the non-systemic opposition and a narrow part of the epistemic community. Moreover, even proponents of the current liberal order insist on the need to reform it, offering more space to Russian specificity and its views on US hegemony, sovereignty and pluralism.

Conclusion

The view that Russia wants to destroy the liberal international order is simplistic. Russia rhetorically supports key liberal normative frameworks, justifies its actions with the liberal order's provisions and criticises the West for non-consistent implementation of those same provisions. Moreover, Russia does not suggest any alternative. Rather, Russia exposes three contradictions in the liberal order: sovereignty vs. intervention, pluralism vs. universality, and democracy vs. American hegemony. Moscow aims to reform the liberal international

---

[60]Valdai Club, *Destruction and New World Order*.
[61]Valdai Club, *Conflict between Universality and Self-Identity*.
[62]Karaganov, *Strategiya dlya Rossii [Strategy for Russia]*; "Buduschii miroporyadok" ["A Future world order"]; and *Chaotisatsiya mezhdunarodnyh otnoshenii i Rossiya. [Chaotisation of international relations]*.
[63]Miller and Lukyanov, *Sderzhannost vmesto naporistosti [Restraint instead of Assertiveness]*.
[64]Kortunov, *Neizbezhnost strannogo mira [Inevitability of a Strange World]*.
[65]Timofeev, *Theses on Russia's Foreign Policy*, 5.
[66]*Ibid.*, 15.

order so as to incorporate its concerns regarding sovereignty and specificity but also to secure for itself a better place in the management of international problems. Therefore, Russia has to be classified as neorevisionist. Two factors support this position; one is Russia's perception that the liberal order does not accommodate its concerns regarding participation in the management of the order and its security; another is the choice of foreign policy over (and as a substitute for) domestic reform. At present there is a strong internal consensus in Russia on this view of the liberal international order.

The fact that Russia uses the liberal order's internal contradictions to justify its foreign policy is crucial because it has several important policy-relevant consequences. First, it allows Russia and the West to engage on the normative terms that both parties share and support. This opens a space for discussion and a search for solutions that are mutually acceptable to the West and the rest of the international community (of which Russia claims to be one of the main representatives). Second, it reveals that for the liberal order to stay *liberal* it has to integrate all major players. The need for this inclusive adjustment of the liberal international order is compounded by the existence of threats affecting all major powers, such as terrorism, nuclear proliferation and climate change. Third, such an adjustment is predicated on Russia shouldering more responsibility for the maintenance and strengthening of the reformed order.[67] A reformed liberal international order will create the necessary context for Russian internal reforms, which in turn will feed Russian support for the reformed order.

Acknowledgements

The research was supported by a grant from the Russian Science Foundation (project no 17-18-01110).

References

Alcaro, R. "The Liberal Order and Its Contestations. A Conceptual Framework". *The International Spectator* 53, no. 1 (2018): https://doi.org/10.1080/03932729.2018.1397878.

Bremmer, I. *The End of the Free Market: Who Wins the War Between States and Corporations?* New York: Portfolio, 2010.

Bounine, I., and A. Makarkine. *Russia: Business and State*, Russie. Nei.Visions No 88. Paris: IFRI, November 2015.

Cadwalladr, C. "Brexit, the ministers, the professor and the spy: how Russia pulls strings in UK". *The Guardian*, 4 November 2017. https://www.theguardian.com/politics/2017/nov/04/brexit-ministers-spy-russia-uk-brexit

Castle, S. "Suspecting Russian Meddling in 'Brexit' Vote, Lawmaker Seeks Inquiry". *The New York Times,* 19 October 2017. https://www.nytimes.com/2017/10/19/world/europe/russia-brexit-arron-banks.html

---

[67]Kortunov, *Neizbezhnost strannogo mira [Inevitability of a Strange World].*

Chandler, D. "International State-building and the Ideology of Resilience". *Politics* 33, no. 4 (2013): 276–86.

Committee to Investigate Russia. *Russian Cyber Attacks*. No date. https://investigaterussia.org/timelines/russian-cyber-attacks

Dunne, T., and T. Flockhart, eds. *Liberal World Orders*. Proceedings of the British Academy. Oxford: Oxford University Press, 2013.

Frear, M., and H. Mazepus. *A New Turn or More of the Same? A Structured Analysis of Recent Developments in Russian Foreign Policy Discourse*, EU-STRAT Working Paper Series No 3. Berlin: EU-STRAT, May 2017.

Fukuyama, F. *The End of History and the Last Man*. New York: Free Press, 1992.

Goldberg, G. "World Chaos and World Order: Conversations with Henry Kissinger. The former Secretary of State reflects on war, peace, and the biggest tests facing the next president". *The Atlantic*, 10 November 2016. https://www.theatlantic.com/international/archive/2016/11/kissinger-order-and-chaos/506876/.

Gromyko, A. *Speech at the conference "Studying EU-Russian Relations: Theories and Methods in Russia and Abroad"*. Saint-Petersburg: SPbGU, 28 June 2017.

Haass, R. "World Order: What Can be Done?" Public Lecture. Cambridge: University of Cambridge, 27 April 2015. https://www.youtube.com/watch?v=42wanbNSR5Q.

Haaze, K. "Kak Putin upravlyaet Rossiei" ["How Putin Governs Russia"]. Lecture. Otkrytaia Rossiya, 17 September 2017. https://openrussia.org/notes/713824/

Higginsmay, A. "Far-Right Fever for a Europe Tied to Russia". *New York Times*, 20 May 2014. https://www.nytimes.com/2014/05/21/world/europe/europes-far-right-looks-to-russia-as-a-guiding-force.html.

Ikenberry, G.J. "The Future of Liberal World Order". *Japanese Journal of Political Science* 16, no. 3 (2015): 450–5.

Ikenberry, G.J. "The Future of the Liberal World Order: Internationalism after America". *Foreign Affairs* 90, no 3 (May-June 2011): 56-68.

International Commission on Intervention and State Sovereignty. *The Responsibility to Protect. Report of the International Commission on Intervention and State Sovereignty*. Ottawa: International Development Research Centre, 2001.

Joseph, J. "Resilience as embedded neoliberalism: a governmentality approach". *Resilience* 1, no. 1 (2013): 38–52.

Kagan, R. *The twilight of the liberal world order*, Report. Washington DC: Brookings Institution, 24 January 2017. https://www.brookings.edu/research/the-twilight-of-the-liberal-world-order/.

Karaganov, S. "Buduschii miroporyadok" ["Future world order"]. *Rossiiskaya Gazeta*, 7 September 2017. https://rg.ru/2017/09/07/karaganov-zapadu-stanovitsia-vs.e-trudnee-naviazyvat-svoi-cennosti.html

Karaganov, S., ed. *Strategiya dlya Rossii. Rossiiskaya vneshnyaa politika: konets 2010h – nachalo 2020h godov [Strategy for Russia, Russian foreign policy: the end of 2010s – beginning of 2020s]* Moscow: SVOP, Rossiya v globalnoi politike, 2016.

Karaganov, S. *Chaotisatsiya mezhdunarodnyh otnoshenii i Rossiya [Chaotisation of international relations and Russia]* Moscow: HSE, 2 November 2011. https://www.hse.ru/video/38279832.html

Klapsis, A. *An Unholy Alliance: The European Far Right and Putin's Russia*. Brussels: Wilfried Martens Centre for European Studies, May 2015. https://www.martenscentre.eu/publications/far-right-political-parties-in-europe-and-putins-russia

Kolesnikov, A. 'Troinoi udar': rossiiskii srednii klass v osazhdennoi kreposti. ['Triple strike': Russian middle class in the fortress under siege] Moscow: Carnegie Endowment for International Peace, 25 February 2015. http://carnegie.ru/2015/02/25/ru-pub-59177.

Kolesnikov, A., and B. Makarenko. "Another Rubber Stamp Duma?", Carnegie Article. Moscow, 6 September 2016. http://carnegie.ru/2016/09/06/another-rubber-stamp-duma-pub-64431.

Kortunov, A. *Neizbezhnost strannogo mira [Inevitability of a Strange World]*. Moscow: RIAC, 15 July 2016. russiancouncil.ru/analytics-and-comments/analytics/neizbezhnost-strannogo-mira/.

Kundnani, H. *What is the Liberal International Order?*, GMF Policy Essay No 17. Washington DC: The German Marshall Foundation of the United States, April 2017 . http://www.gmfus.org/publications/what-liberal-international-order.

Lavrov, S. *Vystuplenie na Primakov Reading Forum "Mir v 2035 godu" [Speech at the Primakov Reading Forum]*. Moscow: IMEMO, 30 June 2017. http://bit.ly/2stC7mI.

Lavrov, S. *Statement and answers to media questions at a joint news conference following talks with Committee of Ministers of the Council of Europe (CMCE) Chairman, Belgian Deputy Prime Minister and Foreign and European Affairs Minister Didier Reynders*, Moscow, 9 April 2015. http://www.mid.ru/press_service/minister_speeches/-/asset_publisher/7OvQR5KJWVmR/content/id/1155333.

Levada. *Mezhdunarodnye sanktsii [International sanctions]* Opinion polls. Moscow: Levada, 15 June 2017. https://www.levada.ru/2017/06/15/16137/

Levada. *Nepoliticheskaya natsiya [A non-political nation]* Opinion polls. Moscow: Levada, 13 April 2017. http://www.levada.ru/2017/04/13/nepoliticheskaya-natsiya.

Levada. *Protestnyi potentsial [Protest potential]* Opinion polls. Moscow: Levada, 11 November 2016. https://www.levada.ru/2016/11/11/protestnyj-potentsial-5/.

Levada. *Kritika i sanktsii [Criticism and sanctions]* Opinion polls. Moscow: Levada, 8 November 2016. htttp://www.levada.ru.2016/11/08/kritika-i-sanktsii-zapada.

Liik, K. *What does Russia want?* ECFR Commentary. London: ECFR, 26 May 2017. http://www.ecfr.eu/article/commentary_what_does_russia_want_7297.

Lobell, S.E., N.M. Ripsman and J.W. Taliaferro, eds. *Neoclassical Realism, the State, and Foreign Policy*. Cambridge: Cambridge University Press, 2009.

Lucas, E. "We must get to the truth about Russia and Brexit". *The Times,* 3 November 2017. https://www.thetimes.co.uk/article/we-must-get-to-truth-about-russia-and-brexit-67brnl608

Medvedev, D. *Berlin Speech at Meeting with German Political, Parliamentary, and Civic Leaders*. Berlin, 5 June 2008. http://archive.kremlin.ru/eng/speeches/2008/06/05/2203_type82912type82914type84779_202153.shtml.

Meister, S. "Russia Blends Cyber Attacks with Information War". *The Cipher Brief,* 17 September 2017. https://www.thecipherbrief.com/russia-blends-cyber-attacks-information-war-west.

Mereminskaya, E. "Gosudarstvo i goskompanii kontroliruut 70% rossiiskoi ekonomiki. FAS priznala gosudarstvo glavnym vragom konkurentsii" ["State and state companies control 70% of the Russian economy"] *Vedomosti,* 29 September 2016.

Miller, A., and F. Lukyanov. *Sderzhannost vmesto naporistosti: Rossiya I novaya mirovaya epoha [Restraint instead of Assertiveness]* Moscow: SVOP, 2017. http://svop.ru/wp-content/uploads/2017/07/report_miller_lukyanov_rus_2.pdf.

Ministry of Justice of the Russian Federation. *Spisok zaregestrirovannyh politicheskih partii [The list of registered political parties]*. Moscow, June 2017. http://minjust.ru/nko/gosreg/partii/spisok

Morozov, V. "Europe: Self-Alignment in Time and Space". *Russia in Global Affairs* 3, no 3 (July-September 2008). http://eng.globalaffairs.ru/number/n_11285.

Ordzhonikidze, M. "Russians' Perceptions of Western Values". *Russian Politics and Law* 46, no. 3 (June 2008): 43–68.

Paterson, T. "Putin's far-right ambition: Think-tank reveals how Russian President is wooing – and funding – populist parties across Europe to gain influence in the EU". *The Independent,* 25 November 2014. http://www.independent.co.uk/news/world/europe/putin-s-far-right-ambition-think-tank-reveals-how-russian-president-is-wooing-and-funding-populist-9883052.html

Polyakova, A. "Strange Bedfellows: Putin and Europe's Far Right". *The World Affairs Journal*, no. 5 (2014). http://www.worldaffairsjournal.org/issue/septemberoctober-2014

Petrov, N. "Rossiya v 2014-m: skatyvanie v voronku" ["Russia in 2013: Falling into a funnel"]. *Pro et Contra* 63, no 3–4 (May-June 2014): 57-72.

Putin, V. *Meeting of the Valdai International Discussion Club*. Sochi, 19 October 2017. http://en.kremlin.ru/events/president/news/55882

Riley, M., and J. Robertson. "Russian Cyber Hacks on U.S. Electoral System Far Wider Than Previously Known". *Bloomberg,* 13 June 2017. https://www.bloomberg.com/news/articles/2017-06-13/russian-breach-of-39-states-threatens-future-u-s-elections

Romanova, T. "Russia: Change or Continuity? The Importation of Western Concepts and their Effect on EU-Russian Relations". In *Globalization and Regime Change in the New Russia and the New Europe*. Lanham, MD: Rowman & Littlefield, 2018 (forthcoming).

Russian Federation. *Concept of the Foreign Policy of the Russian Federation (approved by President of the Russian Federation Vladimir Putin on November 30, 2016)*. Moscow, 30 November 2016. http://www.mid.ru/en/foreign_policy/official_documents/-/asset_publisher/CptICkB6BZ29/content/id/2542248.

Russian Federation. *Concept of the Foreign Policy of the Russian Federation, approved by President of the Russian Federation V. Putin*. Moscow, 12 February 2013. www.mid.ru/nsosndoc.nsf/1e5f0de28fe77fdcc32575d900298676/869c9d2b87ad8014c32575d9002b1c38?OpenDocument.

Russian Federation. *Concept of the Foreign Policy of the Russian Federation, approved by the President of the Russian Federation D. Medvedev*. Moscow, 12 July 2008. archive.kremlin.ru/eng/text/docs/2008/07/204750.shtml.

Russian Federation. *Concept of the Foreign Policy of the Russian Federation, approved by the President of the Russian Federation V. Putin*. Moscow, 28 June 2000. http://www.fas.org/nuke/guide/russia/doctrine/econcept.htm.

Russian Federation. "Conceptsiya vneshnei politiki Rossiiskoi Federatsii" ["Concept of the Foreign Policy of the Russian Federation"]. *Diplomaticheskiy vestnik*, Special Issue, January 1993.

Sakwa, R. "Dualism at Home and Abroad: Russian Foreign Policy Neorevisionism and Bicontinentalism". In *Russia's Foreign Policy: Ideas, Domestic Politics and External Relations*, edited by D. Cadier and M. Light: 65–79. Basingstoke: Palgrave, 2015.

Sakwa, R. "The problem of the 'International' in Russian identity formation". *International Politics* 49, no. 4 (2012): 449–65.

Sakwa, R. "Russia and Europe: Whose Society?" *Journal of European Integration* 33, no. 2 (2011): 197–214.

Scott, M., and D. Torres. "Catalan referendum stokes fears of Russian influence. Online activities designed to cast doubts on Europe's democratic processes, experts warn". *Politico*, 29 September 2017. https://www.politico.eu/article/russia-catalonia-referendum-fake-news-misinformation/

Sorensen, G. *A liberal world order in crisis: choosing between imposition and restraint*. Ithaca: Cornell University Press, 2011.

Suslov, M. "'Crimea Is Ours!' Russian popular geopolitics in the new media age". *Eurasian Geography and Economics* 55, no. 6 (2014): 588–609.

Timofeev, I. *Theses on Russia's Foreign Policy and Global Positioning (2017–2024)*. Moscow: CSR and RIAC, June 2017.

Trenin, D. *A Five-Year Outlook for Russian Foreign Policy: Demands, Drivers, and Influences,* Carnegie Task Force White Paper. Moscow: Carnegie Endowment for International Peace, 18 March 2016. http://carnegie.ru/2016/03/18/five-year-outlook-for-russian-foreign-policy-demands-drivers-and-influences/ivkm.

Valdai Club. *Destruction, Creation and the New World Order*. Sochi, 18 October 2017. http://valdaiclub.com/events/posts/articles/destruction-creation-and-the-new-world-order-day-2/

Valdai Club. *The Conflict between Universality and Self-Identity*. Sochi, 18 October 2017. http://valdaiclub.com/events/posts/articles/session-4-universalism-self-identity/

India's Role in a Liberal Post-Western World

Samir Saran

ABSTRACT

After a period of significant gains, achieved largely through the establishment of institutions that promoted international liberalism, the global order today finds itself at a crucial juncture. Rising inequality, the proliferation of nationalist politics, technology-induced disruptions and the resurgence of zero-sum geopolitics, are all beginning to shake the foundations of the global governance architecture built assiduously over the past 70 years. It is clear that the liberal order, as it is frequently referred to, will not be able to sustain its influence in the 21st century unless it finds new torchbearers in Asia, where politics and economics are scripting a story very different from that of post-war Europe. To some, it is evident that India, which has successfully combined economic growth with its own liberal traditions, will indeed be the heir to and guarantor of this system as an emerging and leading power.

The financial crisis of 2008 and years of conflict in South and West Asia have left the Atlantic powers with little appetite to serve as arbiters of political stability and guarantors of economic growth.[1] Consequently, the void that this shift has created is being filled by rising and regional powers, many of whom have different ideological moorings than their predecessors. Therefore, on many occasions these rising powers are in contest with the institutions of global governance set up in the aftermath of the Second World War. These institutions, which espoused democratic values, open trade and a rule-based international order, were successful at promoting peace and ensuring high economic growth for much of the late 20th century. However, today we witness a growing clamour for closed borders, selective globalisation and the increasing relevance of rightwing politics across the world. The 2016 presidential elections in the United States, the United Kingdom's decision to exit the European Union, and China's attempt to create a new playbook for Asia and Europe through the Belt and Road Initiative represent a growing threat to the liberal international order and detract from the international system's ability to find new suitors.

The world is on the cusp of something new. It is unclear what will replace the international liberal order or who will be instrumental in shaping it. Therefore, to understand

---

[1] This article builds on some of the ideas explored in previous writings. See Saran, "New Delhi Consensus" and "Globalism, Radicalism and Populism"; as well as Saran and Malik, "Asia's New Normal" and "Currents of Disruption".

India's future in this changing world, this article will posit three primary questions. First is a discussion of the strength of the liberal order and a prognosis on its future. Second, as this century is increasingly implicated by developments in Asia, the article will ask which nations are most likely to shape its politics. And, finally, it ponders if India can be a significant actor and whether it will be able to propagate international liberalism.

Accordingly, this article is organised into three parts. The first examines the current dynamics playing out in the Asian continent and its implications for India. This is followed by a part that explores the currents of disruption in the liberal order and India's perspective on this. Finally, the third argues that India can sustain the liberal order and offers a unique governance model regionally and for the world.

The dynamics of the 'Asian century'

Following the global financial crisis of 2008 and the US' subsequent reluctance to engage proactively with the processes of globalisation, Asia has seen an uneasy multi-polar governance structure. Various actors seek to fill the vacuum that was earlier occupied by the United States, with China leading the race. Other regional powers like India, Russia and Japan are also competing within this common space to shape a cohesive governance system.

How the Asian century, with its lack of a unifying economic, political or security architecture, ultimately takes shape will play a strong role in determining India's position in the larger world order. The quest for regional leadership in Asia is shaped by several competing visions, and the strategic, political and economic churning in the Asia-Pacific is creating a climate of uncertainty and flux.

On issues of economic governance, China seeks to consolidate its position through mega agreements like the Regional Comprehensive Economic Partnership (RCEP) and its ambitious Belt and Road Initiative (BRI).[2] India also seeks to play an active role in determining the region's economic architecture with initiatives like the International North South Transport Corridor (INSTC), the Bay of Bengal Initiative for Multi-Sectoral Technical and Economic Cooperation (BIMSTEC) and the Bangladesh, Bhutan, India, Nepal (BBIN) Initiative.[3]

The digital front will also witness a normative contest as Asian giants seek to realise the potential of the internet as a tool for domestic development. China has sought to establish sovereignty over its internet space, distinct from the 'multistakeholderism' that is envisioned by liberal countries such as the United States and India.[4] China is already well ahead of the race in building its capacity to influence norms in this respect. For example, it is the world's largest e-commerce market, accounting for more than 40 percent of the value of e-commerce transactions worldwide.[5]

The global commons is another ground for contestation. Traditionally, the United States provided security and governance in the Indo-Pacific. Today, however, China's geopolitical ambitions and America's own domestic issues are forcing states in Asia to question its continued preponderance in the region. This uncertainty is forcing states to increase militarisation

---

[2]Grieger, "One Belt, One Road".
[3]Nayyar, "India's Asian Integration Strategy".
[4]Srikumar, "BRICS Cyber Sovereignty".
[5]Woetzel *et al., China's Digital Economy.*

in order to protect their sovereignty, strategic interests and rights over important mineral resources.

Demographics will be another key challenge for Asian states as they move into the 21st century. Technological change is increasingly exposing the hollowness of large unskilled pools of labour, and reducing the comparative advantage enjoyed by many states as a result of low wages.[6] In the coming decades, some Asian states will need to grapple with the challenge of providing jobs for their burgeoning young, while others will have to provide old-age security to rapidly ageing populations – and this will have to be done while struggling to transition from low and middle-income to high-income economies.

As the contours of these forces slowly shape up, three possibilities emerge for Asia, each with its own consequence for India.

Scenario one – The US opts for offshore balancing

The first possibility is that the United States adopts a strategy of 'offshore balancing' in Asia. In this scenario, the US would supplement regional powers like India and Japan in order to improve their capacity to check hegemonic rising powers such as China and to ensure a rule-based order in Asia.

If the United States chooses to aid India in its efforts for regional primacy, two effects will become apparent. The first is that it will become significantly harder for China to strong-arm India and indeed other countries in the neighbourhood. Already, evidence of this entente is evident; the United States is increasingly exporting defence equipment to India and is participating in the annual Malabar navy exercises, meant to shape a maritime security order in the Indian Ocean region.[7] Second, the US will complement India's 'Act East' strategy with its own existing partnerships in Asia. Already, the Logistics Exchange Memorandum of Agreement (LEMOA) offers India access to American military facilities in South East Asia. A close partnership with the United States will give India the opportunity to establish itself as a significant player in the emerging Asian architecture.[8]

However, this will not be an easy transition. For one thing, India continues to maintain its position of 'strategic autonomy' and domestic politics make any formal alliance with the United States difficult. It is also unclear if India can overcome its domestic hurdles to take up this mantle. It has not engaged in deep military reforms, meaning that it continues to employ an essentially 20th century armed forces structure. Similarly, its economic reforms have been insufficient to create dependencies between itself and other Asian states in the same manner as China. Furthermore, the US is continuing to focus on its own geopolitical ambitions in the region and, as a result, its lessening but continued support to Pakistan and its economic co-dependence on China will limit its flexibility in dealing with India.

Scenario two – A great power competition takes off in Asia

The second option is that Asia begins to witness a great power competition. In this scenario, India, Japan, China, the US, and possibly Indonesia and Russia compete for power and influence. Already the world is seeing signs of this in the Indian Ocean region. China's

---

[6]Saxer, "Future of Work in Asia".
[7]White, "US-India Defense and Security Ties".
[8]Pardesi, *American Global Primacy*.

aggressive maritime forays and infrastructure projects in Myanmar, Sri Lanka and Djibouti are all sources of concern for New Delhi. Similarly, China is flexing its muscles in the South China Sea, threatening its neighbours with war if they do not acquiesce to Chinese sentiments.[9] Japan, meanwhile, is going through a period of domestic flux and is increasingly being threatened externally. The newfound nuclear capabilities of North Korea, and continuing disputes with China over the Senkaku Islands and with Russia over the Kuril Islands are forcing it to reconsider its pacifist constitution. As the current resident power in the Indo-Pacific, the United States finds itself in an increasingly untenable security position as China continues to undermine its influence economically and militarily.

These trends are also reflected in the increasing level of militarisation in the region. In 2016, Asia witnessed the fastest growth in defence spending in the world. China is currently the largest spender in the region with an estimated USD 215 billion, amounting to almost half the total spending in Asia. The second largest country in the region, India, spends almost a quarter of that amount at USD 55 billion.[10] Not only the larger states in the region, but also the smaller ones, such as the Philippines and New Zealand, increased their defence spending in the last two years.

Scenario three – The US acquiesces in Chinese hegemony

The third option is American acquiescence in Chinese hegemony in Asia. While China would continue as the only military and economic powerhouse in the region, it is possible that Asia would see a future with several sub-political groupings. The Association of Southeast Asian Nations (ASEAN), South Asian Association for Regional Cooperation (SAARC), Shanghai Cooperation Organisation (SCO), and other economic and political groups would likely proliferate, creating their own dynamics. America's withdrawal from the Trans-Pacific Partnership (TPP) may be a first indication of this possibility.

However, this is unlikely to be a sustainable order, led, as it would be, by relatively resource-poor Asian countries. Most of these regional groupings place limited emphasis on promoting human rights and democracy and continue to stay rooted in concepts of sovereignty and non-interference. In this scenario, the US would remain distantly engaged with these sub-systems, without being invested in their continuity or affiliated to their membership.

As economic power increasingly concentrates in Asia, an illiberal Asian order fraught with contestation and conflict would prove to be problematic for the international system as a whole. As Donald Trump reinforces his 'America first' rhetoric with policy, Asian states which were dependent on America for leadership, security and economic ties would now find themselves having to deal with the rise of China and a protectionist world trading regime on their own.

It is within the changing dynamics of Asia and the world order that India will have to reinvent itself as it seeks to fuel its own political ambitions and economic growth.

---

[9] Wood, "China to Philippines".
[10] Tian *et al.*, "World military expenditure 2016".

Currents of disruption in the international liberal order

The liberal order itself is embattled by several challenges. The wave of anti-globalisation sentiment provoked by increasing income inequality is threatening dominant economic models that have sustained growth since the Second World War. Consequently, slow economic growth, immigration from fractured parts of the world, and radical non-state actors such as the Islamic State in Iraq and Syria (ISIS) are fuelling populism and xenophobia in public discourse. Moreover, automation and artificial intelligence are challenging states' ability to provide meaningful employment and social stability. Finally, the world is also witnessing the rise of geopolitics, as revisionist powers such as Russia and China increasingly assert their influence in contested regions.

The international liberal order rested on two pillars. The first pillar contained the economic aspect that included competition, open markets and free trade. The second pillar embodied democracy and its values, comprising the rule of law and human rights. Today, both these pillars are buffeted by several interrelated currents.

The backlash against globalisation

The first one is the complex dynamics of globalisation today. Growing financial and institutional interdependence has made traditional policy levers ineffective, reducing the control national governments have over their policies. In the EU for instance, citizens often feel like decisions are taken in Brussels with limited intervention from national governments. In the same vein, jobs and economic growth in the United States are often tied to decisions in Beijing or the World Trade Organisation (WTO).

Additionally, globalisation has led to a proliferation of non-state actors such as transnational corporations, NGOs and militant groups who often crowd out national governments, making it difficult for them to design effective policies. A case in point is the opacity with which the Trans Pacific Partnership (TPP) negotiations took place, leading many activists to claim that the trade treaty benefited corporations as opposed to American citizens.[11]

Furthermore, while globalised economies have promoted the free and rapid flow of labour, capital and information, they have also led to a significant concentration of wealth amongst the few. A recent study shows that between 2005 and 2014, real income in developed countries stagnated or fell for more than 65 percent of households, composed of close to 540 million people.[12] This economic stagnation also explains why public perception of the matter is pessimistic; a Pew Research Center survey shows that 49 percent of Americans think that US involvement in the global economy is a bad thing because it lowers wages and costs jobs.[13]

In essence, globalisation has driven multiple wedges into society, between skilled and unskilled workers, between global professionals and local industry, between urban and rural dwellers, and between elites and ordinary citizens.

Despite these trends in the West, developing countries continue to view globalisation favourably. In part, this is because they have become the new drivers of economic growth

---

[11]Sundaram, "Who would TPP benefit?".
[12]McKinsey Global Institute, *Poorer Than Their Parents*.
[13]Drake and Doherty, "U.S. Role in the World".

and now account for over two-thirds of the world's GDP.[14] Consequently, the Bretton Woods system that formed the basis of globalisation is also facing a backlash from powers such as India and China, who believe that their rising status has not been adequately acknowledged. These countries are responding to their lack of influence by creating new institutions, like the Asian Infrastructure Investment Bank (AIIB) and the New Development Bank (NDB).

Increasingly, China is scripting a new story for globalisation. This is evident from President Xi Jinping's speech at the 2017 World Economic Forum, where he shunned protectionism and called for a new wave of globalisation distinct from that driven by Western powers.[15] President Xi is portraying the ambitious Belt and Road Initiative as the new driver of globalisation for developing and underdeveloped countries in Africa and Asia.[16]

However, these rising powers do not have the same kind of resources or reach needed to uphold the international order that the Atlantic powers do. These countries are naturally constrained by domestic inequities and development gaps, rendering them incapable of wielding their economic and political capital in the manner that a great power would.

Moreover, it is unclear whether emerging powers will necessarily see value in such normative aspects of the international liberal order as democracy and human rights. China, for example, has notoriously sought to save UN funds by scaling back on its human rights division.[17] It has also developed autocratic relationships with countries like Turkey, which has promised to clamp down on anti-China media.[18] In addition, China has regularly used trade and economic sanctions to punish countries that refuse to acquiesce to its political visions.[19]

These developments have a bearing on India's place in the liberal order. Indian policy-makers see open economic policies as central to India's ambitions in the coming decades. In fact, the 2017 Economic Survey explicitly noted, "Given that India's growth ambitions of 8-10 percent require export growth of about 15-20 percent, any serious retreat from openness on the part of India's trading partners would jeopardize those ambitions."[20] It is no wonder then that, after taking stock of developments in America and Europe, India called for a coalition of middle-income countries to shore up support for globalisation at the 2017 G20 summit in Hamburg.[21]

The rise of populism in public discourse

The second trend is the rise of populism, xenophobia and radicalism in public discourse. Ongoing insurgencies in the Middle East and North Africa have witnessed the rise of militant Islamic groups such as Al-Qaeda, ISIS and Boko Haram, which have spawned offshoots in South Asia in areas like Pakistan, Kashmir, Philippines, Myanmar and the Uyghur region of China. Similarly, the spate of 'lone wolf' attacks in Germany, Britain and France reveal that radicalism is now an idea that is being exported around the world.

---

[14]Dadush, *The future of globalisation*.
[15]Anderlini and Wang, "Xi Jinping".
[16]Vangeli, "New wave of globalisation".
[17]Charbonneau, "UN Human Rights Posts".
[18]"Turkey promises to eliminate anti-China media reports", *Reuters*, 3 August 2017.
[19]Chellaney, "China's Weaponization of Trade."
[20]Government of India, *Economic Survey*, Vol 1, 2016-17, 6. http://indiabudget.nic.in/es2016-17/echap01.pdf
[21]"India calls for middle-income country coalition to revive globalization", *Economic Times*, 8 June 2017.

Consequently, liberal values are being challenged by older visions of power based on identity, reinforcing Samuel Huntington's view that the global order would be premised on a "clash of civilizations".[22] For example, according to the Gallup Coexist Index, 58 percent of French Muslims "very strongly" identify with their religion, compared with only 23 percent of the French public.[23] Similarly, a poll in Britain revealed that British Muslim values differ wildly from public opinion on issues such as homosexuality, gender equality and terrorism, with nearly a quarter of respondents supporting the introduction of Sharia law in some areas of Britain.[24]

Religion and culture are not driving illiberal politics in just the Middle East. Francis Fukuyama has written that in an era of nationalist politics in the West, the "greatest challenge to liberal democracy comes not so much from overtly authoritarian powers such as China, as from within".[25] Fukuyama wrote these words in light of President Donald Trump's refusal to endorse the TPP, criticism of the North Atlantic Treaty Organisation (NATO) and bellicose anti-Muslim rhetoric. These positions constitute an outright challenge to the foundational principles of the international order such as free trade, shared defence partnerships and liberal values.

Similarly, anxiety linked to immigration and slow economic growth is intersecting in a toxic manner in Europe, having manifested itself most spectacularly in the United Kingdom's exit from the European Union.[26] This anxiety is slowly spreading throughout the continent. Despite the fact that some populist parties have lost elections in France, Netherlands and Austria, they continue to gain traction across Europe. Marine La Pen, for example, captured a third of the vote in France's election and Greet Wilders' Freedom Party is the second largest party in the Netherlands.[27]

Exacerbating all of these trends is a fragmented media and internet landscape. The diffusion of power that the information communication revolution brought about in the 1990s has spurred the growth of several competing narratives that are increasingly employed in confrontational manners.

Fake news, twitter bots, Russian influence campaigns, big data and artificial intelligence converged to make the 2016 US presidential elections one of the most divisive in history. For the first time, the potentially anti-democratic nature of social media was on full display as it polarised citizens like never before by creating echo chambers and biased feedback loops. In fact, a 2014 study by the Pew Research Center that tracked US Twitter discussions found that political topics were debated in polarised groups that largely interacted separately.[28] Even in Europe, populist parties like the *Alternative für Deutschland* (AfD) in Germany and Marine La Penn's *Front National* in France have all bolstered their anti-Europe and anti-immigration messages effectively on platforms such as Facebook and Twitter.[29]

In India, the impact of identity and technology on social cohesion can be immense. In a country where religious polarisation continues to occur, and whose young population is

---

[22]Huntington, "The clash of civilizations?", 22.
[23]The Co-exist Foundation, "The Gallup Coexist Index".
[24]Frampton *et al.*, "Unsettled Belonging".
[25]Fukuyama, "US against the world?".
[26]Inglehart and Norris, *Trump, Brexit, populism*.
[27]Maher, "Populism in Europe".
[28]Smith *et al.*, "Mapping Twitter Topic Networks".
[29]Hendrickson and Galston, "Why are populists winning online".

one of the fastest growing constituencies adopting the internet, failing to keep pace with the rapid mobilisation which technology allows might lead to increased social instability.

Ghosts in the machine

The third trend relates to fundamental technological shifts. Developments in artificial intelligence (AI), robotics, big data and the internet of things are heralding what many refer to as the 'fourth industrial revolution'. The consequences of these shifts are still uncertain and how nations shape their economic and political institutions to cope with them will have a significant impact on the continued success of the world order.

Erik Brynjolfsson and Andrew McAfee[30] contend that technology will destroy jobs faster than it will create them. According to them, the fact that incomes are stagnating despite increasing productivity from industry signals that humans are increasingly becoming irrelevant in producing additional wealth. Because of this, investment will continue to prioritise high-skilled individuals, capital and new technologies, instead of focusing on employees, leading to a hollowing out of the middle class. Evidence from around the world is confirming their hypothesis – various studies estimate that automation will threaten 77 percent of all jobs in China,[31] 56 percent of jobs in the ASEAN countries,[32] and 47 percent of jobs in the United States over the next few decades.[33]

Anecdotal evidence of this trend is forthcoming even in India, where companies have already begun to announce that they are going to replace jobs with robots over the next few years.[34] Developments in robotics have made such shifts in production relatively cheap. According to the International Federation of Robotics, 2100 industrial robots were sold in India in 2014, and estimates suggest that this number could rise to 6000 by 2018.[35] Similarly, studies predict that while the information technology (IT) and business process outsourcing (BPO) sectors may generate limited jobs for high-skilled employees, overall the industry will see a net decrease in employment generated due to gains in AI by 2022.[36]

Industry experts and governments have mooted the idea of a Universal Basic Income to cushion against the disruptive forces of new technologies. However, income stability does not necessarily translate into productivity. It remains an open question whether or not nations will manage to maintain social cohesion in an era in which jobs will continue to haemorrhage. Nevertheless, experience does reveal that India is capable of skilling its population to engage with new technology. For example, India benefited immensely from the internet revolution around the turn of the century. Having invested in higher education, it capably created a large cadre of skilled workers for the service industry, resulting in new jobs and economic growth. One interesting anecdote reflecting this ability is the extent to which Western companies were reliant on Indian skill to fix the Y2K 'Millennium' bug in 1999.[37] For Indian policymakers, this experience will have to provide a roadmap for coping with new disruptions.

---

[30]Bernstein and Raman, "The great decoupling".
[31]World Bank, *Digital Dividends*, 129.
[32]Chang and Huynh, *ASEAN in Transformation*.
[33]Frey and Osborne, *The Future of Employment*.
[34]"Raymond to replace 10000 jobs with robots in the next 3 years", *Economic Times*, 16 September 2016.
[35]Pearson, "Robot invasion".
[36]Fersht, "Automation impact".
[37]Goldenberg, "Boom time in India".

Unemployment is not the only consequence of these disruptive forces. As political and economic power continues to diffuse, the notion of public goods will have to be revisited as well. While the state has traditionally provided these goods, behemoths like Uber, which is increasingly integrating with public road networks, are slowly reversing this trend. At the same time, governments and forums like trade unions have very little control over the policy implications of their actions. For example, questions about whether or not Uber is a transport service or an internet intermediary have plagued regulators across continents.[38] Similarly, the plight of its drivers and the scope of national labour laws are still being debated.[39]

Moreover, ethical, moral and legal principles will have to be revisited as artificial intelligence begins pervading our daily lives. Various studies have revealed that AI replicates the racial bias present in humans,[40] posing stark implications for equality. Further, in a globalised economy, it is still unclear which jurisdiction will apply its laws to actions related to artificial intelligence. Consider, for example, if a driverless car crashes in Dublin, whom will this act be attributed to: the Irish government, the car's original code writers in California, or a software programmer in Hyderabad to whom maintenance is outsourced?[41] Attributing liability to transnational corporations through domestic laws is not a new challenge; however, the scale of this conundrum will likely expand exponentially.

The return of geopolitics

Fourth, geopolitical and geo-economic trends are being exacerbated by revisionist powers like China and Russia. Russia's intervention in Georgia and its subsequent annexation of Crimea and intervention in Ukraine raised hackles in Europe and the United States. Similarly, China's aggressive actions across its borders, most prominently in the South China Sea are posing security challenges to the US and other democracies like Japan, South Korea and India. The Middle East has transformed into an unrelenting cycle of strife and war with the Syrian civil war being host to several proxy struggles between Iran, Saudi Arabia, Russia and the United States.

For India as well, the threat in its neighbourhood is clear. China's infrastructure activities along its borders have enticed countries like Nepal and Bangladesh to hedge their relationships with India. Similarly, the China-Pakistan Economic Corridor, which passes through Pakistan-Occupied Kashmir, is a direct affront to India's sovereignty. China's development of the ports of Hambantota in Sri Lanka and Gwadar in Pakistan are seen in New Delhi as a part of China's 'string of pearls' intended to limit India's ambitions of being an Asian power.

What then are the implications of all these trends? For one thing, the globalisation spurred by the Atlantic powers in the 20th century to stimulate economic growth in nations that were devastated by the Second World War is over. In an era of rapid technological change and slower economic growth, the same imperatives no longer exist. Second, while globalisation connected communities and societies together, they were not necessarily homogenous and had little in common. Digital spaces were supposed to bring people together; instead, the internet has polarised individuals like never before. Finally, it is clear that the international

---

[38]Bhatia, "Uber".
[39]Prassal, "Uber, Mechanical Turks".
[40]Devlin, "AI programs".
[41]Saran and Malik, "Currents of Disruption".

liberal order is in need of new torchbearers. These torchbearers will emerge from Asia, Africa and Latin America, countries whose shared values and commitment to human rights and trade will help sustain the liberal order regionally. Their rise will be neither smooth nor inevitable. If disruptors today find the cost to destabilise the global system rather low, its custodians realise that it is expensive to fix the mess they leave behind.[42]

Towards a 'New Delhi Consensus'

Considering all the factors that are buffeting the international liberal order, how does India see itself in the world? Over the next decade, India is well on its way towards becoming a multitrillion-dollar economy and the political narrative India frames around this growth will go a long way towards shaping any world order. Ever since the economic reforms of 1991, India has combined liberal values with the market economy. In this regard, India's rise has been exceptional in Asia, considering that most other states have turned authoritarian in one way or another.

The success of this model has prompted Indian policymakers to recalibrate India's role in the world. In March 2015, Foreign Secretary S. Jaishankar delivered a speech in which he declared that India was intent on playing the role of a "leading" instead of a "balancing" power in Asia.[43]

However, in a complex and multipolar world, India will find that balancing its external ambitions and its own domestic shortcomings will be a difficult challenge. To place the importance of India's rise as a liberal country in context, it is important to understand the impact its political-economic decisions will have globally. The Millennium Development Goals were largely successful because of China's rapid rise and its ability to lift millions of its citizens out of poverty. Similarly, the Sustainable Development Goals agreed by the global community in 2015 will essentially be the narrative of India doing the same, but in a very different world and context. If India succeeds in its endeavour, it will have a development model replicable by large portions of the developing world.

This is what "great powers" do; they provide solutions and roadmaps for others. India as a leading power must take this challenge and deliver on it, for its own sake, and to help achieve the global ambition of a better world.[44]

What then are the characteristics that would shape a 'New Delhi Consensus'?

A sustained democratic project

To start with, India is likely to pursue a developmental model that combines democracy and liberal values with high growth, setting a template for other emerging economies.

The economic liberalisation of 1991 unleashed India on its path towards higher growth. From an abysmal 3.5 percent annual growth in the 1980s to a consistent growth rate of 7 percent since the beginning of 2000, India has lifted millions out of poverty owing to greater integration with the world economy and domestic reforms.[45] Alongside this extraordinary economic growth, India has also successfully retained the liberal democratic architecture

---

[42]Saran, "Globalism, radicalism and populism".
[43]Jaishankar, "Speech at India-US 2015".
[44]Saran, "India as a leading power".
[45]Anklesaria, *Indian Economic Reform*.

it gave itself in 1947. Barring a brief period of emergency in 1975, India has successfully conducted elections, peaceful transfer of power, and a broad-based devolution of social and economic rights. The numerous political parties, civil society organisations and diverse media that dot the Indian landscape evidence the vibrancy of its democracy.[46]

Furthermore, India is keenly aware of the benefits of a more globalised world. Despite India's eagerness to establish new multilateral institutions, such as the BRICS, it continues to see value in supporting institutions such as the United Nations. India's willingness to allow civil society and businesses to shape its policy is also indicative of the reflexive attraction it feels towards liberal internationalism. Civil society organisations in India, for example, have been instrumental in pushing the agenda of multistakeholderism in internet governance,[47] distinct from the notion of cyber sovereignty propounded by nations like China and Russia.

However, if India is legitimately to claim its inheritance of the liberal international order, it must first address the complex development challenges it faces domestically. India's new world is not without its contradictions – indeed, the country's political, social, and economic development has been neither coherent nor smooth.

A by-product of India's stunning economic growth is heightened inequality. In India, the richest one percent owns 58 percent of the country's wealth, while the poorer half jostles for a mere 2 percent of national wealth.[48] Indeed, a 2015 Pew Research Center survey found that less than three percent of the total population of India has incomes that can be classified as middle class.[49] Economic problems aside, India continues to grapple with a myriad of social challenges, including the prevalence of caste inequality and episodic bouts of religious tensions.

Yet, despite the endemic malpractice amongst its political class, widespread poverty and challenges of state capacity, democracy is thriving in India. In fact, several surveys in India have found that Indians consider democracy preferable to any other kind of government; they support the right to a fair trial, free expression, the right to vote, and free media.[50]

Arguably, India's democratic path is more relevant to the developing countries of Asia, Africa and the Middle East. Many countries in these regions continue to suffer from colonial legacies, ethnic rivalry, and large unskilled populations. India's constitutional model of protecting individual and group rights, the devolution of political power to local government and its multiparty system to reconcile various political interests is far better suited to these parts of the world.

A unique cultural ethos

Second, if India is to embrace and inherit the liberal international order, it must offer a distinctly non-Western ethos and way of functioning. The pre-conditions which allowed democracy to thrive in Western countries, such as capitalist modes of production fuelled by industrialisation, largely secular societies and an entrenched bureaucratic class are absent in large parts of the developing world.

[46]"Freedom in the world 2017", Freedom House, 2017, https://freedomhouse.org/report/freedom-world/freedom-world-2017
[47]Colin *et al.*, "Interactions and Policy-Making".
[48]Chakravarty, "The richest 1% of Indians".
[49]Kochhar, "Poverty's Plunge".
[50]Medcalf, "Facing the future".

In a world that is increasingly fractured along religious and ethnic fault lines, with xen-ophobia and populism infiltrating even the more liberal bastions of the West, India has much to offer by way of multiculturalism. As these countries now begin to comprehend the challenges of managing multi-ethnic societies, it is worth noting that India has done so for centuries. This ethos of plurality, diversity and multiculturalism is distinctly Indian and has carried over into Independent India, with its Constitution recognising religious rights and freedoms. Despite this variety of cultures and religions that have inhabited India, the great democratic project has largely continued uninhibited.

Like in many other parts of the world, instances of identity-based polarisation are visi-ble in India. While this is not a new phenomenon, it is unlikely to form the central feature of India's social existence. The strength of India's institutions and the tenacity of its civil society have ensured that, irrespective of the political party in power, India as a country is largely resilient to the anti-Islamic and anti-Semitic sentiments that prevail in many parts of the world. Against the backdrop of rising nationalism and populist politics around the world, Foreign Secretary S. Jaishankar asked, "Can India be different by being different?"[51] The foreign secretary was highlighting that India, more than any other country, is uniquely situated in its ability to manage the inherent contradictions and conflicts that arise in multicultural societies. All political parties in India strive to manage these contradictions and seek to arrive at a golden median in order to ensure that India's diverse communities co-exist peacefully.

Some detractors claim that the contemporary political climate, real or imagined, chal-lenges the fine cultural equilibrium that has defined India. Unfortunately, their criticism stems from a belief that pluralism is a direct by-product of, and perhaps made possible by the adoption of Western-style democracy. India's cultural ethos, however, predates current political structures. Even under foreign rule – whether it was the ravaging hordes of west Asia or the brutal colonial powers of Europe – India's syncretic culture remained resilient and robust. As Shashi Tharoor eloquently states, what truly defines India is the idea of "an ever-ever land – emerging from an ancient civilization, united by a shared history".[52] India's pluralism, then, stems from a unique civilisational consensus – one that is likely to survive troubled times.

In terms of foreign policy, the Indian government has emerged as a prominent votary of the values embodied by the liberal order. At various speeches abroad, Prime Minister Narendra Modi himself has emphasised the importance of "shared democratic values". He has highlighted the importance of globalisation for economic growth and his government has repeatedly stressed the importance of a rule-based international order in various joint documents with the United States and Japan.[53] It is clear that despite India's inherent social contradictions and occasional government apathy, the Indian state is unlikely to forsake the liberal values that have contributed to its success for so long.

Nevertheless, despite the successes of its own democratic model, India has largely been reluctant to export it in the same way that Western powers have. India's foreign policy discourse is still dominated by the country's traditional insistence on the principles of non-intervention and national sovereignty, which are by-products of the Nehru era. While Western countries might express dismay over India's reluctance to promote democracy

---

[51]Saran, "New Delhi Consensus".
[52]Tharoor, "India at 70".
[53]Hall, "Narendra Modi", 128.

overtly abroad, their own ventures have not borne much success. If anything can be gleaned from America's disastrous interventions in Vietnam, Iraq and Afghanistan, it is that democracy and liberal values cannot be imposed from above.

This is not to say, however, that India has not made any such efforts. India has been a member of the 'Community of Democracies' since 2000 and is the second most important sponsor of the UN Democracy Fund, a small UN agency that works with NGOs in the field of democracy assistance.[54] India also annually contributes USD 50,000 to the International Institute for Democracy and Electoral Assistance, which is committed to democratic capacity building around the world.[55]

Located as it is in an unstable neighbourhood, India cannot afford to be evangelical about promoting democracy. Instead, India is attempting to strike a balance: it seeks to respect the various social contracts between state, society and business while promoting democracy and nation building where it can. For example, whereas it has been critical of human rights violations in its neighbouring states, such as Sri Lanka and Myanmar, it has refused to side with the West on issues like sovereignty and the use of force.[56]

The Modi government has similarly been pragmatic in its approach towards unstable states around India's periphery. Yet, this caution must not lead to the presumption that India cannot sustain liberalism in its neighbourhood. Instead, it suggests that the liberal order will have to recalibrate some of its propensity to intervene on breach of values. India seeks to offer a bottom-up model for democracy as opposed to the moral highhandedness of the West.

India's constructive role in global governance

Third, India is emerging as a key player in issues of global governance and development. However, unlike the Atlantic powers that sought to underwrite their own hegemony through the United Nations and multilateral trading regimes, India has championed the cause of developing and least developed countries through multipolarity and multilateralism. The founding generations of independent India were adamant about basing its foreign policy on moral principles, advocating the dissolution of military blocs, solidarity amongst developing countries, and non-alignment.

This is why India rarely sees the global commons in extractive terms and is less inclined to exercise state power and force to dominate them. In fact, through the 1950s and '60s, India participated in the negotiations for the Outer Space Treaty, the United Nations Convention on the Law of the Seas, and the Antarctic Treaty, and placed a special emphasis on protecting and preserving the "common heritage of mankind".[57] Its own actions in the neighbourhood are reflective of its inherent tendencies towards promoting good governance and rule of law in the commons. While revisionist powers like China are now seeking to militarise the Indian Ocean, India has been a net provider of security in the region. The Indian Navy patrols the Internationally Recommended Transit Corridor near the Gulf of Aden, and closer to home, India has often been the first responder and primary provider of aid during disasters like the Indian Ocean tsunami, Cyclone Sidr and Cyclone Nargis.[58]

---

[54]"Democracy Fund", Permanent Mission of India to the UN, https://www.pminewyork.org/pages.php?id=11.
[55]"Supporting Democracy Abroad – India", Freedom House, 17 December 2014, http://www.refworld.org/docid/5497f82715.html
[56]*Ibid.*
[57]Mohan, "Rising India", 135-6.
[58]Xavier and Baruah, *Brussels and Delhi.*

Most importantly perhaps, India has played a pivotal role in climate change negotiations under the United Nations Framework on Climate Change. Traditionally, India fought for more carbon space in order for developing countries to complete their own industrialisations. However, Prime Minister Narendra Modi chose to abandon this narrative, instead highlighting the civilisational and cultural importance of environmental preservation in the Indian ethos. By the time the Paris Conference took place in December 2015, India had already announced its nationally determined target of reducing its carbon intensity by around 35 percent by 2030 and had declared its intention to deploy up to 175 GW of renewable energy by 2022 in order to offset its use of conventional energy resources for growth.[59]

Indeed, India will be uniquely situated in its ability to transition into a high-income economy without the benefits of low-cost and unsustainable modes of energy production. If it can achieve a replicable model, India will have set the stage for millions of citizens from across the developing world to improve their economic conditions sustainably.

A non-interventionist development paradigm

Finally, as India charts its way towards a multitrillion-dollar economy in the coming decades, it will also begin supplying global public goods. Already, India's total development assistance in 2015-16 reached close to USD 2.5 billion dollars, surpassing several traditional OECD donors in 2015.[60] For now, India has focused on its own neighbourhood, with countries like Bhutan, Afghanistan, Nepal and Maldives being the largest recipients of its assistance. However, India is also emerging as a primary development partner for Africa – almost half of all lines of credit extended by India over the past decade were to Africa,[61] touching close to USD 8 billion in 2017.[62] In 2015, the Indian government pledged an additional USD 10 billion dollars to Africa over five years.[63]

If India is to emerge as a supplier of finance and aid, it will have to abandon the philosophical moorings of 'south-south' cooperation that has historically determined its aid. While the global south will inevitably be the largest recipient pool, India will have to begin reframing its development aid in broader geographic terms. The first geographical area must encompass India's immediate neighbourhood; the second would cover its extended neighbourhood, reaching out across Asia and the Indian Ocean, and the third would include geographies that may be distant, but relevant to the global commons.[64]

What is remarkable about India's foreign aid, however, is not the amount it lends, but the manner in which it does so. Unlike Western aid, India's development cooperation is recipient-led and projects are determined on the basis of priorities set by the recipient country. No conditions are attached to the assistance; and the government, as opposed to civil society organisations, is the main conduit for implementing projects.[65] Having made no attempts to pursue exceptionalism – unlike the United States and China – India's development story will be embraced with vigour by foreign markets and governments alike.

---

[59]Government of India, *India's Intended Nationally Determined Contribution*, http://www4.unfccc.int/submissions/INDC/Published%20Documents/India/1/INDIA%20INDC%20TO%20UNFCCC.pdf
[60]Zhang and Shivakumar, "Dragon versus Elephant", 260-1.
[61]Gokaran *et al., India and Africa,* 35-8.
[62]Pattanayak, "India's Lines of Credit".
[63]"Modi sweetens Africa ties with $10bn credit line", *Times of India,* 30 October 2015.
[64]Saran and Aneja, "Economic diplomacy".
[65]Saran, *India's Foregin Aid.*

Conclusion

Today, the Atlantic powers are showing signs of fatigue and are slowly disengaging from their responsibility in upholding the liberal international order. Globalisation, populism, technology and geopolitics have all come together to contest the traditional pillars of the international order. What the international order needs are new drivers and torchbearers, whose growth and normative values can sustain its appeal around the world.

It should be clear then that there is only one legitimate heir to the global liberal order of any consequence: India. New Delhi alone can pursue the expansion of regional and global economic linkages while staying true to the ideals that drive them.[66]

If anything, Prime Minister Narendra Modi has taken great effort to develop on these principles. India's leadership role on matters of global governance (such as climate and internet regimes) and the government's 'Neighbourhood First' policy emphasises the desire to cultivate a New Delhi Consensus. Unlike the Beijing Consensus which is heavily state reliant or the Washington Consensus which does not see the state as a necessary intermediary, India will acknowledge the importance of state, civil society and business in framing a consensus around its role in the liberal order.

The history of India is a saga of the progress of society and of social and community institutions, with or without a strong state and sometimes in spite of the state. We cannot afford to forget that essence while constructing the New Delhi Consensus.[67]

References

Anderlini, J., and Wang Feng W. "Xi Jinping delivers robust defence of globalisation at Davos". *Financial Times*, 17 January 2017. https://www.ft.com/content/67ec2ec0-dca2-11e6-9d7c-be108f1c1dce

Anklesaria, S. *Twenty-Five Years of Indian Economic Reform*, Policy Analysis No. 803. Washington: CATO Institute, 26 October 2016.

Bernstein, A., and A. Raman. "The great decoupling: An interview with Erik Brynjolfsson and Andrew McAfee". *Harvard Business Review*, June 2015. https://hbr.org/2015/06/the-great-decoupling.

Bhatia, G. "Uber Runs into Legal Headwinds in Delhi and Luxembourg". *Bloomberg Quint,* 15 May 2017. https://www.bloombergquint.com/opinion/2017/05/15/uber-runs-into-legal-headwinds-in-delhi-and-luxembourg

Chakravarty, M. "The richest 1% of Indians now own 58.4% of wealth". *LiveMint*, 24 November 2016. http://www.livemint.com/Money/MML9OZRwaACyEhLzUNImnO/The-richest-1-of-Indians-now-own-584-of-wealth.html

Chang, J., and P. Huynh. *ASEAN in Transformation, The future of jobs at risk of automation*, Working Paper No. 9. Geneva: International Labour Organisation, Bureau for Employers Activities, 2016.

Charbonneau, L. "China Pushes to Cut UN Human Rights Posts". *Human Rights Watch*, 7 June 2017. https://www.hrw.org/news/2017/06/07/china-pushes-cut-un-human-rights-posts.

Chellaney, B. "China's Weaponization of Trade". *Project Syndicate*, 26 July 2017. https://www.project-syndicate.org/commentary/china-weaponization-of-trade-by-brahma-chellaney-2017-07

---

[66]Saran, "Globalism, radicalism and populism".
[67]Saran, "New Delhi Consensus".

Colin, A., R. Subramaniam and V. Gagnon. "Interactions and Policy-Making: Civil Society Perspectives on the Multistakeholder Internet Governance Process in India". Philadelphia: Internet Policy Observatory, 2015.

Dadush, U. *The future of globalisation*, Policy Brief -17/18. Rabat, Morocco: OCP Policy Centre, May 2017.

Devlin, H. "AI programs exhibit racial and gender biases, research reveals". *The Guardian,* 13 April 2017. https://www.theguardian.com/technology/2017/apr/13/ai-programs-exhibit-racist-and-sexist-biases-research-reveals.

Drake, B., and C. Doherty. "Key findings on how Americans view the U.S. role in the world". Washington DC: Pew Research Center, May 2016.

Fersht, P. "Automation impact: India's services industry workforce to shrink by 480,000 by 2021". *Horses for Sources*, 3 July 2016. https://www.horsesforsources.com/indias-services-industry-set-to-lose-640000-low-skilled-jobs-to-automation-by

Frampton, M., D. Goodhart and K. Mahmood. "Unsettled Belonging: A survey of Britain's Muslim communities". *Policy Exchange*, 2 Dec 2016.

Frey, C., and M. Osborne. *The Future of Employment: How Susceptible are Jobs to Computerisation?*, Working Paper. Oxford: Oxford Martin Programme on Technology and Employment, 2013.

Fukuyama, F. "US against the world? Trump's America and the new global order". *Financial Times*, 11 November 2016. https://www.ft.com/content/6a43cf54-a75d-11e6-8b69-02899e8bd9d1

Gokaran, S., W. Sidhu and S. Godbole. *India and Africa: Forging a strategic partnership.* New Delhi: Brookings India, 20 October 2015.

Goldenberg, S. "Boom time in India as the millennium bug bites". *The Guardian,* 30 December 1998. https://www.theguardian.com/world/1998/dec/30/millennium.uk

Grieger, G. "One Belt, One Road: Chinas regional integration initiative". Brussels: European Parliamentary Research Service, July 2016.

Hall, I. "Narendra Modi and India's normative power". *International Affairs* 93, no. 1 (2017): 113–31.

Hendrickson, C., and W. Galston. "Why are populists winning online? Social media reinforces their anti-establishment message". *Techtank*, Brookings Institute, 28 April 2017.

Huntington, S. "The clash of civilizations?" *Foreign Affairs* 72, no. 3 (Summer 1993): 22–49.

Inglehart, I., and P. Norris. *Trump, Brexit and the rise of populism: Economic have-nots and cultural backlash*, Faculty Research Working Paper 16-026. Cambridge, MA: Harvard Kennedy School, August 2016.

Jaishankar, S. "Speech at India-US 2015: Partnering for Peace and Prosperity". New Delhi, 16 March 2015. http://www.vifindia.org/speeches-video/2015/march/19/india-u-s-2015-partnering-for-peace-and-prosperity-2

Kochhar, R. "Despite Poverty's Plunge, Middle-Class Status Remains Out of Reach for Many". Washington DC: Pew Research Center, 8 July 8 2015.

Maher, R. "Why is populism still a threat in Europe". *World Economic Forum*, 12 June 2017. https://www.weforum.org/agenda/2017/06/populism-is-still-a-threat-in-europe-heres-why

McKinsey Global Institute. *Poorer Than Their Parents. A New Perspective on Income Inequality*, Report. New York: McKinsey Global Institute, July 2016.

Medcalf, R. "Facing the future, Indian views of the world ahead, India Poll". Sydney and Melbourne: Lowy Institute for Foreign Policy and the Australia India Institute, 2013. https://www.lowyinstitute.org/publications/india-poll-2013

Mohan, C. "Rising India: Partner in Shaping the Global Commons?". *The Washington Quarterly* 33, no. 3 (Summer 2010): 133–48.

Nayyar, D. "India's Asian integration strategy". *East Asia Forum,* 7 March 2017. http://www.eastasiaforum.org/2017/03/07/indias-asian-integration-strategy/

Pardesi, M. *American Global Primacy and the Rise of India.* Asia Pacific Issues No. 129. Honolulu: East-West Centre, March 2017.

Pattanayak, B. "India's lines of credit to Africa touches $8 billion". *Indian Express,* 24 May 2017. http://www.financialexpress.com/economy/indias-lines-of-credit-to-africa-touches-8-billion/682818/

Pearson, N. "Robot invasion undercuts Modi's quest to put Indians to work". *Bloomberg,* 10 August 2015. https://www.bloomberg.com/amp/news/articles/2015-08-09/india-robot-invasion-undercuts-modi-s-quest-to-put-poor-to-work

Prassal, J. "Are Uber, Mechanical Turks and other 'crowdwork' platforms employers?". *Oxford Business Law Blog,* 9 March 2017. https://www.law.ox.ac.uk/research-and-subject-groups/research-collection-law-and-technology/blog/2017/02/are-uber-mechanical

Saran, S. "Building a New Delhi Consensus". *Reflections*, Observer Research Foundation, New Delhi, 18 March 2017.

Saran, S. "Globalism, radicalism and populism on Raisina Hill". *ORF online,* 16 February 2017. http://www.orfonline.org/expert-speaks/globalism-radicalism-populism-raisina-hill/

Saran, S. "India as a leading power: Shaping the development narrative at home and abroad". Observer Research Foundation, New Delhi, 7 April 2017.

Saran, S. *India's Foreign Aid: Prospects and Challenges.* Cambridge, MA: Harvard University, 2014.

Saran, S., and A. Malik, "Currents of disruption: Not just a new world order, but a new world". *The Interpreter*, Lowy Institute, 7 April 2017.

Saran, S., and A. Malik. "Asia's new normal: Making multilateralism work with multipolarity". Observer Research Foundation, New Delhi, 4 June 2016.

Saran, S., and U. Aneja. "Economic diplomacy and development partnerships: Rethinking India's role and relevance". *ORF Expert Speak*, October 2016. http://www.orfonline.org/expert-speaks/india-economic-diplomacy-development-partnerships/

Saxer, M. "The future of work in Asia". Observer Research Foundation, New Delhi, 14 February 2017. http://www.orfonline.org/expert-speaks/the-future-of-work-in-asia/

Smith, M. A., L. Rainie, B. Shneiderman and I. Himelboim. "Mapping Twitter Topic Networks: From Polarized Crowds to Community Clusters". Pew Research Centre, 20 February 2014.

Srikumar, M. "Should BRICS rally around China's call for cyber sovereignty?". Observer Research Foundation, 7 June 2017. http://www.orfonline.org/expert-speaks/should-brics-rally-around-china-call-for-cyber-sovereignty/

Sundaram, J. "Who would the TPP really benefit?". *World Economic Forum*, Davos, 3 June 2016. https://www.weforum.org/agenda/2016/06/who-would-the-tpp-really-benefit

The Co-exist Foundation. "The Gallup Coexist Index 2009: A Global Study of Interfaith Relations", 2009.

Tian, N., A. Fleurant, P. Wezeman, and S. Wezeman. "Trends in world military expenditure 2016". *SIPRI Fact Sheet*. Stockholm: SIPRI, April, 2017.

Tharoor, S. "As India turns 70, Shashi Tharoor reflects on what makes us India". *The Quint,* 15 August 2017. https://www.thequint.com/voices/opinion/as-we-turn-70-shashi-tharoor-reflects-on-what-makes-us-indian-nation

Vangeli, A. "Is China the potential driver of a new wave of globalisation". *The Conversation*, May 2017. https://theconversation.com/is-china-the-potential-driver-of-a-new-wave-of-globalisation-71575

White, J. "A low velocity, high inertia relationship: What's next for US-India defense and security ties". Centre for Advanced Study of India, University of Pennsylvania, 31 July, 2017. https://casi.sas.upenn.edu/iit/joshuatwhite

Woetzel, J., J. Seaong, K. Wang, J. Manyika, M. Chui and W. Wong. "China's digital economy a leading global force". New York: McKinsey Global Institute, August 2017.

Wood, L. "China to Philippines: 'We'll go to war over South China Sea'". *Washington Times,* 23 May 2017. http://www.washingtontimes.com/news/2017/may/23/china-philippines-well-go-war-over-south-china-sea/

World Bank. *Digital Dividends, World Bank Development Report 2016.* Washington DC: World Bank, 2016.

Xavier, C., and D. Baruah. *Brussels and Delhi: converging interests in the Indian Ocean*, Working Paper. Berlin and New Delhi: Global Public Policy Institute and Carnegie India, March 2017.

Zhang D., and Shivakumar, H. "Dragon versus Elephant: A Comparative Study of Chinese and Indian Aid in the Pacific". *Asia & the Pacific Policy Studies* 4, no. 2 (Summer 2017): 260–71.

From an Area of Contestation to a Contested Area: The Liberal International Order in Eastern Europe and the South Caucasus

Laure Delcour

ABSTRACT

While espoused by the newly independent states after the collapse of the Soviet Union, the liberal order has not taken root in interstate relations and is now openly contested in Eastern Europe and the South Caucasus. However, the challenges presented (primarily by Russia) to the international order also trigger growing contestation, in several Eastern European and South Caucasus countries, of an existing regional order premised on Russian hegemony. Therefore, the picture that emerges from these multiple contestations is not an alternative regional order, but rather overlapping orders in a fragmented region.

As compared to the two other areas examined as part of this Special Issue, Eastern Europe and the South Caucasus stand out in two respects. First, unlike most of their counterparts in the Middle East and Asia-Pacific, none of the Eastern European and South Caucasus countries were independent states throughout most of the 20th century.[1] Instead, they were all republics of a single country, the Union of Soviet Socialist Republics (Soviet Union or USSR), which existed until late 1991 and also comprised Russia and Central Asian republics. Second, the Soviet Union was the major rival of the United States (US) for several decades, even though it shared some of the liberal normative frameworks (for instance, multilateralism), as highlighted in Riccardo Alcaro's introduction.[2] In other words, Eastern Europe and the South Caucasus were part of a country that contested the liberal order, and opposed its guarantor, for most of the second half of the 20th century.

However, in contrast to some other parts of the post-Soviet space, Eastern Europe and the South Caucasus have turned into a contested area, where (as illustrated by the 2008 conflict in Georgia, the 2014 annexation of Crimea and subsequent intervention in Eastern Ukraine) Russia challenges the liberal international order and its guarantors. This suggests that Eastern Europe and the South Caucasus lack an established order, understood as a set of rules and practices guaranteed by a major power. Such an absence is in contrast to the Baltic countries which, upon joining the European Union (EU) and North Atlantic Treaty Organisation (NATO), became part of the Western order.

---

[1] These countries are Belarus, Moldova, Ukraine, Armenia, Azerbaijan and Georgia.
[2] Alcaro, "Liberal Order and its Contestations".

This article seeks to explore how these distinctive features have played out in developing a vision of order in the region since the collapse of the Soviet Union. It asks whether and to what extent the countries of Eastern Europe and the South Caucasus, upon becoming sovereign states, have embraced the normative frameworks of the liberal international order. The article starts by tracing the process of adherence to, and contestation of, the liberal normative frameworks since the collapse of the Soviet Union. The second section then seeks to identify the actors and factors behind the growing contestation of the international order. Finally, the concluding section briefly examines the implications of the challenges raised to the liberal world order in Eastern Europe and the South Caucasus.

As the article shows, while espoused by the newly independent states in the early 1990s, the liberal order has not taken root in interstate relations and is now openly contested in the region. However, the challenges presented (primarily by Russia) to the international order have also triggered growing contestation in several Eastern European and South Caucasus countries of an existing regional order premised on Russian hegemony. Therefore, the picture that emerges from these multiple contestations is not an alternative regional order, but rather overlapping orders in a fragmented region.

The liberal international order in Eastern Europe and the South Caucasus: from integration to contestation

In this section, I examine the extent to which the normative frameworks of the liberal international order have been adhered to and applied in Eastern Europe and the South Caucasus since the collapse of the Soviet Union. I highlight the shifting dynamics of (attempts at) integration in, and contestation of the liberal order over the past 25 years.

The collapse of the USSR, a consecration of the liberal international order?

During most of the 20th century, the regional order prevailing in Eastern Europe and the South Caucasus differed sharply from the liberal international order. This is not only because the Soviet Union was based upon different ideological premises and challenged US power, but also because in essence the regional order was imposed on all its constituents.

In the early 1990s, the demise of the Soviet Union seemed to consecrate the principles underpinning the liberal order. As was stated by the former German Chancellor Helmut Kohl, "Our ideas are spreading across the whole European continent".[3] The newly independent states formed as a result of the USSR's collapse indeed engaged in wide-ranging political and economic transformations toward democracy and market economy, identified as building blocks of the liberal international order. In a similar vein, the values and principles underpinning this order emerged as the key normative frameworks to organise and regulate links between the former Soviet republics. Interstate relations were firmly anchored in internationalist values, for instance in the Alma-Ata Declaration, which laid down the founding principles of the organisation that was created to manage relations between the newly independent entities, the Commonwealth of Independent States (CIS):

> the relations between which will develop on the basis of mutual recognition and respect for state sovereignty and sovereign equality, the inalienable right to self-determination, principles

---

[3]Quoted in Delors, *Le nouveau concert européen.*

of equality and non-interference in internal affairs, the rejection of the use of force, the threat of force and economic and any other methods of pressure, a peaceful settlement of disputes, respect for human rights and freedoms, including the rights of national minorities, a conscientious fulfilment of commitments and other generally recognised principles and standards of international law.[4]

References to these principles were reiterated and expanded in the Charter of the CIS. Adopted in 1993, this document especially emphasised equality among CIS members.[5]

Commitment to the values of internationalism came hand in hand with accession to multilateral organisations and the commitment to abide by multilateral rules. All the former Soviet republics formally joined the United Nations (UN) in 1991-92 and throughout the 1990s, most of them adhered to key regional institutions emanating from the liberal order, such as the Organisation for Security and Cooperation in Europe (OSCE) and the Council of Europe. Therefore, the re-ordering of the region was clearly structured around the normative frameworks of the liberal international order.

Crucially, the breakdown of the Soviet Union (and the related collapse of the communist ideology) seemed to confer an absolute conceptual and moral legitimacy on the liberal order, embodied by the United States, the European Union and other Western countries and organisations. Interestingly, acknowledgement of the Western model's supremacy transpired from the narratives of leaders in both Europe and the post-Soviet space. For Jacques Delors, then President of the European Commission, "it is not the East that drifted towards the West, but the West that attracted the East (...)".[6] This was mirrored in the discourse of the new Russian leaders, in particular President Boris Yeltsin and Minister of Foreign Affairs Andrey Kozyrev, who called for Russia's return to the "community of civilised states", just as if seven decades of communist rule were to be considered an abnormal period in Russian history.[7] In essence, the then Russian political elite saw their country as "an organic part of the Western civilisation, whose 'genuine' Western identity was hijacked by Bolsheviks and the Soviet system".[8] The sense of belonging to Europe (thereby espousing the normative frameworks of the liberal order) was shared by some other Eastern European countries, most prominently Ukraine which, like Russia, regarded the EU as a "civilisational entity".[9]

Therefore, the demise of the Soviet Union gave rise to a univocal moment characterised by the uncontested supremacy of the liberal order and the aspirations of Eastern European and South Caucasus countries to integrate into this order. This suggested that interstate relations in the post-Soviet space would develop in line with the normative frameworks of this order.

A limited embeddedness in the liberal international order

However, this moment (interpreted by some as the "end of history"[10]) was short-lived. While the liberal international order was not openly contested in the region until the late 1990s, interstate relations reflected the principles and practices of liberal internationalism only to a very limited extent.

---

[4]Alma-Ata Declaration, http://gaidar-arc.ru/file/bulletin-1/DEFAULT/org.stretto.plugins.bulletin.core.Article/file/2880 (in Russian), http://www.operationspaix.net/DATA/DOCUMENT/3825~v~Declaration_d_Alma-Ata.pdf (in English).
[5]Article 1, Charter of the CIS, in Brzezinski and Sullivan, *Russia and the Commonwealth of Independent States*.
[6]Delors, *Le nouveau concert européen*.
[7]Delcour, "Towards a Global Europe?".
[8]Tsygankov, "Russia in Global Governance".
[9]Dragneva and Wolczuk, *Ukraine Between the EU and Russia*, 30.
[10]Fukuyama, "The End of History".

Even though they were enshrined in the CIS founding documents, principles underpinning *internationalism* such as respect for sovereignty, rejection of the use of force, peaceful settlement of disputes and respect for human rights were repeatedly infringed throughout the 1990s. The bloody conflicts that burst out between Armenia and Azerbaijan over Nagorno-Karabakh, as well as between Georgia and its break-away region of Abkhazia, and to a lesser extent between Moldova and Transnistria offered blatant examples of human rights violations in the South Caucasus, for instance with respect to refugees and displaced persons. These unresolved conflicts have continued to question the very essence of state sovereignty, a cornerstone of internationalism that figured prominently in the bilateral and multilateral agreements binding post-Soviet countries. They have also pointed to the limitations of the *multilateral* rules and mechanisms set up with a view to settling conflicts, be it under the auspices of the UN in the case of Abkhazia or the OSCE in the cases of South Ossetia and Nagorno-Karabakh (for the latter, through the Minsk Group).

Regionalism offers the best illustration of the limited application of the normative frameworks underpinning the liberal international order. This is perhaps unsurprising, given that regionalism "is nothing other than internationalism and multilateralism on a smaller scale".[11] After the Soviet Union collapsed, how to organise interstate relations emerged as a crucial question in Eastern Europe and the South Caucasus. Persisting economic and societal links between former Soviet republics prompted the preservation of some forms of regional cooperation. However, Eastern European and South Caucasus countries were reluctant to engage in new regional organisations after gaining or recovering their sovereignty, especially at a time when they were confronted with the daunting tasks of building functioning states and embarking on deep economic reforms. Therefore, since the early 1990s regionalism has been fraught with tensions between integration and disintegration in the post-Soviet space.[12] A number of regional cooperation/integration initiatives were launched,[13] however, many of these were ineffective or some simply stalled. For instance, in spite of ambitious statements and initiatives, the CIS did not develop as an effective vehicle for economic (re-)integration.[14] A defining feature of this framework was the variable geometry principle which enabled member countries to cherry pick and participate only in those agreements in which they had an interest (286). Notably, two countries (Ukraine and Turkmenistan) did not ratify the CIS Charter, even though the charter defines a member country as one that has ratified it. In addition, other mechanisms significantly limited the obligations imposed on member countries. These included reservations (which were used extensively), withdrawal provisions and exemption clauses, paving the way for very broad interpretations of commitments made (292-5). Thus, "sovereignty sensitivities" (319) *de facto* limited regionalism.

The evolution of *interdependencies* throughout the 1990s also illustrates the tensions between integration and disintegration. Despite the huge disruptions that followed the collapse of the USSR, the post-Soviet republics remained closely linked to the former centre, Russia, in both economic (trade and energy flows) and societal (migration) terms.

---

[11]Alcaro, "Liberal Order and its Contestations".
[12]Libman, "Regionalism and Regionalisation in Post-Soviet Space".
[13]Wirminghaus counted 39 initiatives of regional integration in the post-Soviet space between 1991 and 2010, of which 36 gave birth to regional organisations. Wirminghaus, "Ephemeral Regionalism", 25.
[14]Dragneva, "Is 'Soft' Beautiful?", 280.

Nevertheless, no effective governance framework (whether regional, intergovernmental or transgovernmental) emerged to frame cooperation on issues of common concern.

Finally, interstate relations in Eastern Europe and the South Caucasus have never become genuinely embedded in the fifth liberal normative framework outlined in the introduction to this Special Issue, namely *democracy*,[15] even though equality among members is formally proclaimed in the Charter of the CIS, among other official documents. In fact, Russia has continuously been the dominant power in the region, even though it has not always acted as such (for instance in the early 1990s, when its capacity to act internationally was severely affected by its own hectic internal transformation process). From the outset of the post-Soviet era, Russia's policy *vis-à-vis* other post-Soviet republics has been highly ambiguous. It is premised upon a vision in which Russia's security is tightly interwoven with the fate of these countries, as illustrated by the concept of 'near abroad' coined by the Russian Ministry of Foreign Affairs. In essence, this concept implies that while Russia recognises the sovereignty of these countries, it regards them as an area of privileged interests where Russia has a special role to play.

Overall, in the wake of the USSR's collapse, interstate relations developed in a highly asymmetrical way through opaque bargains that were mostly reached bilaterally. The pervasiveness of informal links, as well as conflicts affecting both the state-building and foreign policy of the countries concerned emerged as major obstacles to the development of rule-based interstate relations premised upon the normative frameworks of the liberal international order.

Growing challenges to the liberal order

In contrast to the early years of the post-Soviet period, the liberal order and its ideational underpinnings have been increasingly challenged in the region since the early 2000s.

Over the past decade, key principles of *internationalism* and *multilateral rules* have been severely undermined in the region. Russia's military interventions in Georgia in 2008 and in Ukraine in 2014 took place in flagrant violation of the principles enshrined in the UN Charter, of which article 2 prohibits "the threat or use of force against the territorial integrity or political independence of any state". Another flare-up of the Nagorno-Karabakh conflict between Armenia and Azerbaijan in 2016 also attests to the ineffectiveness of multilateral mechanisms in the region. This is despite the frequent references to the normative frameworks of the liberal order in the foreign policy narratives of East European and South Caucasus states. President Putin justified Russia's intervention in Ukraine with international law and principles.[16] Thus, this suggests the emergence of alternative interpretations of international rules, rather than a mere contestation of them.

The evolution of *regionalism* highlights similar trends. Upon being launched,[17] the Eurasian integration process, broadly depicted as the most ambitious regional project since the early 1990s, claimed to draw inspiration from the liberal order in both institutional (as reflected in the emulation of the EU's framework) and ideational terms. According to President Putin, Eurasian integration would be based upon "universal integration principles as an essential part of Greater Europe, united by shared values of freedom, democracy, and

---

[15] Alcaro, "Liberal Order and its Contestations".
[16] Averre, "The Ukraine Conflict", 706.
[17] The Eurasian Customs Union was launched in 2010 and the Eurasian Economic Union in 2015.

market laws".[18] It was thus designed as an "open project" that does not stand "in opposition to anyone". In addition, the construction of a Common Economic Space, to be followed by the creation of the Eurasian Economic Union (EAEU), would be beneficial for all participating countries.[19] However, this was contradicted by the way the Eurasian project subsequently advanced with respect to both the enlargement process and the deepening of integration.

Pressure emerged as a crucial instrument for bringing new countries of Eastern Europe and the South Caucasus into the Eurasian project and deterring them from closer links with the EU. In 2013, Russia exerted so much pressure on Armenia that the country finally gave up association with the EU and joined the EAEU instead. Indeed, the Armenian political elites had explicitly ruled out EAEU membership given the limited benefits it would offer,[20] and instead favoured deep economic integration with the EU, regarded as a model for the country's modernisation. Similarly, the repeated use of technical standards as punitive trade measures between EAEU members and the reintroduction of custom checks between Russia and Belarus in early 2017, clearly signalled the subordination of general principles and rules to the specific interests of the member states.[21]

The fourth liberal ideational framework, *interdependencies*, has increasingly been hollowed out. This is not only due to the above-mentioned shortcomings of regionalism. These have been compounded by the weakness of transnational networks and non-governmental actors (for instance, civil society and businesses) which play a role in policymaking in some other regions. In the absence of any effective governance framework (whether formal or informal) that would steer cooperation towards addressing regional issues, interdependencies have increasingly produced negative spillover effects in Eastern European and South Caucasus countries. In particular, the lack of effective governance mechanisms, combined with the high interdependencies with Russia, has increasingly exposed these countries to the destructive effects of external shocks.

Last but not least, the fifth normative framework of the liberal order, *democracy* (understood as the right of "all states to representation and participation in international [and regional] decision-making"),[22] has been stripped to the bone in the region. Interstate relations are pursued in a highly asymmetrical way, through opaque bargains that are mostly reached bilaterally, as is the case in the energy sector. There, the role of intermediary companies has hindered transparency in gas trade between Russia and Ukraine or Moldova, while reinforcing Russia's leverage and creating a "rent of energy dependency",[23] that is, rent-seeking opportunities for domestic actors (closely interwined political elites and business circles) that contribute to perpetuating dependency on Russian energy.

Thus, while overwhelmingly espoused by the newly independent states in the early 1990s, the liberal order appears only weakly rooted in Eastern Europe and the South Caucasus, if at all. As was blatantly exposed during the conflict in Ukraine, the normative frameworks upon which this order is premised are openly challenged in the region. However, while marking the end of the post-Cold War order in Europe,[24] the sequence of events that unfolded in

---

[18]Putin, "New integration project for Eurasia".
[19]*Ibid.*
[20]Grigoryan, "Armenia: Joining Under the Gun".
[21]Dragneva and Wolczuk, *The Eurasian Economic Union*.
[22]Alcaro, "Liberal Order and its Contestations".
[23]Balmaceda, *Energy Dependency, Politics and Corruption*, 97.
[24]Averre and Wolczuk, "Introduction: The Ukraine Crisis".

Ukraine opened an era of unpredictability and triggered uncertainty over both the objectives and scope of the challenge to the international order.[25]

Unpacking contestations in Eastern Europe and the South Caucasus

In this section, I analyse what exactly is being contested in Eastern Europe and the South Caucasus, by whom and as a result of which factors. I ask to what extent the challenges to the international order in the region reflect a contestation of ideas or authority.

As argued in the literature, contesters of the liberal order may challenge the ideas and rules upon which it is built.[26] Such ideational contestation can stem either from normative beliefs or strategic calculations. Countries can challenge the international liberal order because they follow other principles: for instance, non-Western actors (e.g. China, Brazil) may have different values deriving from their own history and preferences.[27] Countries can also challenge the liberal order because they reap limited gains from participation in it. This is despite the fact that the liberal order is premised on a high degree of openness and generalised (even if loose) rules of behaviour, and should thereby have paved the way for more equal representation and benefits for all countries.[28] I argue that it is mainly the latter motivation – a perception of losses resulting from participation in the international order – that has fuelled contestation in Eastern Europe and the South Caucasus, primarily Russia.

Indeed, since the collapse of the Soviet Union none of the Eastern European and South Caucasus countries has openly challenged the validity and legitimacy of the principles embedded in the international liberal order. On the contrary, they have consistently declared themselves to be playing by the multilateral rules. This is clearly reflected in Russia's official narrative, in which multilateral institutions and international rules hold a central role.[29] Other countries in the region, such as Azerbaijan, have invariably mentioned multilateral principles (in this case, territorial integrity) and to UN resolutions when referring to the conflicts in which they are involved.

Therefore, what is contested (primarily by Russia) is not so much the validity of the core principles of the liberal international order as their interpretation and application by the guarantors of this order, namely the US and the West at large. This is vividly illustrated by divergences over the principle of sovereignty. Russia has stuck to a traditional interpretation of sovereignty, premised on a territorialised understanding of this principle, thereby supporting a restrictive interpretation of the UN Charter in this respect.[30] This is in sharp opposition to the broader and more dynamic interpretation backed by the West, which has favoured foreign intervention in specific cases, *inter alia* in the name of the responsibility to protect. Thus, the dissent between Russia and the West has developed over the interpretation of multilateral principles, as well as the balance to be found between seemingly opposite norms.

---

[25] Averre, "The Ukraine Conflict".

[26] For instance, free-market capitalism has been criticised by rising powers, among others. As pointed out by Newman and Zala, the 2012 Delhi declaration expressed a "collective desire" for "responsible macro-economic and financial policies". Newman and Zala, "Rising Powers and Order Contestation", 9.

[27] Acharya, *End of American World Order*.

[28] Ikenberry, *Liberal Leviathan*.

[29] Romanova, "Russia's Neo-Revisionist Challenge".

[30] Allison, "Contested Understandings of Sovereignty", 1.

While framed in normative terms, this opposition is largely rooted in strategic calculations over the gains and losses stemming from application of the liberal international order. In essence, Russia views the liberal international order as "discriminatory and disadvantageous" to itself.[31] What the country contests, then, is the domination of the West in this order, which provides Western countries and organisations with greater leverage in interpreting the rules. For Russia, many Western-led interventions (for instance, in Yugoslavia in 1999 and Iraq in 2003) were in clear breach of international law as they were not backed by a multilateral mandate; however, they triggered only limited criticism because of the West's hegemony. Thus, in exposing the contradictions of the liberal order[32] Russia questions the Western monopoly of the interpretation of multilateral principles.

Taking the critique one step further, Russia claims that this monopoly has enabled the West to exploit the frameworks and arrangements of the international order with a view to advancing its own interests in Eastern Europe and the South Caucasus. In Russia's views, the West has used the post-Cold War order (in particular, the European system of security governance) to marginalise Russia on the continent. This is because NATO, not the OSCE, (of which Russia is a member), has emerged as the central institution of this system. Since the mid-1990s, Russia's relations with NATO have been fraught with mistrust.[33] In particular, Russia regards NATO's eastward enlargement (especially the planned expansion to Ukraine and Georgia) as an aggressive attempt to expand the bloc's sphere of influence.[34] Likewise, the EU's European Neighbourhood Policy (ENP) and above all, the Eastern Partnership launched in 2009 are perceived as endeavours to marginalise Russia while seeking to deepen the EU's links with Eastern European and South Caucasus countries. In this vein, the exclusion of Russia clearly signals the EU's failure to "embody a vision embracing the whole continent".[35] Therefore, Russia criticises the West for its failure to "deepen the structures and practices of liberal internationalism within the framework of a shared continental vision".[36] Thus, the central question that has inspired contestation by Russia is not "what rules", but rather "who makes the rules",[37] and, one may add, "whom do they benefit". Contestation is premised upon the perception that normative frameworks are interpreted and applied on an *ad hoc* basis for the sole benefit of the West.

This vision that underpins Russia's contestation of the liberal order is nevertheless challenged within Eastern Europe and the South Caucasus. For several countries in the region (primarily Georgia and Ukraine), the liberal international order and its guarantors are regarded as a protection against Russia's hegemonic behaviour. This is because the normative frameworks of the international order (among others, equality and openness) offer assurances against Russia's use of its asymmetric bargaining power. Notably, in the liberal order equality in interstate relations is premised upon the acceptance of, and compliance with common principles,[38] goals and collectively recognised forms of interactions.[39] By contrast, Russia has been only barely constrained by the loose regional arrangements that have developed in the post-Soviet space since the early 1990s. Although the Eurasian Economic

---

[31]Makarychev, *Self-Inflicted Marginalization*, 1.
[32]Romanova, "Russia's Neo-Revisionist Challenge".
[33]Averre, "The Ukraine Conflict".
[34]Karaganov, "Europe and Russia".
[35]Sakwa, "The Death of Europe?", 554.
[36]Sakwa, 566, quoted in Averre, "The Ukraine Conflict", 707.
[37]Romanova, "Russia's Neo-Revisionist Challenge".
[38]Makarychev, *Self-Inflicted Marginalization*, 2.
[39]Averre, "The Ukraine Conflict", 702.

Union emerged as a more ambitious and legally-binding endeavour, Russia retains the role of gate-keeper in the integration process as a result of the strongly intergovernmental decision-making.[40] Likewise, the bilateral agreements (whether in trade, energy or migration) have imposed only limited restrictions on Russia's actions.

Therefore, "it is only in the framework [of the liberal order] that Russia can be challenged in its near abroad policy (…) based upon imperial legacies".[41] Thus, at the end of the 1990s, resistance to regional integration and criticism of Russia's policies by Georgia, Moldova, Ukraine and Azerbaijan were increasingly combined with an explicit desire for closer links with the West. The establishment of GUAM as a consultative forum in 1997, and especially its transformation into a regional organisation named GUUAM, Organisation for Democracy and Economic Development, in 2001 provides perhaps the best illustration of this tight connection.[42] Like many of their predecessors in the post-Soviet space, these regional initiatives have had very limited tangible outcomes.

Nevertheless, domestic developments in the two countries that were the most reluctant to take part in Russia-driven regional initiatives, Georgia and Ukraine, epitomise the growing contestation of the regional order. These domestic political changes have had important regional implications as they have exacerbated Russia's concern over a loss of influence. The so-called Rose and Orange revolutions (which took place in Georgia in 2003 and in Ukraine in 2004, respectively) were regarded by Russia as attempts by the West to replace the legitimate authorities with Western-friendly leaders, thereby attracting these countries into the West's sphere of influence and moving them away from Moscow. A decade later, the ousting of Ukrainian President Viktor Yanukovych following mass protests on the Maidan Square stirred up Russia's anger over what it regarded as a coup backed by the West. Despite the primacy of domestic factors in explaining political changes, with the military interventions in Georgia (2008) and Ukraine (2014), Russia responded to what it perceived mainly as a Western expansionist agenda in Eastern Europe and the South Caucasus.[43] This is clearly demonstrated by the sequencing of events: Russia's intervention in Georgia took place only a few months after NATO's Bucharest summit, during which NATO spoke for the first time of Georgia and Ukraine as "potential members" (even though the organisation did not grant them Membership Action Plans). Likewise, Russia's annexation of Crimea and support to rebels in Eastern Ukraine happened a few weeks after a new political team came to power and prioritised the signature of the Association Agreement with the EU. From Russia's perspective, the military interventions in Georgia and Ukraine were needed to undermine these countries' integration in Western structures, thereby alleviating Russia's feeling of "existential insecurity".[44]

This suggests that Russia's actions are driven by different principles and rules depending upon the level considered.[45] Internationally, Russia still refers extensively to, and follows, multilateral rules and institutions, even though it contests the use of these rules and institutions by the West. Regionally, Russia's narrative and (to an even greater extent) actions are primarily guided by its own interests (even though these are frequently clothed in a discourse

---

[40]Dragneva and Wolczuk, "The Eurasian Economic Union".
[41]Makarychev, *Self-Inflicted Marginalization*.
[42]Initially composed of Georgia, Ukraine, Azerbaijan and Moldova, it was joined by Uzbekistan in 2001.
[43]Delcour and Wolczuk, "Spoiler or facilitator of democratization?", 460.
[44]Makarychev, *Self-Inflicted Marginalization*, 3.
[45]Allison, "Russia and international legal order", 528.

emphasising either common history and "blood-based relations",[46] or mutual benefits). The concept of sovereignty offers perhaps the best illustration of this discrepancy. While it is adamant in defending a strict conception of sovereignty internationally, "Moscow has never treated the sovereignty of [Eastern European and South Caucasus] countries as inviolable".[47] It is the violation of their territorial integrity that has further fuelled Georgia's and Ukraine's distancing from a regional order characterised by Russian coercive dominance.

Thus, this section has shed light on two intricate processes: the rejection, in several Eastern European and South Caucasus countries, of existing domestic and regional orders (premised on illiberal elites and Russia's hegemony, respectively), combined with a clear commitment to the international liberal order; and the contestation by Russia (acting as the guarantor of the regional order) of the international order, which is regarded as an instrument of Western expansionism in the post-Soviet space.

Overlapping orders in a fragmented region

In this concluding section, I briefly examine the implications of the challenges to the liberal world order in Eastern Europe and the South Caucasus. Arguably, contestation of the world order can result in the emergence of alternative normative visions and institutional arrangements in any region. Thus, the effects of contestation hinge crucially on its ability to envisage new normative frameworks that can claim broad legitimacy and gain the support of powerful coalitions of actors.

In challenging the Western interpretation of international principles, Russia "claims to play a role of a bearer of universal trends".[48] As stated by a Russian analyst, "in demanding a change in the rules of the game, [Russia] actually speaks for the entire Non-West".[49] However, Russia's "grandiose appeal for new rules"[50] is not underpinned by the framing of an alternative normative agenda. This is evidenced, for instance, by the arguments used to justify the annexation of Crimea: Russia has referred to the right of self-determination of the Crimean peninsula, yet another founding principle of the international liberal order. Whatever the validity of this argument, this indicates that Russia positions itself within the existing normative frameworks of this order. Likewise, Russia's key regionalist project, the Eurasian Economic Union, is grounded in the principles of the liberal order, even while some aspects of the integration process highlight clear breaches of these norms and rules.[51] The EAEU as a whole has not emerged as a normative contender. Thus, while bearing major implications for the international liberal order, Russia's initiatives do not reflect a "substantive revisionist legal agenda".[52]

In a similar vein, in contesting Western hegemony Russia has not garnered the support of a coalition of countries, whether regionally or worldwide. In Eastern Europe and the South Caucasus, none of Russia's closest allies (not even Belarus, a member of all Russia-driven regional initiatives) has followed Moscow in its recognition of Abkhazia's and South

---

[46]Makarychev, *Self-Inflicted Marginalization*, 3.
[47]Busygina, *Russia-EU Relations and Common Neighbourhood*, 107-8.
[48]Makarychev, *Self-Inflicted Marginalization*, 3.
[49]Karaganov, "Europe and Russia".
[50]Allison, "Russia and the international legal order", 528.
[51]As illustrated, for instance, by the reintroduction of customs checks between Russia and Belarus. See Dragneva and Wolczuk, "The Eurasian Economic Union".
[52]Allison,"Russia and the international legal order", 542.

Ossetia's independence and the annexation of Crimea. In fact, Russia's violations of Georgia's and Ukraine's territorial integrity have caused "deep unease" even among the countries that share Russia's restrictive understanding of sovereignty, such as Azerbaijan.[53] Therefore, while several countries in the region (primarily Belarus and Azerbaijan) do not embrace the West's interpretations of the principles underpinning the liberal order and have joined Russia (for instance, within the Council of Europe) in criticising these interpretations, they remain suspicious of Russia's contestations of the international order. This is because they regard them to be an expression of Russia's "'hard' hegemony"[54] in the region, that is, "a system of domination based on coercion, but exerted in a more subtle way" and camouflaged under the veil of common interests or values.

Therefore, the picture that emerges is not of an alternative regional order, but rather of overlapping orders in a fragmented region. In recent years, the Eastern European and South Caucasus area has been widely depicted as a region divided between those countries seeking to integrate into the Western hub (e.g. Georgia, Ukraine) and other countries maintaining close ties with Russia (e.g. Belarus). However, such a division overlooks important nuances. First, as a result of Russia's actions, dividing lines now pass *through* countries such as Georgia (with South Ossetia and Abkhazia), Moldova (with Transnistria) and Ukraine (with Crimea), thereby fragmenting the area. Second, none of the Eastern European and South Caucasus countries fully endorse the authority of either Russia or the West and many of them seek close ties with both. This is perhaps best illustrated by the examples of Armenia and Moldova. While being a member of the Eurasian Economic Union since 2015, Armenia has sought to maintain close links with the EU as a result of the high resonance of the EU's model in the country,[55] and signed a Comprehensive Enhanced Partnership Agreement in late 2017. Conversely, although Moldova has engaged in political association and deep economic integration with the EU, the country's population remains split over foreign policy choices.[56]

Thus, the complexities of engagement with regional projects (deriving from multiple identities and preferences) translate into the creation of inner and outer circles of integration (whether in the Eurasian project[57] or in Western initiatives such as the EU's Eastern Partnership) and overlapping arrangements. In addition, some of the institutions in the broader region (e.g. the OSCE) include most Eastern European and South Caucasus countries together with the West, thereby still offering an inclusive and pluralist platform for security governance. However, they are now permeated by the divergences between Russia (backed by some other post-Soviet countries) and the West, and lack credibility due to their mixed record in recent conflicts (for instance, in Ukraine).[58] Crucially, the shared norms upon which they are premised are increasingly contested by Russia (720).

Overall, developments in Eastern Europe and the Caucasus (and more broadly, the Eurasian continent) reflect the emergence of a "negotiated order" (717). While the normative frameworks of the international order are challenged in an increasingly blunt way, the main contester, Russia, does not offer any substantial alternative. Therefore, the current order in Eastern Europe and the South Caucasus is characterised by "multiple and fluid sets

---

[53]*Ibid.*, 532.
[54]Destradi, "Regional powers and their strategies", 918.
[55]Delcour, "Between the Eastern Partnership and Eurasian Integration".
[56]*Ibid.*
[57]Samokhvalov, "The new Eurasia".
[58]Averre, "The Ukraine Conflict", 714.

of relations" (717) that are shaped by interests rather than norms and values. A corollary of this is the high degree of unpredictability characterising governance in the region.

References

Acharya, A. *The End of the American World Order*. London: Polity Press, 2014.

Alcaro, R. "The Liberal Order and Its Contestations. A Conceptual Framework". *The International Spectator* 53, no. 1 (2018). doi: https://doi.org/10.1080/03932729.2018.1397878.

Allison, R. "Russia and the post-2014 international legal order". *International Affairs* 93, no. 3 (2017): 519–43.

Allison, R. "Contested understandings of sovereignty, the use of force and the wider international legal order: the political context". European Leadership Network conference, 2015. https://www.europeanleadershipnetwork.org/wp-content/uploads/2017/10/ELN-Narratives-Conference-Allison.pdf.

Averre, D. "The Ukraine Conflict: Russia's Challenge to European Security Governance". *Europe-Asia Studies* 68, no. 4 (2016): 699–725.

Averre, D., and K. Wolczuk. "Introduction: The Ukraine Crisis and Post-Post Cold War Europe". *Europe-Asia Studies* 68, no. 4 (2016): 551–5.

Balmaceda, M. *Energy Dependency, Politics and Corruption in the Former Soviet Union: Russia's Power, Oligarch's Profits and Ukraine's Missing Energy Policy, 1995–2006*. London: Routledge, 2008.

Busygina, I. *Russia-EU relations and the Common Neighborhood*. London: Routledge, 2017.

Brzezinski, Z., and P. Sullivan. *Russia and the Commonwealth of Independent States: Documents, Data, and Analysis*. New York: M.E Sharpe, 1997.

Delcour, L. "Towards a Global Europe?" In *The Global 1989. Continuity and Change in World Politics*, edited by G. Lawson, C. Armbruster and M. Cox: 135–55. Cambridge: Cambridge University Press, 2010.

Delcour, L. "Between the Eastern Partnership and Eurasian Integration: Explaining Post-Soviet Countries' Engagement in (Competing) Region-Building Projects". *Problems of Post-Communism* 62, no. 6 (2015): 316–27.

Delcour, L., and K. Wolczuk. "Spoiler or facilitator of democratization? Russia's role in Georgia and Ukraine". *Democratization* 22, no. 3 (2015): 459–78.

Delors, J. *Le nouveau concert européen*. Paris: Odile Jacob, 1992.

Destradi, S. "Regional powers and their strategies: empire, hegemony, and leadership". *Review of International Studies* 36, no. 4 (2010): 903–30.

Dragneva, R. "Is 'Soft' Beautiful? Another Perspective on Law, Institutions and Integration in the CIS". *Review of Central and East European Law* 29, no. 3 (2004): 279–324.

Dragneva, R., and K. Wolczuk. *The Eurasian Economic Union: Deals, Rules and the Exercise of Power*, Chatham House Research Paper. London: Royal Institute of International Affairs, May 2017.

Dragneva, R., and K. Wolczuk. *Ukraine Between the EU and Russia. The Integration Challenge*. London: Palgrave, 2015.

Fukuyama, F. "The End of History?" *The National Interest* 16 (1989): 3–18.

Grigoryan, A. "Armenia: Joining Under the Gun". In *Putin's Grand Strategy: the Eurasian Union and its Discontents*, edited by S.F. Starr, and S. Cornell. Washington: Central Asia-Caucasus Institute & Silk Road Studies Program, 2014.

Ikenberry, G. J. *Liberal Leviathan. The Origins, Crisis and Transformations of the American World Order*. Princeton: Princeton University Press, 2012.

Karaganov, S. "Europe and Russia: Preventing a New Cold War". *Russia in Global Affairs*, 7 June 2014. http://eng.globalaffairs.ru/number/Europe-and-Russia-Preventing-a-New-Cold-War-16701.

Libman, A. "Regionalism and Regionalisation in the Post-Soviet Space: Current Status and Implications for Institutional Development". *Europe-Asia Studies* 59, no. 3 (2007): 401–30.

Makarychev, A. *Self-Inflicted Marginalization? Illiberal Russia in search for its own identity*, CIDOB Notes121. Barcelona: CIDOB, June 2015.

Newman, E., and B. Zala. "Rising Powers and Order Contestation: Disaggregating the Normative from the Representational". *Third World Quarterly*, published online November 2017.

Putin, V.V. "Новый интеграционный проект для Евразии — будущее, которое рождается сегодня" [A new integration project for Eurasia - a future that is being born today]. *Izvestia*, 3 October 2011.

Romanova, T. "Russia's Neo-Revisionist Challenge to the Liberal International Order". *The International Spectator* 53, no. 1 (2018). doi: https://doi.org/10.1080/03932729.2018.1406761.

Sakwa, R. "The Death of Europe? Continental Fates after Ukraine". *International Affairs* 91, no. 3 (2016): 554–79.

Samokhvalov, V. "The new Eurasia: post-Soviet space between Russia, Europe and China". *European Politics and Society*, published online, 27 January 2016.

Tsygankov, A. "Russia in Global Governance: Multipolarity or Multilateralism?" In *Contemporary Global Governance: Multipolarity vs New Discourses on Global Governance*, edited by D. Lesage and P. Vercauteren: 51–62. Frankfurt/Brussels: Peter Lang Publishing Group, 2009.

Wirminghaus, N. "Ephemeral Regionalism: the Proliferation of (Failed) Regional Integration Initiatives in Post-Soviet Eurasia". In *Roads to Regionalism*, edited by T. Börzel, L. Goltermann, M. Lohaus and K. Striebinger: 25–44. Farnham: Ashgate, 2012.

The Middle East's Troubled Relationship with the Liberal International Order

Paul Salem

ABSTRACT

The Middle East has had a complex relationship with the so-called liberal international order. Many peoples and elites of the region welcomed the promise, and promises, of the liberal order after the collapse of the Ottoman Empire, and sought to integrate into it; for other peoples and elites, there have been negative reactions and resistance to it. Today, a majority of countries are integrated, at least nominally, into the global order, while some are decidedly still in systemic challenge with it. The Middle East has also had difficulty in cohering as a region; the condition today is one of collapsed regional order and proxy conflict.

There has been considerable scholarship about the troubled interaction and integration of the new states of the post-Ottoman Middle East into the international order that emerged and evolved in the 20th and 21st centuries.[1] Raymond Hinnebusch offers, perhaps, the most rigorous examination.[2] He deploys neo-realist, structuralist, pluralist, and constructivist approaches to explore and understand the various facets of Middle Eastern states' relationships with, and interactions within, the evolving international order, from the fall of the Ottoman Empire to the dawn of the current century. Hinnebusch emphasizes that "the Middle East has been profoundly shaped by the international system, or more precisely, the great powers, which dominate its developed 'core'". L. Carl Brown also underscores the degree to which the Middle East became a "penetrated system".[3]

Hinnebusch employs the realist perspective to explain how Middle Eastern states were drafted into global power conflicts, but also how the realist security dilemmas of regional states often pitted them against each other.[4] He warns, however, about the "a-historical tendency" in neo-realism to "assume states systems to be unchanging, made up of cohesive

---

[1] The Middle East is treated as encompassing the countries of North Africa, the Levant and Arabian Peninsula, as well as Turkey and Iran.

[2] Hinnebusch, *International Politics of Middle East*.

[3] Brown, *International Politics and Middle East*, 16-8.

[4] George Joffe provides a detailed account of the boundary disputes among Middle Eastern states in his chapter "Disputes over state boundaries". Paul Noble also emphasizes the persistence of "realist-style security concerns" and the "*multidimensionality* of the area's security problems", in his chapter "From Arab to Middle Eastern System?".

rational actors".[5] From the structuralist perspective, many authors underscore the "core-periphery" relationship that emerged between the dominant Western-Northern metropoles and the economically and politically dependent Middle Eastern countries.[6] Pluralism's insight is in disaggregating the state and looking at non-state, sub-national, or transnational movements that impact the regional and international relations of the Middle East; this approach has grown only more relevant in recent years as armed non-state actors and violent transnational movements have become major players. The constructivist approach looks beyond power and economic relations to examine the influence of values, identities, ideologies and other 'soft forces'. Much of the work within this approach,[7] emphasizes the impact of these 'soft' forces, particularly in intra-regional competition and conflict, as well as in challenges to state stability and legitimacy.

In this article, I will draw on the approaches and insights explored in the available scholarship, as well as interrogate the recent historical and political record. I will attempt to respond to the questions framed by the editor of this volume and will follow his suggested format of examining 'outside-in' and 'inside-out' perspectives.[8] In doing so, I will be hewing close to a constructivist approach, insofar as this issue investigates the relevance and impact of liberal 'norms, values, and principles' in international relations. I will also include a fair amount of historical analysis to avoid the "a-historical tendencies" that Hinnebusch warned against.

Indeed, the Middle East has had a complex and varied relationship with the so-called liberal international order. Many peoples and elites of the region welcomed the promise, and promises, of the liberal order after the collapse of the Ottoman Empire, and sought to integrate into it; for other peoples and elites, and in different time periods, there have been negative reactions and resistance to it. Today, a majority of countries are integrated, at least nominally, into the liberal international order, while some, like Iran, are still in some systemic challenge with it. The framer of this issue also seeks an examination of the forces of regionalism; I will argue that even though there was some measure of regionalisation in previous decades, the condition today is one of collapsed regional order. This article will look at the dynamics and evolution of the Middle East's interaction with the principles and realities of the liberal order, as well as the principles and realities of regionalism.

Outside-in: The Middle East's integration into, and resistance to, the liberal international order

The births, betrayals, and betrothals of a troubled relationship

Fitful beginnings

The liberal international order was born twice in the Middle East; the first, after World War I, stillborn; the second, after World War II, more enduring.

---

[5]Hinnebusch, *International Politics of Middle East*, 1.
[6]Cammet *et al.*, *Political Economy of the Middle East*; Brown, *International Politics and Middle East*; Bromley, "From Tributary Empires"; Owen, *Middle East in World Economy*.
[7]See, for example, Barnett, "Institutions, roles and disorder"; Salame, "Integration in the Arab World; Ajami, *The Arab Predicament*.
[8]Alcaro, "The Liberal Order and its Contestations".

The people of what we now call the Middle East had grown increasingly exposed during the 19th century to some of the ideas which would eventually make their way into the liberal order.[9] The currents of nationalism in Europe, that would become tributaries to the idea of self-determination in the liberal order, had a particularly strong resonance among Arab populations beginning to harbour ambitions of breaking free from Turkish Ottoman rule.[10] Indeed, the Arab revolt against the Ottomans during World War I was based on a British commitment to Hussein bin Ali, Sharif of Mecca that his revolt would give birth after the war was over to a unified and independent Arab state encompassing the Levant and part of the Arabian Peninsula. This promise was betrayed in a secret side agreement between the British and the French, and later in the Paris Peace Talks; the promised Arab regions were eventually divided up between the two colonial powers. Nor did the postwar arrangements loosen the colonial grip on Egypt and the countries of North Africa.[11] The British had also given a wartime commitment, under the Balfour Declaration, to offer up post-Ottoman Palestine as a national home for the Jewish people.[12]

The Ottoman empire was the big loser in the First World War, but the new Turkey led by Mustafa Kemal embraced the promise of a Western-facing modern Turkish nation state within the proposed liberal international order. It fought for, and secured, Turkish national independence. Postwar Iran also avoided direct colonial rule, although the British maintained a strong influence in the country through their control of the burgeoning oil industry there. The Kurds had high hopes for the post-Ottoman order, but all their appeals for statehood and independence before and during the Paris Peace conference came to naught.

In the end, although the Western allies waged World War I with lofty promises to the local populations of a coming liberal order in which they would enjoy self-determination and independence, these promises, at least in the Arab and Kurdish contexts, were betrayed. In effect, what emerged after World War I, even in the context of the League of Nations, with regard to much of the Middle East, was not a liberal order but an organised and legally dressed up form of Western imperialism to replace Ottoman imperial rule.[13]

Given the role that the US would play in building and sustaining the second and more successful iteration of the liberal international order after World War II, it is interesting to note that in the immediate post-World War I period, Arab public opinion had a fairly positive impression of the US in terms of its distinctness from the European colonial agenda. Unlike Britain and France, the US was seen as having no colonial or imperial past in the Middle East, no territorial ambitions, and had become known in decades past as a distant alternative society of democracy and economic opportunity to which thousands of Ottoman subjects had emigrated.

This public impression did not take account, of course, of the deeper changes in the international system, and the gradual penetration of American energy and security interests that would become clearer over time. The temporary positive impression was buttressed in the postwar period by President Woodrow Wilson's 14 Points, which emphasized the right of self-determination, and by the King-Crane Commission. The latter was supposed to be

---

[9]See Hourani, *Arabic Thought in Liberal Age*, 67-102.

[10]See, for example, Dawn, "From Ottomanism to Arabism", 375-6.

[11]Brecher, "French Policy Toward the Levant", 641-3.

[12]"European imperialism also laid the seeds for the Arab-Israeli conflict by granting support for the establishment of a Jewish state in Palestine while making simultaneous commitments to the Palestinians." Cammet *et al.*, *Political Economy of Middle East*, 95.

[13]Bromley, "From Tributary Empires", 46-52.

a joint French, British, Italian and American commission emanating from the Paris Peace Conference to survey opinion in, and make recommendations about, the non-Turkish areas of the former Ottoman empire. As it turned out, the European members withdrew from the commission as its findings would likely conflict with their governments' colonial designs, so the US went ahead with it alone. Although the findings were not made public at that time, it was clear to Arab and Kurdish publics that the US favoured some form of independence for the non-Turkish territories, while the Europeans insisted on a colonial arrangement.

Born again

The second coming of the promise of a liberal international order after World War II initially had a more favourable reception in, and outcome for, the region. The major victors of the Second World War, the US and Union of Soviet Socialist Republics (USSR), both had strong anti-colonial policies, the interwar mandates in the Levant were abrogated, and seven Middle Eastern states (Iran, Turkey, Iraq, Syria, Lebanon, Saudi Arabia and Egypt) were founding members of the United Nations. The Lebanese delegate, Charles Malik, was a member of the drafting committee, along with Eleanor Roosevelt and others, of the UN's Universal Declaration of Human Rights. The new international order, delineated in the founding charter of the United Nations, indeed promised a liberal international order where once colonised peoples could achieve self-determination and statehood on an equal footing with former colonial and imperial powers. And the US still held a very positive appeal as a principled non-colonial democratic power that had stood up for the region after the First World War, and delivered independence to many colonised countries after the Second. The newly independent Arab states accompanied participation in the new liberal international order by attempting a regional order through the establishment of the League of Arab States in 1945.[14]

But the romance, both with the international order and the regional order, as well as with the US, was short-lived. The establishment of the state of Israel in 1948, and the support from the US, Soviet Union, and liberal order for it, in the face of widespread Arab opposition, quickly recast the international order in old colonial terms. The USSR soon repositioned itself on the Arab side, and Arab public opinion swung decidedly in an anti-Western and anti-American direction. A revolt and coup in Egypt in 1952 brought young army official and Arab nationalist Gamal Abdel Nasser to power and, from the mid-1950s to the late 1960s, he led a wide pan-Arab movement in opposition to the Western dominated liberal order, bringing Egypt and other Arab countries into closer alignment with the USSR and Warsaw Pact countries. He championed principles raised by the liberal order, such as self-determination, but championed them for Palestinian rights and Arab unity in the face of an international order that he charged had denied them.[15]

The attempt at regional order represented by the League of Arab States was also shattered, as Egypt and Saudi Arabia soon found themselves enmeshed in proxy wars throughout the region that toppled governments and led to various proxy civil wars, most notably in

---

[14]Arab leaders were hesitant to grant much power to the League, and rather viewed it as a means to avoid calls for Arab unity rather than a means to achieve it. This hesitance is exemplified in the weak organisational structure of the league. For more, see Dakhlallah, "League of Arab States".

[15]Advocated by Egypt, as well as Syria and Iraq, pan-Arabism spread throughout the region following a number of radical leftwing movements in the 1950s, apparently making the reversal of Arab fragmentation imposed by the mandate period an attainable goal. *Ibid.*

Yemen, and briefly in Lebanon in 1958. Nasser had another regional order in mind: one led by Egypt and organised according to leftist Arab nationalist principles.[16] Nasser's Egypt also vowed to defeat Israel, which he regarded as a Western colonial implant, and this led to two wars in 1956 and 1967.[17]

The struggles for national self-determination, led by Yasser Arafat and the Palestine Liberation Organisation (PLO) against Israeli domination of Palestine and by the National Liberation Front (FLN) against French domination of Algeria enflamed anti-colonial passions linked to the liberal international order, and merged with other nationalist and leftist struggles against the US-led order, such as those in Cuba, Vietnam and Mao's China.

Arab return, Iranian rupture

Israel's victory over Egypt and other Arab armies in the 1967 war marked the end of the leftist Arab nationalist defiance of the liberal order. Egypt had also been exhausted by its Cold War with Saudi Arabia throughout the region and its failed attempts at Arab unity with Syria. Under Anwar Sadat, Nasser's successor, Egypt marched gradually and decidedly to take its place as a member of the US-led order, a position it has maintained since then. With Egypt's shift, other once radical states, like Syria and Algeria, also gradually reintegrated into the global order.[18]

While Arab states were returning to the fold, the Iranian revolution of 1979 and the Islamic Republic that emerged from it took Iran, both in theory and practice, out of the US-led order. The Islamic Republic decried the US as the 'Great Satan' and called for Islamic revolution throughout the largely Western- and liberal order-aligned Muslim world, and called for the establishment of an Iranian-led Muslim regional order that would maintain the jihad against the US-led international order.

While Arab states acquiesced to the liberal international order, an offshoot of the Islamist movement in the Arab world took on the mantle of fighting the US and complicit Arab states. In Egypt, this led to the assassination of the main accomplice in their eyes, President Sadat. In Afghanistan, an army of Sunni jihadists was forged with support from the US and Saudi Arabia to fight the Soviet invasion there. That army then turned its sights on the US, Europe, Saudi Arabia, and later Iraq, Syria, Yemen, Libya and other countries in an attempt to weaken the US and dismantle the international and regional order of which it sat atop. Their dream, which recently flickered briefly again in Iraq and Syria, was to re-establish a caliphate over the Islamic world and revive a global jihad of the Muslim world against the world of unbelief – mainly the 'crusader' West.

The collapse of the USSR and the end of the Cold War after 1990 brought a moment of unrivalled American hegemony. But instead of promoting a transition toward a more liberal order in the Middle East, this period started with the first major US military ground deployment in the Middle East, in the war to push Iraqi ruler Saddam Hussein's army out of Kuwait, and continued with a consolidation of US geopolitical influence in the region in collaboration with the region's authoritarian regimes. A glimmer of liberal transition

---

[16]See Barnett, "Institutions, roles and disorder"; Kerr, *The Arab Cold War*; Sela, *End of Arab Israeli Conflict*.
[17]Under Egyptian leadership, Arab nationalists pursued the goal of achieving pan-Arabism as the key to liberating Palestine. Opposition to Western military alliances with Arab regimes brought pro-Soviet and Arab nationalist movements into closer alignment.
[18]Fradkin and Libby, "Learning From Sadat", 32.

– quickly snuffed out – would have to wait two more decades, and would be fuelled by the region's restive youth.

Crisis and collapse

The Sunni jihadist army would define world events in the first decades of the 21st century and impact the region's relationship to the liberal international order. The attacks of 9/11, 2001, managed to commandeer US foreign and security policy in favour of massive and draining military engagements in Afghanistan and Iraq – and in the case of Iraq, seemingly against the principles of multilateralism and international law that the US was supposed to uphold. The liberal flag of 'bringing democracy to Iraq' was raised unconvincingly after accusations that Saddam had vast weapons of mass destruction (WMD) capabilities and was supporting al-Qaeda proved empty. While al-Qaeda was dealt a severe blow in Afghanistan, the reckless war and its aftermath in Iraq strengthened both opponents of the liberal international order: Iran and Sunni jihadists.

The dismantling of the Iraqi state also destroyed what was left of a precarious state-based Arab regional order. The uprisings of 2011 landed another blow with states in Yemen and Libya collapsing, and those in Syria and Iraq foundering. Iran gained dominance in Iraq and Syria and a foothold in Yemen, and an al-Qaeda offshoot, the Islamic State of Iraq and Syria (ISIS), declared a Caliphate in 2014. Its ideologically thoroughgoing rejection of the principles and realities of the post-Ottoman state system and the principles of the international order that gave birth to it presents perhaps the most virulent challenge to the modern international regional order. ISIS has been driven out of its capital and its main cities; its impact is greatly-diminished, but it will live on in various parts of the Levant and the wider Middle East, and will survive as a virulent ideology.

While the Arab states, at least those that have not collapsed, continue to cling to the liberal international order, Iran continues to define itself in opposition to it, and ISIS and al-Qaeda continue to lead a struggle against it.[19] Indeed, the case of Iran is interesting. The majority of the population seems to favour a reintegration into the international order, but the hardline elites that control national security policy, represented by the Supreme Leader and the Islamic Revolutionary Guards Corps (IRGC), still favour an oppositional position. President Hassan Rouhani, who has been elected twice on what could be interpreted as an integrationist agenda, secured a nuclear deal with the international community, but otherwise has been unable, or unwilling, to push harder for a normalisation of Iran's foreign policy and entanglements, especially toward the US and in the Middle East. Of course, Iranian hardliners have been given a boost by the rise of hardliners in the US under the Trump administration.

While the Middle East's integration into the liberal international order and the region's own regional integration might be at their lowest ebb, the Kurds have been trying to move in the other direction, acting on the liberal principle of self-determination – raised a century ago, but never honoured in their case – to claim independence for the Kurdish region of northern Iraq. Yet again, their ambitions continue to be thwarted.

---

[19]Stein emphasizes this point with Iran's refusal to accept the international order, maintaining its so called 'axis of refusal'. This lies within Iran's identity as an opponent to Western imperialism. See Stein, "Ideological Codependency and Regional Order", 676–80.

Principles and practice in the Middle East

While the foregoing gives a historical contextualisation of the ebbs and flows of outside-in interactions between the liberal international order and the Middle East, the following section looks at the ideational-normative conceptions articulated in this issue's framing article as conceptual pillars of the liberal international project, and interrogates their impact and resonance within the Middle Eastern context.

Internationalism

The 20th century brought a historic shift of worldview in the Middle East. The prevalent view in previous centuries was one in which most people viewed themselves as part of an imperial order defined by the Muslim Umma,[20] and in fundamental contradiction with other societies and empires that had profoundly different values. The prevalent view that gained increasing traction in the 20th century was one in which people regard themselves as members of nation states within an international order of nation states,[21] and an international order that expresses and aspires to – although it often violates it in practice – certain widely shared international values.

Societies in the Middle East only began to take the West seriously in the 19th century, after the Napoleonic invasion of Egypt and the clear Western ascendance in science, technology and warfare. For a millennium before that, there was a sense of centrality, superiority and complacency that Muslim societies and empires were superior to the West and East in most ways that counted.[22] Nor was there, in previous centuries, any conception of a 'global order' in the modern sense of the term. Only with European global exploration and expansion from the 15th to the 19th centuries did that reality of a global expanse, eventually requiring a global order, emerge. The First World War decisively showed that a powerful array of world powers existed outside the Muslim world, and handily defeated its principal imperial power.

The Middle East of the 20th century internalised the new global scope of power relations, and hence can be said to have internalised internationalism as a guiding perspective. The major disputes with the emerging international order were in many cases on the liberal international order's own terms: the Kurds and Palestinians demanded that the order honour its commitment to self-determination; the Algerians battled against the continued French colonisation of their land; Arab nationalists demanded national self-determination in a unified Arab state; Iranians and Arabs wanted the US and others to honour the principle of non-interference in other states' affairs – principles that were violated, for example, in the US-backed coup against the Iranian prime minister in 1953.

A number of states and proto-states in the region still have some differences of principle with the liberal international order. As stated above, Iran is a hybrid example of a state that is both part of and in contradiction with it; and ISIS challenges the very principle of a nation state and is at war with both the regional and international order.

---

[20]'Ummah' refers to the Islamic community, commonly intended as the community of Muslims throughout the world. The vision of a global Islamic community remains very much alive in the political and social discourse of Islamist movements. Within this perspective, and on the contradiction between the Muslim Ummah and other societies, see Nasr, "Islamic Unity".
[21]Harik, "Origins of Arab State System", 22-3.
[22]Lewis, *What Went Wrong?*, 3.

Institutionalism

As mentioned above, several Arab states were present at the birth of the UN and many of the new order's global multilateral institutions. For the region's governments, this often accorded them some much needed political legitimacy, and in some cases gave them recourse to political and financial support in times of difficulty. The UN has played significant roles in attempting mediation and conflict resolution in the Arab-Israeli conflict and in various civil wars in the region, and UN peacekeeping forces have been important in several conflict arenas. The international financial institutions, mainly the International Monetary Fund (IMF) and the World Bank, have been key players with governments in the region in challenging or influencing public economic and financial policy, and in participating in long-term development. As many have argued,[23] this has not counteracted the powerful impact of unbalanced core-periphery relations on Middle Eastern economies and societies.

The relations with international institutions have also been fraught as Middle Eastern states and publics have often wanted the UN Security Council (UNSC) to take more decisive action against Israeli occupation, or have blamed international financial institutions like the IMF for economic hardships at home. But even states seemingly in conflict with the liberal international order, like the Islamic Republic of Iran or the regime of Syrian President Bashar Assad since the uprising of 2011, have clung to their seats in the UN and other international organisations as a means to maintain their international legitimacy and leverage. Only during the days of Nasser did several states in the region actively seek to join an alternative set of multilateral institutions represented, separately, by the Warsaw Pact and the Non-Aligned Movement.

Regionalism

The establishment of the League of Arab States in 1945, after centuries of Turkish rule, and two decades of European rule, was an attempt to create an 'international' order at the regional level among the newly independent states of the region. But this attempt at regionalism was troubled from the start; it was light and weak, and challenged at many stages in ensuing years. Most importantly, it was a conception of regionalism that included only Arab countries and, by definition, excluded other regional states like Turkey, Iran and Israel, which would be born three years later. The League was also established by conservative Western-leaning governments which would all be discredited, and some overthrown, after the poor Arab showing in the 1948 conflict that concluded with the defeat of Palestinian Arabs and the establishment of the state of Israel.[24] The Arab League was paralysed during the Arab Cold War between Nasser's Egypt and a conservative Saudi Arabia, with each country trying to pull the league toward its own vision for the region. While the Arab League envisioned a regional order defined by independent sovereign states lightly coordinating within a weak set of multilateral institutions, Nasser envisioned a much deeper integration, either through unification of countries – as happened between Egypt and Syria between 1958 and 1961 – or through a Warsaw Pact type of ideological, political and security reality in which Egypt would lead and dominate a group of affiliated Arab states.[25]

---

[23]Cammet *et al., Political Economy of Middle East*; Brown, *International Politics and Middle East*; Bromley, "From Tributary Empires"; Owen, *Middle East in World Economy.*
[24]For more on the travails of this emerging Arab state system, see Maddy-Weitzman, *Crystallization of Arab State System.*
[25]The Arab League was designed as a bulwark against full integration, with the belief that full integration of states came at the expense of independent state sovereignty. See Mohamedou, "Arab Agency and UN Project".

But after Nasser's death and Egypt's separate peace with Israel in 1979, the Arab states reverted to the original conservative and limited ambitions of the Arab League as a body where sovereign states could meet occasionally, address some common concerns, and attempt to resolve differences and avoid conflict. As Arab regimes grew less legitimate and more repressive, the Arab League was also a venue where Arab leaders could meet as an oligarchy to make a show of television legitimacy, and rail about Israel or other issues for public consumption. Although Arab League bureaucrats had ambitions to deepen the multilateral institutional infrastructure of the Arab region with open trade zones, common infrastructure projects, and educational, cultural, and economic institutions of various sorts, the political regimes of the Arab states, as well as crony capitalist elites benefiting from national monopolies, effectively resisted real regionalisation or the proliferation of regional multilateral institutions that could in any way impinge on their authoritarian rule in their own countries. The Arab League never evolved into anything more than an occasional meeting of Arab heads of state.

The Arab League's attempt to maintain and represent a minimal common agenda among Arab states disintegrated in stages. The first blow was Egypt's signing of a separate peace with Israel in 1979 against unanimous Arab objections. The second was Syria's alignment with the Islamic Republic of Iran against widespread Arab backing of Iraq in its 1980-88 war with Iran. The third was Iraq's unprovoked invasion and attempted annexation of Kuwait in 1990. And after the US invasion of Iraq in 2003 and the uprising in Syria after 2011, there is no longer any Arab regional order to speak of. Iran is now the dominant player in Iraq, Syria and Lebanon, and has a strong foothold in Yemen. While the old Arab order is in ruins, there is no new regional security or political architecture to take its place.[26]

At a sub-regional level, the Arab monarchies of the Gulf established the Gulf Cooperation Council (GCC) in 1981. The GCC has had some success in coordinating policy among the six members, but has succumbed to internal division in crisis several times, including the current standoff with Qatar that has left that country blockaded by its GCC neighbours.[27]

Interdependence

The first elites that inherited power in the region after World War II accepted the relations of economic, political and security interdependence that linked their local governments to the centres of global power. But the revolutionary elites that unseated them in many countries in the aftermath of 1948 rejected this interdependence. They sought to unlink their countries' economies from the global metropoles through policies of rapid industrialisation, protectionism, import substitution and autarky. And they sought to supplant their political and security dependence on Western powers by building relations with the Soviet Union and the Soviet bloc. For many years, while Saudi Arabia, Jordan, Lebanon, Tunisia and Morocco accepted and tried to build on the new global realities of interdependence, Egypt, Syria, Iraq and Algeria, among others, went the other way. But as the Soviet Union declined and the limits and burdens of partnering with the Socialist bloc became apparent, first Egypt, then other formerly Soviet bloc-integrated countries came back to the liberal fold, seeking economic support and a role in a US-dominated world order.[28]

---

[26]In Salem and Harrison, *From Chaos to Cooperation*, the authors examine pathways to building a more inclusive and sustainable regional order.
[27]Naheem, "The Dramatic Rift".
[28]For more on Egypt's move back into the liberal international order, see Jawaad, *Middle East in New World Order*, 168-73.

Again, post-revolution Iran is an outlier in this narrative. Partly by choice, but largely by the hardship and isolation ensuing from the war with Iraq, followed by years of isolation and sanctions imposed on it by the US, Iran made a virtue of isolation, and built up its own economic and security resources without real interdependence with the global order. To be sure, they struck deals with various outside players, including China, Russia and even North Korea in some areas and, after the nuclear deal with the international community in 2015, they seek more investment from European countries, but the basic model of the hardliners has remained one of self-reliance and non-interdependence. Yet, this is a matter of great debate within Iran, and President Rouhani was elected both times to represent the argument that Iran needed to open up to the global economy and accept the quid pro quos of economic interdependence if it sought to grow further.

The integration of most of the region's countries into the global economy has been uneven with main exports concentrated in raw materials (oil and gas), and imports including almost everything else. Only Israel and Turkey (after 2000) have been able to develop a serious non-energy export capacity to help balance their economic relations with the rest of the world. Some tiny Gulf states, like the United Arab Emirates (UAE) and Qatar, have been able to plot an interesting course of development based on becoming global trade and financial hubs. Whether a populous country like Saudi Arabia can make the transition from a rentier to a productive economy – the principal aim of the Saudi Vision 2030 – remains to be seen. Crown Prince Muhammad bin Salman, the champion of Vision 2030, understands that economic goals will also require social and cultural change. His recent decision to allow women to drive and his move against the religious right are part of an attempt to weaken the religious shackles of the past and enable young Saudi men and women to be more mobile and productive members of the economy.

Nevertheless, the level of intra-regional economic integration remains very low. Intra-regional trade is the lowest of any region in the world, and intra-regional infrastructure as well as the homogenisation of customs and regulations or the creation of regional common markets are negligible. This is partly because governments do not trust their neighbours and fear the flows and dynamics that would be unleashed by regional integration; and partly because there is low complementarity among regional economies, with many of them seeking to export and import the same range of goods.[29]

International democracy

The liberal international order implies that all states, big and small, have a right to participate in international decision-making on a more or less equal footing. This principle was embraced by most states in the region after the Second World War, as it gave them a say in international affairs that most had not enjoyed in any form previously. It also gave them some leverage in the global order that was otherwise dominated by American, European and Asian powers, with not a Muslim world power among them.[30] The principle was used as a point of contention for Palestinians and Kurds clamouring to have their right to international representation and participation respected.

Within the region, this principle is represented in the Arab League, where states, large and small, enjoy comparable decision-making power, as the League adopted decision-making

---

[29]Hoekman, *Intra-Regional Trade*.
[30]Deudney and Ikenberry, "The Nature and Sources".

by consensus. This despite the fact that, in various time periods, Egypt and Saudi Arabia and, more recently, Qatar and the UAE, have enjoyed outsize sway in the organisation. But the Arab League is limited in membership, and there is no regional organisation that brings together all the states of the region, which would have to include, in addition to the Arab states, Turkey, Iran and Israel.

Of course, the form of 'democratic' participation implied by the liberal international order applies to relations among states, and does not suggest or impose democratisation as a form of internal organisation. Nevertheless, members of the new liberal order did commit to basic principles of abiding by the rule of law, respecting basic principles of human rights, and safeguarding their own populations. While few Middle Eastern countries paid much heed to the niceties of human rights or the sanctity of the rule of law, let alone the aspirations of democracy, most governments between the 1950s and 1970s achieved fairly significant progress in terms of human development in education, public health, housing and economic growth.[31] This slowed significantly from the 1980s onwards as public deficits grew, public services declined and income inequality increased, while demographic growth continued apace.

In terms of major breaches of human security by governments, there have been several, perhaps starting with the Hafez Assad regime's brutal putting down of a rebellion in Hama in 1982, to Saddam Hussein's treatment of Iraqi Kurds and Shiites after 1991. After the uprisings of 2011, both Libya's Muammar Qadhafi and Syria's Bashar Assad declared war on large swathes of their own population. In complex and very different ways, each of these major breaches ended up having significant international and regional consequences.

While the liberal international order does not presume or require that its members be democratic themselves, it has generally benefited from and been sustained by the leadership of a democratic United States and a democratic Western Europe; and today a majority of the UN's members are democracies.[32] In contrast, the Arab League has been a league of authoritarian states. Lebanon, a broken and imperfect democracy, was the only non-authoritarian country in the mix for several decades. Today, one might add Tunisia and a broken Iraq on the 'transitioning' or 'non-authoritarian' side of the ledger.

Not only did the Arab League have no major democratic members, the coalition was a mutually reinforcing club for authoritarian forms of government. When uprisings took place in Central and Eastern Europe, a pro-democratic regional organisation – the European Union (EU) – was there to provide a pathway and support for democratic transition. When the Arab uprisings erupted in 2011, the main members of the Arab League were most concerned about how to *stop* these waves of public empowerment. By 2014, they had managed to roll back the waves of change in Egypt and Bahrain; while Syria, Yemen and Libya have since moved not toward transition, but disintegration.

From the above discussion, it should become apparent that the Middle East has had a complex but impactful interaction with the five main conceptual frameworks of the liberal international order. Some have been internalised, others rejected, and others interpreted partially or selectively, but they have all played a role in shaping the narratives and frameworks surrounding the region's relationship with the liberal order.

---

[31]Cammet *et al., Political Economy of Middle East.*
[32]Deudney and Ikenberry, "The Nature and Sources".

Inside-out: the Mideast disorder today – emanating impacts

Today there is no regional order in the Middle East. It is the most dis-organised region within the international order. Not only are regional powers in proxy conflict, but several key states have collapsed, and hundreds of armed non-state actors, including major trans-national terrorist groups like ISIS and al-Qaeda have risen and managed to run large swathes of territory in Syria and Iraq. While ISIS has recently been beaten back from major cities like Mosul and Raqqa, its presence and threat remain significant. Far from supporting the international liberal order in any constructive way, the Middle East region has drawn global powers, such as the US and Russia, into local conflicts on opposite sides, provided space for the export of terrorist threats around the globe, and produced a massive flow of refugees to Europe. This has shaken the European Union, contributed to the British referendum vote on exiting the EU (Brexit), and injected a nationalist option into European and American politics that sits uncomfortably alongside (when it is not clearly opposed to) liberal principles.

The inability of the international community to act in a unified manner to stop the bloodshed in Syria signalled a historic low point for the international order, and the bloody campaign by the Assad regime against its own population has done away with the nascent international principle of the 'responsibility to protect'.

The Middle East today can be described as broken into zones of chaos and zones of influence with fast-moving lines of conflict. Part of this is due to internal uprisings and conflict, but in the cases of Iraq, Libya and Syria, external international (that is extra-regional) intervention from the West and Russia has played a major role. The zones of chaos extend over most of Libya, large areas of northern and eastern Syria, parts of western Iraq, and parts of Yemen. There, armed non-state actors and some major terrorist groups predominate. As mentioned previously, the old Arab state order has collapsed. Iran now has a strong zone of influence that extends from Tehran, through Basra, Baghdad, Mosul, Aleppo and Damascus to Latakia, Tartous, Beirut and the Mediterranean. It also has a significant foothold in the Yemeni capital Sanaa and the important Red Sea port of Hudayda. Turkey, which had strong ambitions before 2011, is left with only a small zone of influence in northern Syria. Saudi Arabia casts a long shadow over the GCC countries (although Qatar is still attempting to chart its own course) and has leverage with Jordan and some with Egypt. Its once dominant influence in Yemen collapsed with the collapse of order there; it is now in direct and proxy conflict with allies and clients in Yemen against the Houthi coalition which has backing from Iran. Egypt, once a regional hegemon, is a shadow of its former self, struggling to contain an insurgency in northern Sinai and threats from the western border with Libya.

The US still has the widest set of partnerships and alliances in the region, but its influence waned under the Obama administration and did not regain a solid purchase and purpose in the first year of the Trump administration. Russia is back in the Middle East after an absence of several decades, and has aligned itself with Iran and the Assad regime; it also enjoys close relations with Israel and has patched up frayed relations with Turkey.

Different regional players have different visions of regional order for the Middle East, but none of the players have enough regional power or sufficient international backing to overcome current divisions and collapses and turn their vision into reality. The vision for the region of Iranian hardliners could be described as a mirror image of the Nasserist vision: a Middle East of revolutionary anti-Western anti-Israeli states (or armed non-state actors), but with an Islamist ideology and aligned under Tehran's ideological, political and security leadership. This vision has no chance of overall success. Iran's appeal does not reach beyond countries with large Shiite or at least non-Sunni Muslim communities, and it has not been able to project power except into countries that have already fully or partially collapsed. The Russian intervention was key in preserving an Iranian client state in Syria, but cannot be leveraged into some grander Iranian ambition over other parts of the Middle East. Iran will be busy over the next years consolidating the costly and precarious gains it has made in the Levant, and may be aiming for a 'Helsinki moment' in which its regional influence is recognised and normalised. Whether it will maintain a foothold in Yemen is hard to say.

Turkey, before the war in Syria, had a vision for regional order in the Middle East that would have been most consistent with the liberal international order. With its policy of 'no problems with neighbours' and its friendly relations with most Arab states as well as Iran and Israel, Turkey was essentially proposing a Middle East regional order that was inclusive of all major states, built on respect for state sovereignty and rule of law, and holding the promise of increased trade, investment and economic prospects. It would have been a new regional order in line with and supportive of the liberal order. Turkey was also encouraging democratisation. President Recep Tayyip Erdogan thought that this vision was on the cusp of realisation in the early months of the Arab spring and took something of a victory tour to Egypt and Tunisia in late 2011. But the vision collapsed in the carnage of the Syrian war, the rise of ISIS, the coup in Egypt, and other regional developments. Erdogan turned combative, partisan and sectarian in his regional foreign policy, and increasingly authoritarian and undemocratic in his rule at home.[33]

Saudi Arabia yearns for a return to the status quo ante of an authoritarian and docile Arab regional order, particularly without Iranian presence, but this order is gone, never to return. The Saudis have continually urged the US to push back, weaken and contain Iran, but Iran's presence in the Levant seems fixed for the time being. Saudi Arabia is focused on challenges closer to home: they have yet to find a way to regain dominance in Yemen and prevent Iranian influence from becoming a permanent presence on their southern border; and they have the continual fear of unrest among the Shiite populations in Bahrain or the Saudi Eastern Province, which would provide opportunities for Iran to project influence into the heart of the GCC and Saudi Arabia itself. Riyadh has shown an eagerness to resolve the Israeli-Arab conflict, which would be a great boon for rebuilding one part of regional order, but they cannot proceed without some form of two-state solution between Israel and the Palestinians.

Israel has no conflict with any of the major Arab states but is focused on the short- and long-term threats from Iran. In the long term, it worries about the future of Iran's nuclear program; in the short term it worries about the massive Hezbollah missile arsenal in Lebanon, and Iran and Hezbollah's expanded influence in Syria. Israel would welcome a normalisation of relations with the Arab states, but recent governments seem unable or unwilling to find a path forward toward a negotiated settlement with the Palestinians. To be sure, a weak and divided Palestinian leadership has not made finding such a path any easier.

Egypt is consumed by its own political, economic and security worries. President Abd al-Fattah Sisi has a straightforward state-based vision for the Middle East – opposed to

---

[33]Gunter, "Erdogan and Decline of Turkey".

armed non-state actors of all kinds and Islamists of all kinds – and is in favour of old-fashioned authoritarianism. But today, Egypt has virtually no influence beyond its precarious borders.[34]

Some major non-state actors like ISIS and al-Qaeda have their own alternative visions of regional order. While al-Qaeda is playing a longer game, ISIS has expressed the basic vision of replacing the modern order of nation states integrated into the global order with an Islamic Caliphate that will eventually extend to the entire Muslim world, and re-establishing an empire that is in permanent conflict with powers and empires of the unbelievers. This vision is being defeated today in Iraq and Syria, and while both ISIS and al-Qaeda will survive as virulent networks and militias in various parts of the region and the world, their vision has no realistic pathway to realisation.

There will be no alternative vision or regional order for the Middle East in the foreseeable future. What the near future holds is a region defined by disorder and conflict, with continued proxy wars and failed states continuing to export refugees and terrorist threats.

The pathway to restoring a semblance of order is not easy, but it is not impossible either. The key breakdown in the Middle East that has fuelled the recent spate of proxy wars, radicalisation, refugees, and the rise of terrorist groups is the collapse of states. The key to restoring a modicum of order is reconstituting failed states. Regardless of the causes of partial or full state collapse in Iraq, Syria, Libya and Yemen, the priority in coming months and years must be to end ongoing civil wars there, find reasonably inclusive political arrangements and then help these broken states reconstitute and rebuild political, security and economic institutions. There is unlikely to be a cooperative regional order in the near future that includes Iran, Saudi Arabia and Turkey, let alone Israel; but it is possible, through mediation, to bring about a de-escalation of proxy conflict between these regional powers. The aspiration of building a truly inclusive and cooperative liberal regional order along the lines of the Association of Southeast Asian Nations (ASEAN), the Organisation of American States (OAS), or the more ambitious EU, will have to remain a distant dream.

Acknowledgements

I would like to thank my MEI intern, Yousuf Eltagouri, for his help in finalising this text. I would also like to thank the editors of this volume and the two anonymous outside reviewers for their helpful comments.

References

Ajami, F. *The Arab Predicament: Arab Political Thought and Practice Since 1967.* Cambridge: Cambridge University Press, 1981.

Barnett, M. "Institutions, roles and disorder: the case of the Arab states system". *International Studies Quarterly* 37, no. 3 (1993): 271–96.

---

[34]Frantzman, "Egypt Confronts Economic Challenges".

Brecher, F.W. "French Policy Toward the Levant 1914–18". *Middle Eastern Studies* 29, no. 4 (1993): 641–63.

Bromley, S. "From Tributary Empires to States System". In *Rethinking Middle East Politics*. Austin TX: Univ. of Texas Press, 1994: 46–52.

Brown, L. C. *International Politics and the Middle East: Old Rules, Dangerous Game*. Princeton, NJ: Princeton University Press, 1984.

Cammet, M., I. Diwan, A. Richards and J. Waterbury. *A Political Economy of the Middle East, 4th ed.* Boulder CO: Westview Press, 2015.

Dakhlallah, F. "The League of Arab States and Regional Security: Towards an Arab Security Community?" *British Journal of Middle Eastern Studies* 39, no. 3 (2012): 393–412.

Deudney, D., and G. J. Ikenberry. "The Nature and Sources of Liberal International Order". *Review of International Studies* 25, no. 2 (April 1999): 179–96.

Dawn, C. E. "From Ottomanism to Arabism: The Origin of an Ideology". In *The Modern Middle East*, edited by A. Hourani, P. Khoury and M. Wilson: 375–94. Berkeley, CA: University of California Press, 1993.

Fradkin, H., and L. Libby. "Learning From Sadat: The Dividends of American Resolve". *World Affairs*, Sept. 2012.

Frantzmen, S. "Egypt Confronts Economic and Security Challenges as it Attempts to Regain Its Position in the Arab World". *Middle East Review of International Affairs* 2, no. 1 (2017).

Gunter, M. M. "Erdogan and the Decline of Turkey". *Middle East Policy* 23, no. 4 (2016): 123–30.

Harik, I. "The Origins of the Arab State System". In *The Foundations of the Arab State*, edited by G. Salame. London: Croom Helm, 1987.

Hinnebusch, R. *The International Politics of the Middle East*. Manchester University Press, 2003.

Hoekman, B. *Intra-Regional Trade: Potential Catalyst for Growth in the Middle East*, MEI Regional Cooperation Policy Paper Series. Washington DC: Middle East Institute, April 2016.

Hourani, A. *Arabic Thought in the Liberal Age: 1798–1939*. Cambridge: Cambridge University Press, 1983.

Jawaad, H. *The Middle East in the New World Order*. Basingstoke: Palgrave Macmillan, 2014.

Joffe, G. H. "Disputes over state boundaries in the Middle East and North Africa". In *The Middle East in Global Change: The Politics and Economics of Interdependence Versus Fragmentation*, edited by L. Guazzone: 58–94. New York: St. Martin's Press, 1997.

Kerr, M. *The Arab Cold War: Jamal Abd al-Nasir and his Rivals, 1958–1970*. London: Oxford University Press, 1971.

Korany, B., and A. E. Hillal Dessouki, eds. *The Foreign Policies of Arab States: The Challenge of Globalization*. Boulder, CO: Westview Press, 1991.

Lewis, B. *What Went Wrong? Western Impact and Middle Eastern Response*. Oxford: Oxford University Press, 2002.

Maddy-Weitzman, B. *The Crystallization of the Arab State System, 1945–1954*. Syracuse, NY: Syracuse University Press, 1993.

Mohamedou, M.-M. O. "Arab Agency and the UN Project: The League Of Arab States between Universality and Regionalism". *Third World Quarterly* 37, no. 7 (2016): 1219–33.

Naheem, M. A. "The Dramatic Rift and Crisis between Qatar and the Gulf Cooperation Council (GCC) of June 2017". *International Journal of Disclosure and Governance*, 13 Sept. 2017.

Nasr, S. H. "Islamic Unity – The Ideal and Obstacles in the Way of its Realization". *Iqbal Review* 40, no. 1 (April 1993): 161–3.

Noble, P. "From Arab System to Middle Eastern System? Regional Pressures and Constraints". In *The Foreign Policies of Arab States, The Challenge of Globalization*, new revised edition, edited by B. Korany and A. E. Hillal Desouki: 67–166. Cairo: American University of Cairo Press, 2008.

Owen, R. *The Middle East in the World Economy, 1800–1914*. London and New York: Meuthen, 1981.

Salem, P., and R. Harrison. *From Chaos to Cooperation: Toward Regional Order in the Middle East*. Washington DC: The Middle East Institute, 2017.

Salame, G. "Integration in the Arab World: The Institutional Framework". In *The Politics of Arab Integration*, edited by G. Salame and G. Luciani: 256–79. New York: Croom Helm, 1988.

Sela, A. *The End of the Arab Israeli Conflict: Middle East Politics and the Quest for Regional Order.* Albany NY: State Univ. of New York Press, 1988.

Stein, E. "Ideological Codependency and Regional Order: Iran, Syria, and the Axis of Refusal". *PS. Political Science & Politics* 50, no. 3 (2017): 676–80.

Order and Contestation in the Asia-Pacific Region: Liberal vs Developmental/Non-interventionist Approaches

Richard Stubbs

ABSTRACT

The United States/European-inspired liberal international order has long been challenged in the Asia-Pacific. During the Cold War years, Washington sponsored a developmental, state-interventionist order to contain the threat from Asian communism. This developmental order persisted even as the end of the Cold War allowed the US to promote a liberal regional order. Moreover, after the Asian Financial Crisis of 1997-98, the US was increasing constrained by its post-9/11 preoccupation with the Middle East, the rise of China, its responsibility for the Great Recession of 2008-09 and the infighting that consumed Washington. While elements of a liberal order can be found in the Asia-Pacific today, they must continue to contend with non-interventionist and developmental values still found in the region.

If an international or regional 'order' is considered the dominant ideological framework within which relatively settled and regularised international affairs are conducted, then the United States- and European-inspired liberal international order, while gaining traction at the global level, has long been challenged in the Asia-Pacific region (East and Southeast Asia). Indeed, during the Cold War years the normative tenants of the liberal international order were eclipsed in the Asia-Pacific region by Washington's dominant goal of containing Asian communism. It was only with the winding down of the Cold War during the late 1980s that the US turned to promoting the key features of the liberal international order in the Asia-Pacific. Essentially, for the US the liberal international order was an aspiration or ideal towards which regional policies and structures should be moved. However, the Cold War era developmental ideological framework continued to be a factor within the region as it battled against the emerging influence of the proponents of the liberal international order. This competition among contending orders or paradigms in the Asia-Pacific will continue well into the future.

The US, aided by the European powers, used its hegemonic status after the Second World War to build a liberal international order. As Riccardo Alcaro points out in his Introduction to this Special Issue, the emerging liberal international order emphasised internationalism, which stressed mutual responsibilities, including protecting human rights around the world; multilateralism to create predictability in a chaotic world; regional arrangements such as the

European Union to promote cooperation; interdependence, which meant the opening up of national economies and the reduction of barriers to trade and capital flows; the kind of governance which subsumed national interests to the interests of the wider international community; and democracy, both within countries and at the international level.[1] These ideas were encapsulated in a series of international institutions such as the International Bank for Reconstruction and Development, later the World Bank; the International Monetary Fund (IMF); the General Agreement on Tariffs and Trade, later the World Trade Organisation (WTO); and such security organisations as the North Atlantic Treaty Organization (NATO). But, while this emerging ideal of a liberal international order was highly influential, it was by no means universal.

Asia-Pacific's Cold War developmental regional order

Ironically, it was Washington that encouraged an alternative developmental order to arise in the Asia-Pacific. After the outbreak of the Korean War in June 1950, the US government became preoccupied with containing Asian communism. Most particularly, American governments were fearful of the People's Republic of China being able to spread out across East and Southeast Asia rather like the Japanese military had been able to take over much of Southeast Asia in December 1941 and January 1942. There was also a concern that individual countries in East and Southeast Asia weakened by the ravages of the Second World War and internal guerrilla warfare might not be able to deal with either the external threat or domestic communist subversion and that, consequently, America's interests in the region would be undermined.

The result of America's determination to contain Asian communism was a series of outcomes that contrasted markedly with the key features of the emerging liberal international order. Military relations in the Asia-Pacific region were dominated by a series of bilateral security arrangements between the US and its main allies – Japan, South Korea, Taiwan, South Vietnam, the Philippines and Thailand. This 'hub-and-spoke' security system was reinforced by the infusion of massive amounts of military aid which ensured the rapid expansion of militaries around the region. South Korea and Taiwan developed among the largest armies in the non-communist world and the Philippines was the site of the two largest military bases outside of the United States. Outsized militaries also meant military dictatorships in all of America's main regional allies except Japan. Washington may have been uneasy at times with the way its allies were governed, but it saw 'strong' governments as crucial to ensuring that Asian communism was kept in check.

America's approach to confronting Asian communism, therefore, put little reliance on promoting the ideas embodied in the liberal international order. Multilateralism was given short shrift. The one major US-sponsored security organisation, the Southeast Asia Treaty Organization (SEATO), which was created in 1954, had only two of its eight members – the Philippines and Thailand – from Southeast Asia and generally "had an inbuilt impotence".[2] It faded and was dismantled in the 1970s. The Association of Southeast Asian Nations (ASEAN), founded in 1967 by five non-communist Southeast Asian countries, has been more durable but has attracted little direct support from the US. Moreover, those seeking

---

[1] Alcaro, "Liberal Order and its Contestations". See also Ikenberrry, "Liberal Internationalism".
[2] Other member countries were Australia, France, New Zealand, Pakistan (including East Pakistan, now Bangladesh), the United Kingdom and the United States. Nairn, "SEATO", 5.

to replace military dictatorships with democratic institutions were largely ignored by the US government during the Cold War years. Similarly, in many of Asia-Pacific's non-communist military dictatorships abuse of human rights was widespread, with the US seemingly unconcerned.

Nor did the region's economies live up to the aspirations of the liberal international order during the Cold War years, despite receiving massive amounts of economic aid from the US. Japan, Taiwan, South Korea and Singapore adopted a neo-mercantilist, 'developmental state' approach to economic development with Malaysia, Thailand and even in some respects Hong Kong also making use of aspects of this economic strategy.[3] Comparatively autonomous, relatively meritocratic, state institutions implemented a plan for economic growth which was coordinated by a central agency. Selected industries were protected through high tariffs and domestic regulations and targeted sectors of the economy, especially export-manufacturing industries, were given subsidies, including cheap credit, and other advantages, such as access to advanced technologies. This emphasis on state management of the economy and barriers to imports contrasted with the market-oriented approach and free flow of trade which was at the heart of the liberal international order's ideological framework. Importantly, Washington tolerated this state-guided economic approach because the prosperity and social stability it produced strengthened America's allies, making it easier for them to confront and contain the threat from Asian communism.

Some commentators, most notably G. John Ikenberry, have suggested that this set of arrangements amounted to a "liberal hegemonic order".[4] However, it is difficult to see the dominance of the US in the hub-and-spoke security system and Washington's failure to exert pressure on Asia-Pacific governments to democratise or safeguard human rights as exhibiting liberal ideals. Similarly, economic policies that favoured domestic firms through import protection and export promotion also undercut the free flow of goods and capital which were key liberal norms. It is therefore, impossible to conceive of the Cold War Asia-Pacific order as a liberal regional order.

Post-Cold War contending regional orders

With the unravelling of the Cold War in the late 1980s, the US started to pressure Asia-Pacific governments to introduce policies which would produce greater economic and political liberalisation. Freed from the need to prioritise the containment of Asian communism, the US government could give full rein to its commitment to democracy and human rights and its wish for a fully open regional economy. But the old developmental Asia-Pacific order persisted. It had provided prosperity and stability for many in the region and, as a result, was appreciated by significant sectors of society including politicians, bureaucrats, business leaders and parts of the general public. They valued what the dominant, guiding role of the state had produced. The two contending ideological frameworks began to face off against each other.[5]

Initially, the US had some success in promoting democratisation. While President Ronald Reagan was personally slow to abandon his 'old friend' President Ferdinand Marcos during the People Power Revolution in the Philippines in February 1986, the US government did

---

[3]Woo-Cumings, *Developmental State*; Stubbs, "Whatever Happened".
[4]Ikenberry, "American Hegemony", 353.
[5]Stubbs, "East Asian Developmental State".

play a role in the final, relatively peaceful, transfer of power to the newly elected president, Corazon Aquino. The example of the fall of President Marcos and the People Power Revolution in the Philippines, combined with increasing pressure from the United States, helped to bring democratic reform to South Korea, Taiwan and, to a limited extent, Thailand in the late 1980s and early 1990s. During the 1990s, US administrations also campaigned for respect for human rights in the region. For example, President Bill Clinton challenged China to give more respect to human rights during his visit to Beijing in June 1998 and Vice President Al Gore chided the Malaysian government for its stand on human rights during a visit to Kuala Lumpur later that year.[6]

However, where the US had most success was in advancing the economic ideals associated with a liberal international order. Using its influence over the IMF, the World Bank and the Organisation for Economic Cooperation and Development (OECD), the US mounted considerable pressure on its allies in the Asia-Pacific to open up their economies through privatisation, deregulation and liberalisation. Although the economic reforms undertaken by Japan and Taiwan were not as far-reaching as the American government might have liked, in other parts of the region, reforms were more extensive. In South Korea, foreign banks were accommodated, a stock market was developed, and regulation of the financial sector reduced, including the liberalisation of capital transfers. The Korean government also gave up many of its monitoring and coordinating powers, leaving more decisions about the development of the economy to the major conglomerates. Similarly, in Thailand, Malaysia and Indonesia import taxes were cut, tariff protection for inefficient sectors and limits on capital movement considerably reduced. Stock markets were also introduced into the major Southeast Asian economies.[7]

US bilateral pressure was complemented at the regional level by American actions in the Asia-Pacific Economic Cooperation (APEC) forum, which was established in 1989. Washington, backed by Australia, Canada and New Zealand, used APEC to push for a formally negotiated, legally-binding agreement which would be systematically implemented over a given period of time and bring about near total liberalisation of the region's economies.[8] In 1993, President Clinton converted the annual meeting of foreign and trade ministers into an annual summit meeting of APEC leaders. He used the first summit in Seattle in November 1993 to press for the adoption and implementation of policies that would lead to open regionalism in the Asia-Pacific. The clear goal was to put in place a liberal regional order.[9]

Yet, despite the best efforts of the US government, creating a liberal regional order in the Asia-Pacific proved to be problematic. The old, Cold War-rooted developmental order had staying power. In Japan, the 'iron triangle' of politicians, bureaucrats and vested business interests ensured that key economic sectors such as agriculture, construction and insurance remained protected.[10] Similarly, in Taiwan and Singapore the state continued to play a significant role in their economies. At the regional level, the ASEAN – and after 1997 the ASEAN Plus Three (China, Japan and South Korea) grouping – provided a counterweight to APEC. ASEAN principles, enunciated in the 1976 Treaty of Amity and Cooperation

[6]Clinton, "President's News Conference"; Landler, "Gore Scolded".
[7]Bowie and Unger, *Politics of Open Economies*; Stubbs, *Rethinking*, 161-72.
[8]Stubbs and Mustapha, "Ideas and Institutions"; Ravenhill, *APEC*.
[9]Higgott and Stubbs, "Competing Conceptions".
[10]Sakakibara, "Interview".

(TAC), included respect for sovereignty and freedom from external interference. This was the basis for criticism of America's interventionist attempts to foster democracy and respect for human rights within Southeast Asia countries.[11]

The US also ran into opposition in pursuit of its goal of promoting regional liberalisation and open regionalism through APEC. Contrary to the American conception of legally mandatory agreements, Asian members favoured a non-binding, voluntary approach to liberalisation which emphasised tackling the easiest issues first. The resulting stalemate, which produced irreconcilable differences over negotiations during the late 1990s involving the Early Voluntary Sectoral Liberalisation initiative, convinced the Anglo-American members that APEC could not be used as the vehicle to implement the economic elements of a liberal regional order.

The 1997-98 Asian Financial Crisis (AFC) proved to be a battleground for supporters of the competing liberal and developmental regional orders as they sought to gain pre-eminence for their vision in the Asia-Pacific region. As the AFC unfolded, a campaign to denigrate the developmental regional order was mounted by senior members of the US administration, such as Treasury Secretary Robert Rubin, and officials at the IMF, such as Michel Camdessus.[12] They asserted that the ideas underpinning the developmental regional order had caused the crisis. One consequence was that the IMF imposed liberal, market-oriented policies on governments that sought its help. On the other hand, many leaders in the Asia-Pacific blamed the US and the IMF for propelling them into the crisis.[13] While the US had pushed hard for financial liberalisation, it had not indicated that there was a commensurate need to monitor and regulate the more open financial system to ensure that the shift in financial and commercial activity presented no threat to the economy. There were also many among the region's elites who thought that the IMF's advice and policies in response to events were so ill-conceived that they had quickly turned the currency crisis of mid-1997 into a deep economic recession and social catastrophe in places like Thailand, Indonesia and South Korea.[14]

These conflicting views of the causes of the AFC and the best way of overcoming the problems it generated meant that those advocating a liberal regional order, while stymied in significant ways, made some progress towards their ideal. Governments in the Asia-Pacific did open up their economies, most notably in South Korea. The Asian Financial Crisis also acted as a catalyst for a series of free trade agreements (FTAs) among the Asia Pacific countries and counterparts around the wider Pacific Rim region, including an ASEAN-China FTA.[15] Equally, China was admitted to the WTO in December 2001. This accession to the WTO required that China reach a separate agreement with the US, which imposed additional conditions on China to ensure foreign companies greater access to the Chinese market.

However, elements of the old developmental order lingered on. Banking regulatory structures and practices in Japan, South Korea and Malaysia were tightened up with bureaucracies bolstered to ensure greater oversight capacity. Governments in the region also embarked on a massive accumulation of foreign exchange reserves.[16] This domestic 'self-insurance policy'

---

[11]Stubbs, "The ASEAN Alternative".
[12]Hall, "Discursive Demolition"
[13]Higgott, "Asian Economic Crisis".
[14]Stiglitz, *Globalization and Its Discontents*, 98-118.
[15]Dent, "Free Trade Agreements".
[16]Hamilton-Hart, "Banking Systems".

was complemented by the Chiang Mai Initiative (CMI), set in motion in May 2000. The CMI, which was converted to the CMI Multilateralisation in 2010, provided for a network of currency swap agreements that member states could rely on, should their currencies once again come under attack.[17] The whole idea of self-insurance was an obvious neo-mercantilist policy which was strongly criticised by the US. Finally, China, despite liberalising parts of its economy to comply with WTO requirements, remained intent on managing the forces of globalisation through state intervention in the economy where necessary. For example, large state-owned enterprises dominated key strategic sectors such as banking, transportation and energy and led China's advance into the wider global economy.[18]

US retreat and China's rise

For the first few years of the twenty-first century, the US was by any measure "the most powerful country on the planet".[19] It should have been able to expand its influence and promote its vision for a liberal regional order in the Asia-Pacific, and in many ways the US was successful in pressing for the liberalisation of markets within the region. However, this was achieved more through a series of bilateral agreements than by way of a multilateral region-wide arrangement. For example, FTAs were completed with Australia and Singapore, and negotiations begun with South Korea and Thailand.

Nevertheless, a series of constraints began to emerge which make it difficult to think of the Asia-Pacific as being totally in the grip of a US-inspired liberal regional order stressing democracy, respect for human rights, open economies and multilateral security arrangements.

First was the dramatic shift in US foreign policy in the wake of the searing events of 11 September 2001. The primacy of foreign economic policy during the 1990s gave way to safeguarding the homeland and defeating the evils of terrorism. The George H.W. Bush administration's concern with the peace dividend, which came with the end of the Cold War, and the Clinton administration's stress on the beneficial effects of the intensification of economic globalisation were seemingly set to one side. President George W. Bush's litmus test for international relations was whether or not a government supported the US in countering global terrorism. Indeed, the FTAs negotiated with Australia, Singapore, South Korea and Thailand were seen as rewards for support on the security front rather than purely economic arrangements.[20] The post-9/11 invasion of Afghanistan and the March 2003 invasion of Iraq gave US policy a Central Asia and Middle East focus that took the attention of top level US officials away from other parts of the globe, including the Asia-Pacific. As American forces became ever more bogged down in Iraq and Afghanistan, the 'war on terror' became almost all consuming for the US. Increasingly, US perspectives on the Asia-Pacific region appeared to regional governments to be distorted by America's preoccupation with its ill-fated wars. Muslims in Southeast Asia, especially in Indonesia, became alienated by US actions in Iraq and the general anti-Muslim tone in US rhetoric,

---

[17]Bank of Japan, "Chiang Mai Initiative Multilateralization".
[18]Eaton, *The Advance of the State*, 79; Hsueh, *China's Regulatory State*, 34-7.
[19]Beeson, "American Ascendency", 3.
[20]Conners, "Thailand", 138; Mustapha, "Threat Construction", 496-7.

and regional governments resented the US government "viewing Southeast Asia through a Middle Eastern lens".[21]

The Bush Administration's prioritisation of security over international economy issues also meant that APEC summits, which could have been used to support liberal economic policies in the region, were generally hijacked by US officials in order to try to get regional endorsement of America's global counter-terrorism strategies.[22] Similarly, senior US officials ignored the general institutionalisation of regional relations that materialised in the wake of the Asian financial crisis. They were indifferent to the rise of the Shanghai Cooperation Organisation, were generally dismissive of the ASEAN Regional Forum and missed the significance of the first East Asian Summit in 2005.[23] With the top Republican politicians so engaged in the Middle East and so disengaged from what was happening on the ground in the Asia-Pacific, it was difficult for US officials in the region, who did understand the trends on the ground, to effectively push a liberal regional order agenda.

Second came the Great Recession of 2007-09. The great recession was the result of the failure to properly monitor and regulate the real estate and financial markets in the US and the United Kingdom. The irony of the fact that people like Alan Greenspan – the Chairman of the Federal Reserve, who had chastised Asia-Pacific governments before and during the AFC for poor financial practices and failing to introduce greater liberalisation of their financial sectors – were widely blamed for creating the conditions which led to the great recession, was not lost on Asia-Pacific governments. For Asia-Pacific leaders, it was not the banking industry that was the problem. Insulated by reform of the financial sectors in the aftermath of the AFC, the governments of the Asia-Pacific region were faced with a trade crisis rather than a financial crisis. The big problem was that exports from Asia-Pacific countries to the US dropped precipitously in absolute terms. For example, South Korea's exports to the US dropped by 23 percent from 2008 to 2009.[24] This downturn in trade with the US weakened Washington's influence in the region.

Importantly, America's legitimacy as the sponsor of a more liberal regional order was severely dented by the way in which the great recession unfolded. The questions that were raised about corporate corruption, the failure to adhere to the rule of law, and government mismanagement all damaged US credibility as the advocate for a more open, liberal regional economy. Washington also found it difficult to get its economy back up and running and, consequently, it took a long time before the US could help the global economy recover from the severe downturn it had precipitated.

One of the reasons why the US was having only mixed success in diffusing liberal regional order values, policies and practices was that China's stock in the Asia-Pacific region was on the rise. China was credited with helping Asia-Pacific economies survive the Asian financial crisis by not having to devalue their currency. Such a move would have undercut the competitive position of China's neighbours and deepened the crisis. From 2001 onwards, the Chinese economy grew increasingly rapidly. From 2003 to 2007, it sustained growth rates of well over 10 percent per year. This massive expansion in the Chinese economy acted as a major catalyst to the economic growth of other Asia-Pacific economies and put China in an increasing positive light around the region. During the great recession, China introduced

[21]Ba, "System Neglect?", 378.
[22]Higgott, "After Neoliberal Globalization".
[23]Ibid.; Pempel, "How Bush Bungled".
[24]Observatory of Economic Complexity, https://atlas.media.mit.edu/en/.

a stimulus package which gave a boost not only to the Chinese economy but also to the economies of many of its Asia-Pacific neighbours. Others in the region followed suit. A common feature of all the regional stimulus packages was greater state intervention and enlarged bureaucracies. In other words, as a result of the great recession, the governments of the Asia-Pacific put increased emphasis on the state-management approach rather than on the market-oriented economic strategy stressed by proponents of a liberal regional order.[25]

In addition, in 2003 China was the first non-ASEAN country to sign on to ASEAN's Treaty of Amity and Cooperation (TAC). As a former Secretary General of ASEAN noted, the TAC's norms for interstate conduct "dovetailed with the Five Principles of Peaceful Coexistence formulated by China in the 1950s".[26] Other members of the Asia-Pacific region quickly followed China's lead. This approach to international relations was in line with the general views that had been circulating in the region for many years and which had emerged in response to the common historical experiences of Western colonial intervention and the pressures of the Cold War. Indeed, they had been formalised in the Final Communique of the 1995 Bandung Conference.[27]

Led by China and ASEAN, then, an alternative approach to the conduct of regional relations, which contradicted in significant ways the interventionist norms of a US/Europe-sponsored liberal regional order, was beginning to surface. Various labels have been devised to highlight that China's domestic economic and foreign policy strategies are distinctive from those of America's liberal international order approach. Some have used the term 'Beijing Consensus' to distinguish it from the US-inspired, market-oriented Washington Consensus, while others have referred to the 'China model'.[28] Overall, there is no agreement as to what either term stands for, but there is a general understanding that a rival approach to the liberal international order is broadly in operation in the Asia-Pacific and it should be acknowledged. As Shaun Breslin argues, "the idea of a China model is more important as a symbol or metaphor than as a distinct or coherent model that might provide a clear guide for development elsewhere".[29] In the wake of the great recession, therefore, a key question arose: given the rise of China and the preoccupation in Washington with the Middle East and getting the domestic economy back on track, could the US continue to advance the ideals of the liberal regional order in an effective way?

Fragmented Washington

The main problem for the US in promoting a liberal regional order in the Asia-Pacific during the years following the great recession was the growing fragmentation of Washington's political elite. This created difficulties for America's allies in the Asia-Pacific region as they were faced with competing and often contradictory pronouncements and policies. Importantly, when the US was most effective in developing the liberal international order, bipartisanship tended to be the norm. As Michael Mastanduno has argued, at its most compelling, US foreign policy was the product of a hegemonic strategy that sought "not to simply dominate" but "to gain the acceptance of other major states for an international order shaped

---

[25]Stubbs, *Rethinking*, 201-2.
[26]Severino, *Southeast Asia*, 279.
[27]Stubbs, "The ASEAN Alternative", 457-60.
[28]Ramo, *The Beijing Consensus*; Kurlantzick, "Why the 'China Model'".
[29]Breslin, "The 'China Model', 1328.

by the United States and consistent with its interests and values".[30] However, this approach was under attack.

The increasingly combative nature of Washington politics had been percolating for some time. The muscular foreign policy of the Republican neoconservatives, who had implemented a pre-emptive war strategy in Iraq in 2003, was developed in direct contrast to the Democratic administration's Wilsonian, liberal institutionalist policies of the previous decade.[31] The failure of the Iraq war highlighted the differences and led to a divided Washington. These divisions were accentuated with the rise of the Tea Party wing of the Republicans. From 2009 onwards, they were a very vocal minority pushing for a curious mixture of isolationism and unilateral military action when absolutely necessary.[32] With Washington's political elite fragmenting, decisions too often became based on domestic political considerations. In other words, foreign policy was the spillover of the vitriolic and often incendiary domestic political battles between Democrats and Republicans – and even within each party – rather than on a clearly thought out strategy rooted in America's liberal values.

The rifts at the centre of American politics grew even deeper during the eight years that President Barack Obama was in the White House. These splits were transmitted to US foreign policy and resulted in mixed signals for US allies as they sought to come up with new solutions to various security and economic threats. Without a domestic consensus on which interests and values to prioritise, it proved very difficult to maintain a coherent foreign policy around which allies in the region could unite.[33] Handcuffed by the visceral divide that characterised Congress and the battle between the Republicans and President Obama, the US proved incapable of the necessary bipartisanship that could fully underwrite a liberal regional order in the Asia-Pacific.

Despite the obstacles faced by the Obama administration, there was an attempt to re-engage with the Asia-Pacific and re-energise hopes for a liberal regional order. In 2011, Secretary of State Hillary Clinton wrote about the "need to accelerate efforts to pivot to new global realities".[34] At the same time, President Obama gave a series of speeches in which he set out a plan to "rebalance" America's focus so as to forge a renewed relationship with governments in the Asia-Pacific region. He emphasised that the US would strengthen military alliances in the region, re-engage with regional organisations such as ASEAN and the East Asian Summit, promote the Trans-Pacific Partnership (TPP) as a regional free trade agreement and support human rights and democracy. His comment to a joint session of the Australian Parliament, that "History is on the side of the free - free societies, free governments, free economies, free people. So let there be no doubt, in the Asia-Pacific in the 21st century, the United States of America is all in", was clearly a rallying cry for those who favoured a liberal regional order sponsored by Washington.[35]

The 'pivot to Asia' did produce several positive results. The US continued to maintain a significant number of troops in bases around the region, most notably in Japan and South Korea, and there were some new military deployments associated with the pivot. Moreover, President Obama developed positive interactions with the region's key multilateral

---

[30]Mastanduno, "Hegemonic Order", 24.
[31]Krauthammer, "The Neoconservative Convergence".
[32]Mead, "The Tea Party".
[33]Cox, "Middlepowermanship", 829-31.
[34]Clinton, "America's Pacific Century".
[35]Lane, "Obama's Speech".

organisations. He attended the East Asian Summits and maintained good relations with ASEAN, which culminated in February 2016 when he invited ASEAN leaders to the first US-ASEAN Summit to be held on US soil. The long-running South Korea-US Free Trade negotiations were finally ratified and went into effect in March 2012. More importantly, negotiations over the TPP, which included Brunei, Japan, Malaysia, Singapore and Vietnam, became central to the pivot's economic strategy.

But the rebalancing effort continued to be hampered by events in the Middle East and Afghanistan, as well as in Washington. The fallout from the original US invasion of Iraq in 2003 rolled on as the Arab Spring crested in 2012; the Syrian civil war escalated; the Iraq crisis worsened as the so-called Islamic State gained a foothold; the Iran nuclear proliferation issue bubbled along; and the drawdown of troops in Afghanistan proved more difficult than expected. Resources were also limited by the partisan wrangling in Washington over the recurring debt ceiling crisis and calls to cut the projected expansion of the deficit. The compromise that was eventually reached – the Budget Control Act of 2011 – curtailed the military budget just as the Obama administration was attempting to implement the pivot to Asia.

With the uncertainties surrounding US foreign policy in the Asia-Pacific region and the steady rise of China, regional governments continued to evaluate their relations with Washington. Some regional governments were concerned that the pivot appeared to directly target China, boosting America's military presence in response to China's increasing assertiveness. The TPP was being sold as a way of ensuring that the US would write the rules of the regional economy, not China.[36] Yet, the problem for Asia-Pacific leaders was that for good or ill their economies were becoming more and more closely tied to that of China and, although America's continued presence in the Asia-Pacific was clearly welcomed, China's growing military capability could not be ignored. Asian leaders felt trapped in the emerging dilemma of possibly having to choose sides.

Therefore, as a result of China's increasing influence in the region after the turn of the century, many governments sought to engage in what has been termed 'hedging'. This strategy entailed engaging in complex, pragmatic relationships with the major powers, but most especially the US and China, through economic and security agreements. The aim of the Asia-Pacific governments was to bring China into the region's main institutions, while balancing China's growing power by enmeshing the US – and other powers such as Japan, India, the European Union and Russia – into the region's affairs.[37] This hedging approach, combined with the limitations of the US pivot to Asia and the domestic and Middle East preoccupations of Washington, clearly diluted America's effectiveness in advocating for a liberal regional order in the Asia-Pacific.

The Trump effect

President Donald Trump has shown no evidence whatsoever of wanting to promote a liberal regional order in the Asia-Pacific. Trump has certainly not been interested in helping to open up Asia-Pacific's national economies, develop a multilateral regional free trade area or encourage the reduction in barriers to regional capital flows. Significantly, one of his

---

[36]The White House, "Statement".
[37]Acharya, "Power Shift"; Goh, "Understanding 'Hedging'".

very first acts after he was sworn in as President in January 2017 was to withdraw the US from the TPP negotiations that had been a central feature of the Obama administration's Asia-Pacific liberalising strategy. Moreover, guided by the neo-mercantilist 'America First' slogan that propelled him into office, Trump threatened to impose tariffs on imports from China and Japan and renegotiate the FTA with South Korea. Certainly, the Trump administration does not see the world in liberal institutional terms in which the US would animate greater international interdependence and support the wider interests of the international community. Indeed, the fact that so many senior posts related to the Asia-Pacific in the State Department and Department of Defense were left unfilled for so long after Trump came to power made it difficult for his administration to develop and project onto the region any coherent strategy.[38]

Nor has the Trump administration sought to protect human rights or promote democracy in the Asia-Pacific. The President struck up a good relationship with the President of the Philippines, Rodrigo Duterte, whose war on drugs claimed thousands of lives and was widely criticised for violating human rights. He also welcomed to the White House the Thai Prime Minister, Prayuth Chan-ocha, who led a coup in May 2014. In Cambodia during 2017, the government of Hun Sen cracked down on the opposition and the independent media ahead of the 2018 national elections. One commentator argued that these actions came at a time when the "US influence is seen as receding in Southeast Asia" and when the Trump administration itself "attacks media and its own political opponents in crude terms".[39] Trump indicated he will travel to the APEC and East Asian Summit meetings in November 2017, but it was not clear if this represented a commitment to multilateralism or was simply an efficient way of conducting bilateral relations and sustaining the hub-and-spoke and containment models that long characterised US relations with its key Asia-Pacific allies and enemies. There were no signs of a liberal regional order being promoted by Trump.

Conclusion

Three points can be drawn from this analysis. First, efforts to establish a liberal regional order in the Asia-Pacific have always been contested. The developmental regional order that arose out of the circumstances of the Cold War was well established before the post-Cold War attempts by the US to spread liberal values and move the region towards a liberal order. In most societies within the region, the post-Cold War period saw a battle between a developmental coalition and an opposing liberal market-oriented coalition with a mix of politicians, bureaucrats, business people and opinion leaders making up each side. The views of these coalitions spilled over onto the way regional economic and security relations were conducted. Importantly, then, at no time has a liberal regional order been pervasive in the Asia-Pacific.

Yet, second, it should not be thought that the quest for a liberal regional order in the Asia-Pacific has been abandoned. Although the Obama administration was hampered by a divided Washington and distracted by events in the Middle East and the Trump administration has made no attempt to support a liberal regional order in the Asia-Pacific, liberal values and elements of a liberal regional order endure in the region. Notably, regional domestic

---

[38]Panda, "Trump Goes to Asia".
[39]Reed, "Hun Sen Tightens Grip".

market-oriented coalitions have been strongly supported by international agencies such as the IMF, the WTO and the OECD, as well as the biennial Asia-Europe Meetings (ASEM), as they pursue a more liberal, open regional economy. And APEC still has the potential to lead a renewed effort to negotiate a regional free trade agreement.[40] Moreover, the EU remains active in "strengthening the foundations of democracy" and fostering respect for human rights through the Informal ASEM Seminars on Human Rights.[41]

Finally, what does the continuing contestation between those who favour a liberal regional order and those who want a more state-directed, developmental regional order mean in practice? Essentially what has emerged is "an amalgam of ideas" as aspects of each paradigm are privileged in different policy circumstances.[42] For example, in economic terms the state tends to be more involved in strategically important areas such as energy production and distribution, financial services and telecommunication, while more market-oriented policies apply to consumer electronics, textiles and garment manufacture, food stuffs and so forth.[43] Liberal economic principles are also in play, in part at least, in negotiations over the Regional Comprehensive Economic Partnership, which includes the ASEAN Plus Three members as well as Australia, New Zealand and India. The patchwork of democratic, authoritarian and hybrid states also means that the democratic dimension of a liberal order is respected in some places and ignored in other parts of the Asia-Pacific. Similarly, respect for human rights including religious, political, environmental and labour rights is mixed at best.

In the future, elements of a liberal regional order will persist in the Asia-Pacific region but they will remain contested. Developmental ideas, some of which are indigenous to the region and rooted in long-established institutions and some of which were the product of the Cold War years, will endure. The influence of each set of ideas will fluctuate depending on the changing context and the fortunes of those championing them.[44] But inevitably they will continue to compete.

Acknowledgements

Thanks to Gregory Chin and Andrew Cooper for their observations on the issues discussed here and to the Social Sciences and Humanities Research Council of Canada, Insight Grant 435-2015-1357, for funding the research on which this analysis is based.

References

Acharya, A. "Power Shift or Paradigm Shift? China's Rise and Asia's Emerging Security Order". *International Studies Quarterly* 58, no. 1 (March 2014): 158–73.

Acharya, A. *Whose Ideas Matter? Agency and Power in Asian Regionalism*. Ithaca: Cornell University Press, 2011.

---

[40] Cooper and Stubbs, "Contending Regionalisms".
[41] See, for example, Asia-Europe Foundation, "16th Informal ASEM Seminar".
[42] Skogstad, "Conclusion", 238.
[43] Hseuh, *China's Regulatory State*, 42; Stubbs, *Rethinking*, 209-10.
[44] Acharya, *Whose Ideas Matter*; Stubbs, "ASEAN Alternative".

Asia-Europe Foundation. "16th Informal ASEM Seminar on Human Rights". Beijing, 8-10 November 2016. http://www.asef.org/projects/themes/governance/3808-16th-informal-asem-seminar-on-human-rights-

Ba, A. "System Neglect? A Reconsideration of US-Southeast Asia Policy". *Contemporary Southeast Asia* 31, no. 3 (December 2009): 369–98.

Bank of Japan. "Chiang Mai Initiative Multilateralization (CMIM) Comes into Effect". Joint Press Release, 24 March 2010. https://www.boj.or.jp/en/announcements/release_2010/un1003e.htm/

Beeson, M. "American Ascendency: Conceptualizing Contemporary Hegemony". In *Bush and Asia: America's Evolving Relations with East Asia*, edited by M. Beeson: 3–23. Abingdon: Routledge, 2006.

Bowie, A., and D. Unger. *The Politics of Open Economies: Indonesia, Malaysia, the Philippines and Thailand*. Cambridge: Cambridge University Press, 1997.

Breslin, S. "The 'China Model' and the Global Crisis: From Friedrich List to a Chinese Mode of Governance?". *International Affairs* 87, no. 6 (November 2011): 1323–43.

Clinton, H. "America's Pacific Century". *Foreign Policy*, 11 October 2011. http://foreignpolicy.com/2011/10/11/americas-pacific-century/

Clinton, W.J. "The President's News Conference with President Jiang Zemin of China in Beijing", 27 June 1998. http://www.presidency.ucsb.edu/ws/index.php?pid=56229

Connors, M.K. "Thailand and the United States: Beyond Hegemony?" In *Bush and Asia: America's Evolving Relations with East Asia*, edited by M. Beeson: 128–44. Abingdon: Routledge, 2006.

Cooper, A.F., and R. Stubbs. "Contending Regionalisms: Hubs and Challengers in the Americas and the Asia-Pacific". *The Pacific Review* 30 no. 5 (September 2017): 615–32.

Cox, R. "Middlepowermanship, Japan, and Future World Order". *International Journal* 44, no. 4 (Autumn 1989): 823–62.

Dent, C.M. "Free Trade Agreements in the Asia-Pacific a Decade On". *International Relations of the Asia-Pacific* 10, no. 2 (May 2010): 201–45.

Eaton, S. *The Advance of the State in Contemporary China: State-Market Relations in the Reform Era*. Cambridge: Cambridge University Press, 2016.

Goh, E. "Understanding 'Hedging' in Asia-Pacific Security". CSIS *PacNet* no. 43, 31 August 2006. https://www.csis.org/analysis/pacnet-43-understanding-hedging-asia-pacific-security

Hall, R.B. "The Discursive Demolition of the Asian Developmental Model". *International Studies Quarterly* 47, no. 1 (March 2003): 71–99.

Hamilton-Hart, N. "Banking Systems a Decade After the Crisis". In *Crisis as Catalyst: Asia's Dynamic Political Economy*, edited by A. MacIntyre, T.J. Pempel and J. Ravenhill: 45–69. Ithaca: Cornell University Press, 2008.

Higgott, R. "After Neoliberal Globalization: The 'Securitization' of US Foreign Economic Policy in East Asia". *Critical Asian Studies* 36, no. 3 (2004): 425–44.

Higgott, R. "The Asian Economic Crisis: A Study in the Politics of Resentment". *New Political Economy* 3, no. 3 (November 1998): 333–56.

Higgott, R., and R. Stubbs. "Competing Conceptions of Economic Regionalism: APEC versus EAEC in the Asia-Pacific". *Review of International Political Economy* 2, no. 3 (Summer 1995): 516–35.

Hsueh, R. *China's Regulatory State: A New Strategy for Globalization*. Ithaca, NY: Cornell University Press, 2011.

Ikenberry, G.J. "Liberal Internationalism 3.0: America and the Dilemmas of Liberal World Order". *Perspectives on Politics* 7, no. 4 (March 2009): 71–87.

Ikenberry, J.G. "American Hegemony and East Asian Order". *Australian Journal of International Affairs* 58, no. 3 (September 2004): 353–67.

Krauthammer, C. "The Neoconservative Convergence". *Commentary*, 1 July 2005. https://www.commentarymagazine.com/articles/the-neoconservative-convergence/

Kurlantzick, J. "Why the 'China Model' Isn't Going Away". *The Atlantic*, 21 March 2013. https://www.theatlantic.com/china/archive/2013/03/why-the-china-model-isnt-going-away/274237/

Landler, M. "Gore Scolded in Malaysia for Defense of Dissenters". *New York Times*, 18 November 1998. http://www.nytimes.com/1998/11/18/world/gore-scolded-in-malaysia-for-defense-of-dissenters.html

Lane, S. "Obama's Speech a Statement of Intent". *ABC News Online*, 17 November 2011. http://www.abc.net.au/news/2011-11-17/brack-obama27s-speech-to-parliament/3678058

Mastanduno, M. "Hegemonic Order, September 11, and the Consequences of the Bush Revolution". In *Bush and Asia: America's Evolving Relations with East Asia*, edited by M. Beeson: 24–41. Abingdon: Routledge, 2006.

Mead, W.R. "The Tea Party and American Foreign Policy: What Populism Means for Globalism". *Foreign Affairs* 90, no. 2 (March/April 2011): 28–44.

Mustapha, J. "Threat Construction in the Bush Administration's Post 9/11 Foreign Policy: (Critical) Security Implications for Southeast Asia". *The Pacific Review* 24, no. 4 (September 2011): 487–504.

Nairn, R.C. "SEATO: A Critique". *Pacific Affairs* 41, no. 1 (Spring 1968): 5–18.

Panda, A. "Trump Goes to Asia: What's on the Line?". *The Diplomat*, 3 October 2017. https://thediplomat.com/2017/10/trump-goes-to-asia-whats-on-the-line/

Pempel, T.J. "How Bush Bungled Asia: Militarism, Economic Indifference and Unilateralism Have Weakened the United States across Asia". *The Pacific Review* 21, no. 5 (December 2008): 547–81.

Ramo, J.C. *The Beijing Consensus: Notes on the New Physics of Chinese Power*. London: Foreign Policy Centre, 2004.

Ravenhill, J. *APEC and the Construction of Pacific Rim Regionalism*. Cambridge: Cambridge University Press, 2001.

Reed, J. "Hun Sen Tightens Grip on Cambodia". *Financial Times*, 19 September 2017, 4. https://www.ft.com/content/8b9f655c-97a6-11e7-a652-cde3f882dd7b?mhq5j=e5

Sakakibara, E. "Interview with Eisuke Sakakibara". *PBS: Commanding Heights*, 15 May 2001. www.pbs.org/wgbh/commandingheights

Severino, R.C. *Southeast Asia in Search of an ASEAN Community: Insights from the Former ASEAN Secretary General*. Singapore: Institute of Southeast Asian Studies, 2006.

Skogstad, G. "Conclusion". In *Policy Paradigms, Transnationalism, and Domestic Politics*, edited by G. Skogstad: 237–53. Toronto: University of Toronto Press, 2011.

Stiglitz, J. *Globalization and Its Discontents*. London: Allen Lane, 2002.

Stubbs, R. *Rethinking Asia's Economic Miracle: The Political Economy of War, Prosperity and Crisis*. 2nd ed. London: Palgrave, 2017.

Stubbs, R. "The East Asian Developmental State and the Great Recession: Evolving Contesting Coalitions". *Contemporary Politics* 17, no. 2 (June 2011): 151–66.

Stubbs, R. "Whatever Happened to the East Asian Developmental State? The Unfolding Debate". *The Pacific Review* 22, no. 1 (March 2009): 1–22.

Stubbs, R. "The ASEAN Alternative? Ideas, Institutions and the Challenge to 'Global' Governance". *The Pacific Review* 21, no. 4 (December 2008): 451–68.

Stubbs, R., and J. Mustapha. "Ideas and Institutions in Asia". In *The Oxford Handbook of the International Relations of Asia*, edited by S.M. Pekkanen, J. Ravenhill, and R. Foot: 690–702. Oxford: Oxford University Press, 2014.

The White House, Office of the Press Secretary. "Statement by the President on the Trans-Pacific Partnership". Washington DC, 5 October 2015. https://obamawhitehouse.archives.gov/the-press-office/2015/10/05/statement-president-trans-pacific-partnership

Woo-Cumings, M., ed. *The Developmental State*. Ithaca: Cornell University Press, 1999.

Contestation and Transformation. Final Thoughts on the Liberal International Order

Riccardo Alcaro

ABSTRACT
The liberal international order, the inseparable mix of US geopolitical power and ideational project of organising international relations along normative frameworks such as internationalism, institutionalism and democracy, is reeling under the pressure of profound systemic changes such as greater interconnectedness and multipolarity. Predictions abound that increasing great power competition, most visibly at play in geographical areas of contested orders, will eventually tear it down. However, even if major actors – the US included – display a selective, irregular and often instrumental commitment to the liberal order, they are still repositioning themselves in that order and not outside of it. In addition, conflict is not the default outcome of order contestation, as hybrid forms of governance are possible even in troubled regions. No doubt, the world of tomorrow will be less American-shaped and less liberal, but transformation is a more plausible future than collapse for the liberal order.

The Introduction to this Special Issue opined that underlying the diverse and animated debate among scholars and practitioners over the nature and shape of tomorrow's world is a widespread expectation that it will be less liberal and less American-shaped. The articles collected in the issue largely vindicate that basic assumption.

Giovanni Grevi summarises the point well when he questions the lingering validity of the equation between modernisation and Westernisation. Grevi sees 'modernisation' as implying economic and technological progress, a reductionist notion of what is 'modern' that would have appalled many European and American intellectuals of the past century. Yet Grevi is on solid empirical ground when he implies that the wealth and power that come from a vibrant economy and technological innovation are now separable from democracy, pluralism and secularism. Francis Fukuyama's bold claim that liberal democracy is the ultimate polity has not stood the test of time – although it might still retain appeal as a normative proposition. The world is less liberal and therefore less 'Western'.

The end of history Fukuyama predicted when the collapse of the Soviet bloc bestowed upon the West an unexpected geopolitical triumph has proven short-lived. In fact, it has lasted no more than the very brief period in history in which one liberal democracy, the

152

United States, exerted unrivalled power around the world. As American power is again being resisted and challenged internationally, so is the liberal ideology that has underpinned its project of organising international relations around its security, economic and normative interests. The world is less American and therefore less liberal.

The articles collected in this issue have gone beyond just validating the above. That American/Western material and ideational power is in relative decline was after all the assumption from which they started off. The question they engage with, directly and indirectly, is the meaning and implications of that adverb, 'less': how much less liberal and less American-shaped is the world becoming, and what does that mean exactly?

The introductory note compared predictions of what tomorrow's world will look like to acts of divination, and the contributors to this Special Issue have wisely abstained from indulging in the exercise. Their analyses nonetheless enlighten our understanding of systemic and agency-related dynamics that are increasingly shaping global politics, thereby providing critical frames of reference for imagining the future. To look into that future, it is necessary to delve a bit more extensively into the process of repositioning of each global player considered in this Special Issue. This involves determining each player's existing position in the liberal international order, assessing the nature and scope of its commitment to that order, and tracing its foreign policy back to the view(s) of order its domestic constituents espouse.

Global repositioning

A common trait emerges from the articles examining the evolving role in global politics of what the Introduction dubbed "global actors": their relationship with the structures and norms of the liberal international order is not linear, but irregular, selective, conditional, or instrumental.[1] Elements of lingering commitment to that order co-exist with claims to reform or re-organise it. In a way, all global players are in some way renegotiating their 'terms' of membership in the liberal project. The articles focus on the actors and therefore have a clear bias towards agency, yet authors recognise that the process of global repositioning of these players reflects deep systemic changes in terms of interconnectedness and distribution of resources.

Economic and financial interconnectedness, the influence of multinational corporations, and digital technology and automation have all reduced the room for manoeuvre of governments. As Samir Saran soberly notes, the disruptive potential of climate change, artificial intelligence (AI), robotics, big data and the 'internet of things' is immense. Automation continues to threaten low-skilled jobs all around the world. Internet platforms such as Uber constrain the ability of government to regulate and guarantee public goods like transport. Income inequality has risen everywhere, with wealth concentration at its historical peak or close to it. The revolution in information and communications technologies has enabled political polarisation driven by identity-informed politics of exclusion. Most worryingly, the variation in the distribution of resources away from the US towards a plurality of actors – a process accelerated by the great recession of 2008-09 – is a tectonic shift that is turning the

---

[1] It is worth recalling that the generous, or at least premature, depiction in the Introduction of most of the players as "global" was not referring to their ability to project power globally but, more modestly, to their extra-regional geopolitical outlook.

153

management of challenges associated with interconnectedness into a function of power competition.

In principle, all major players recognise the need to address the aforementioned challenges cooperatively. However, their primary focus is less on the challenges themselves than on making sure that governance arrangements protect their security and economic potential – and secure their influence. Consequently, they tend to accord preference to the elements of the liberal order that they perceive as directly serving their policy goals and to promote alternative governance mechanisms whenever the existing order is deemed to be biased against them. An additional complicating factor is that engaging in geopolitical competition, a consequence of greater emphasis on nationalist themes, has become politically expedient. In the cases of China and Russia, the process of national repositioning in the global context is inextricably linked to calculations related to the survival and continued rule of the illiberal regimes in power. The retrenchment into narrow-minded, nationalist-leaning worldviews observable in so many places reveals, but also feeds, a general dissatisfaction with the existing order – critically, including the order's original founder and guarantor, the United States.

The *America* that emerges from John Peterson's analysis is a *tormented liberal champion*. To be sure, that the US has always had a troubled relationship with the normative-institutional framework, to the creation of which it contributed the most and which is largely an emanation of its power, is no big news. US leaders have traditionally interpreted the role of guarantor of the liberal international order as encompassing a right to derogate from liberal rules and practices whenever it is required by the national interest or what they perceive as such. The difference today is that the proposition that the liberal order may no longer be an emanation of US power, but in fact a constraint on it, has regained full legitimacy.

A growing number of American citizens are sceptical about the US' global engagement having ultimately benefitted their lives or their country's fortunes. Some, probably a few, see the liberal international order's structures as having impeded the consolidation of an enduring US hegemony when US power was unrivalled, as in the 1990s and early 2000s – an idea that informed much of the foreign policy of the George W. Bush administration, particularly during the president's first term. Many others are suspicious of the alleged advantages of global engagement and would like the US simply to tend to its own business. For people like President Donald Trump, this process invariably entails revisiting a number of "bad deals" – free trade agreements, defence alliances, climate arrangements – that have allegedly harmed the US because they have let other countries free ride on America's military or financial commitments. While the scepticism is widespread, even dominant on the right side of the political spectrum, doubts also abound in the progressive camp, especially among leftwing working class voters and the educated young. Unquestionably, liberal internationalism as the ideological superstructure of a US-centred international system has less appeal for Americans today than it has ever had since the end of World War II (WWII).

Even the foreign policy elites, among whom there was long a bipartisan consensus that global engagement was indeed in America's long-term interest, are now torn between diverging opinions. Liberal internationalists want to use the US' lingering strength to co-opt the rising powers to act as responsible stakeholders in maintaining global stability and the key institutions, regimes and practices of the liberal order, a proposition that former President Barack Obama elevated to a sort of doctrine. On the other hand, the nationalists accept multipolarity and advocate the full normalisation of US foreign policy, whereby the country should abandon any pretence of leading the world and instead use its military and economic edge to pursue aggressively 'better deals' than the ones it is now supposedly involved in.

These are evidently oversimplifications of a more varied debate, yet they lay bare the extent of the differences in perspectives from which American foreign policymakers draw their assumptions. The debate does not even unfold along political lines as supporters of both positions can be found among Republicans and Democrats or, more specifically, as elements of the internationalist and nationalist agendas co-exist, often not entirely coherently, in the same administration. The result is an uncertain and at times confusing foreign policy in which observers struggle to see any clear direction.

If the US were a mid-size country, such oscillations would be of minimal practical consequence. Yet, as recalled in the Introduction, the United States is still very much a systemic power despite its weaker hold on global supremacy. This means that it is still capable of moving the system of international relations (rather than simply moving *in* the system) by way of the sheer magnitude of its power, hard and soft alike. The conclusion is that the stabilisation of global politics and the nature of the underlying settlement among global players is conditional on the American foreign policy establishment finding an enduring consensus on what role the US should play in the world. Absent this, the other pieces of the global puzzle are unlikely to fall into place.

Those regions that have traditionally relied on the partnership with Washington to orientate their foreign policy, most notably *Europe*, have consequently been forced to review their options to safeguard whatever security and economic benefits they have gained from US commitments to the liberal order's norms and structures. Such an inherently defensive nature of Europe's global repositioning is a dominant theme in Michael Smith and Richard Youngs' analysis. In their eyes, Europe has turned into an *unsure, 'selective' liberal advocate*.

For historical and geopolitical reasons, Europe's commitment to internationalism has traditionally been very much connected to its Atlanticism. After all, the Europeans turned the page on centuries of almost uninterrupted warfare only after the US security umbrella turned them all into loyal allies and supporters of the liberal order. Undoubtedly, that support has been internalised over the years, particularly thanks to the radical experimentation in regional integration the Europeans embarked on when they first established common, and partly supranational, institutions. The fact remains though that America's dwindling commitment to the liberal order poses a new set of challenges for the Europeans, who do not possess the same political and military resources as the Americans do to back liberal institutions and promote liberal practices. In addition, Europe has also experienced a return of nationalism, with populist forces increasingly questioning such key principles of Europe's post-WWII liberalism as open markets and borders, as well as pooled sovereignty. The combination of limited resources and a shrinking base of popular support are the external and internal background, respectively, of the increasingly selective defence of the liberal international order Smith and Youngs ascribe to contemporary Europe.

They see evidence of this across a wide spectrum of policy areas. Long a champion of an open and free trade system, the EU has increasingly opted for bilateral arrangements. A peculiarity of the latter is that, under the heading of 'free trade', the EU has in fact injected a degree of 'soft mercantilism' into its trade and economic relations. The Union has made use of regulatory standards and sectoral exclusions to diminish imports, anti-dumping measures to protect against aggressive external competition, and limits on foreign investments in 'strategic' sectors to preserve key assets. The politicisation of trade – no longer a

155

purely technocratic matter but an issue subject to political considerations – is part of the explanation for the EU's toying with soft forms of protectionism. But strategic calculations, such as concerns about fair competition practices or the influence that external powers (China and, in the energy field, Russia) may gain through investments, matter as well. In short, the Europeans rely on their main asset – the size of the common market – to play a power game through the political use of rules and regulations.

Hints of Europe's evolving global power game are increasingly visible in the pursuit of 'triangulations' in areas other than trade and economic regulations, whereby Europe shifts its alignment with this or that global player depending on the issue at hand. NATO and a strong partnership with the US is still very much the preferred choice to ensure Europe's defence and keep a revanchist Russia at bay. A quasi-antagonist in Europe, Russia is nonetheless seen by several European governments as an inescapable interlocutor when it comes to fighting jihadi extremism, eventually stabilising the Middle East or, more concretely, defending the nuclear deal with Iran, which Europe sees as critical to the stability of the Gulf and the endurance of the nuclear non-proliferation regime. Following President Trump's decision to withdraw from the Paris Accord on climate change, Europe has found a willing partner for the fight against global warming in China. Yet, Europe sides with the US in denying China the status of full market economy. Had the talks over a Transatlantic Trade and Investment Partnership been finalised, the relationship with the US would have given the EU an almost unassailable advantage over China and other rising economies in the regulatory field.

Overall, Europe's global repositioning is about generating patterns of selective cooperation – where possible, enshrined in formal rules and regimes – on issues of critical importance. Nevertheless, the notion that spreading liberal values and norms, including democracy, contributes to European interests has lost steam. This is most evident in Europe's approach to its surrounding regions to the east and south, where the ambition of turning neighbouring countries into a 'ring of friends' increasingly aligned with EU standards and values has given way to a preference for stability. According to Smith and Youngs, Europe is undergoing a transition from a cooperative interdependence paradigm to a competitive interdependence paradigm. The EU as such is involved in the process as the Union is increasingly framed as a means to protect European borders as well as citizens' welfare and security rather than a liberal transformative force of global politics.

In a way, as Shaun Breslin explains, *China* is also engaging in selectively committing to liberal order structures and norms. The commonality, however, is superficial. Whereas Europe is a liberal polity forced by a lack of resources and uncertain domestic support to downgrade its commitment to the norms and structures of the liberal order, China is an illiberal state whose massive financial firepower allows it to pick and choose whatever bits of the liberal order suit its growing ambitions best. Whereas reactiveness and a desire to protect existing gains define Europe's global repositioning, China is proactive and hungry for 'conquest'. Deng Xiaoping's recommendation to keep a low profile no longer applies. The leadership of the Communist Party now sees China as a *confident trailblazer* in a world full of uncertainties.

The People's Republic has embraced liberal practices such as participation in multilateral cooperation and global trade; yet it has shown scarce attachment to liberal principles such as non-discriminatory trade, political pluralism, human rights, responsibility to protect. Lately, the Chinese government has made an explicit attempt at eliminating the apparent contradictions of its global posture. In the words of President Xi Jinping, China's successful experience as a non-liberal capitalist country committed to global stability and trade has opened a "trail" that other countries in the world may follow to advance their economies while safeguarding their independence – that is, while resisting calls to align with the liberal powerhouses of the West.

Breslin insists that China's global repositioning is loosely happening within the contours of the liberal international order. Despite the fuss about the 'Chinese characteristics' of the country's development, there is no doubt that the People's Republic is much more aligned with liberal regimes and practices today than when it was a communist country for real and not only in name. China sees its strenuous defence of sovereignty and the principle of non-intervention as fully in line with international law, both customary and treaty-based. Its veto-wielding permanent seat in the Security Council is no longer just a shield but also a device to shape international relations, partly by obstructing undesired Western policies (for instance, sanctions against friendly governments such as Sudan's), partly by cooperating with Western powers on issues of mutual concern (Iran and North Korea, to cite just two examples). In a similar vein, Chinese-led development institutions like the Asia Infrastructure Investment Bank (AIIB) are a way of restraining Western power (the US is not part of the AIIB, although most EU states are) while remaining anchored in the liberal order structures; after all (and contrary to expectations), the AIIB has developed projects in cooperation with institutions dominated by the US and its allies, such as the World Bank and the Asian Development Bank. Beijing's successful campaign to get more voting power in the International Monetary Fund (IMF) is further proof that China's quest for influence is predicated on its continued participation in the structures of the liberal order.

This, however, does not tell the full story. China's activism within the institutions of the liberal order is outpaced by its activism outside of them. China has worked on extending its military projection at sea far off its coasts to push back against US clout in Northeast Asia, the Strait of Taiwan and Southeast Asia. This explains China's refusal to pull the rug out from under North Korea, a key buffer between China itself and the US ally South Korea, as well as its assertiveness in the South China Sea, where it has placed military facilities on artificial islands built in disputed waters. Chinese leaders see the neighbourhood as critical to national security, but also as a launch pad for expanding Chinese influence globally. In cooperation with Russia, China has managed to rein in American influence in Central Asia, a key region for the development of the infrastructure that is supposed to enable the expansion of land trade along a new 'Silk Road' connecting East Asia to Europe. Similarly, the building of ports and other commercial and military facilities in countries such as Bangladesh, Myanmar, Sri Lanka and Djibouti aims at securing control over the sea routes to the Persian Gulf and the Mediterranean – the maritime Silk Road. China has long set its eyes on other regions as well, such as Africa and Latin America, all of which have experienced massive Chinese economic penetration.

China's activity in development and infrastructure mixes elements of pressure or even coercion (as investments bring influence) with elements of spontaneous cooperation (unlike Western aid, China's help comes free of conditions that beneficiaries respect sound governance standards). Foreign direct investments, especially in infrastructure, by state-run enterprises awash with cash but opaque in terms of governance further complement China's power. With money pouring in, even EU member states feel the pressure not to go the extra mile to lambast China for promoting unfair competition, restricting access to its own market or cracking down on political freedoms. The geopolitical design of China's development, infrastructure and investment policies is a re-orientation of trade and investment routes as well as political ties towards China, to make it the economic hub of the Asia-Pacific, the source of massive investment and trade with Europe, Africa, North and South America, and the pillar of the global economy.

Russia is arguably the global player that has developed the most conflictual relationship with the structures and principles of the liberal international order. In her contribution, Tatiana Romanova traces the origins of Russia's issues with the liberal order back to geo-politics, culture and history, as well as domestic politics. In Moscow, dissatisfaction with post-Cold War settlements curbing Russian influence, especially in the former Soviet space, is widespread. Lately, Russia's leadership has emphasised the unique nature of Russian civilisation, with the narrative of a conservative and patriotic nation permanently engaged in a fight to preserve its identity from cultural interferences from east and especially west. This nationalistic discourse has enabled President Vladimir Putin to create a mutually legit-imising dynamic between an ambitious, even hazardous foreign policy and his increasingly illiberal rule.

Romanova nonetheless warns against assuming that Russia is bent on destroying the liberal order. The trappings of democracy, elections and public opinion remain the ultimate source of political legitimacy, which in theory leaves room for the government to re-align with liberal discourse should it eventually achieve its ultimate objectives: regime security, national power, global recognition. While the pursuit of these objectives entails a consider-able dose of revisionism, the latter concerns Russia's place within the global (liberal) order, not the order itself. According to Romanova, Russia can be seen as a *restless neorevisionist*.

Russia is convinced that the success of its strategy is conditional on the delegitimation of America's hegemonic foreign policy, which Russia fears the most when it takes the form of support for ostensibly liberal (pro-Western) forces in the former Soviet republics. When the institutions of the liberal international order are compatible with its worldview, however, Russia is more than happy to support them (at the same time, nothing delights Russian diplomats more than denouncing US unilateralism as inconsistent with the liberal mul-tilateral project). The United Nations Security Council, in which it holds a veto-wielding permanent seat, fits perfectly with Russia's vision of a multipolar, or multicentric, system of great power interactions.

Critical to performing 'polar' functions is exclusive control over each pole's neighbour-hood and shared control over regions where great power influence is more balanced. This explains why Russia sees competition with the US and its allies in the former Soviet space as a zero-sum game, while the Middle East or other theatres are less critical to its secu-rity and therefore considered areas of potential accommodation. In Russia's eyes, regional arrangements should be organised around the interests of the dominant pole(s) rather than advancing any constitutionalisation of the international system. In these terms, Russia's view is inherently illiberal or at least non-liberal. That said, Russia is not opposed to regional settlements, provided they are backed by consensus among the great powers, and recognises the need for cooperative management of cyber, environmental, terrorism, and non-pro-liferation issues.

This profoundly state-centric and power-based view of global politics also infuses Russia's view of economic relations. An often-neglected component of Russia's neorevisionism is its attempt to disentangle itself from economic interdependence so as to reduce its vulnerability to external shocks and pressure. The Russian government has not only adopted retaliatory forms of trade protectionism (for instance, in response to US and EU sanctions adopted after its aggression in Ukraine), but has also greatly expanded the role of state-owned enterprises in the economy (according to Romanova, 70 percent of Russian GDP can now be traced back to the state, whereas it was only 35 percent in 2005).

In the end, for Russia the question of 'what rules' should apply to global politics is always a function of 'who rules' global politics – something which Russian leaders assume all global players share, whether they say it openly or not. Their opposition to the liberal order is first and foremost opposition to an exclusionary US hegemonic design of which Russia is just an appendix. Yet Russia appreciates the order emanating from US power and the liberal international system and is therefore unwilling to undermine it fully. Its neorevisionism lies in its plan for a co-opted (or controlled) neighbourhood and a multilateral system of formal and informal arrangements that constrain US power while leaving room for great powers to cooperate on issues of mutual interest. However, so long as this objective is not secured, Russia is willing to act as a spoiler by inflicting damage on the US and its allies, creating confusion and fomenting divisions within NATO and the EU, as well as delegitimising liberal discourse and practices.

A common tactic employed by Russia and China to push back against the US' global clout is to denounce liberal discourse as the rhetorical cloak in which America wraps its hegemonic designs. Another regularly heard accusation is that of applying double standards, whereby international rules are invoked selectively depending on whether they suit US (or European) interests. The result is that substantive discursive struggles over the meaning and implications of internationalism, institutionalism or liberalism are somewhat downgraded to rhetorical skirmishes between geopolitical rivals. This makes the case of *India*, a non-Western democracy experiencing sustained economic growth, especially interesting. As Samir Saran argues, with Western power on a declining curve and China embodying an illiberal development model, the importance of India's combination of 'non-Westernism' and liberalism cannot be understated. Indeed, the profile of India that comes out of Saran's analysis is singular. For Saran, India is the only *liberal alternative* (to the West).

While India holds a restrictive view of sovereignty and non-intervention similar to that of Russia and China, its approach to multilateral cooperation is broader and more inclusive. Unlike China and Russia, India is not obsessed with the centrality of states – witness its openness to include non-governmental organisations in international policymaking processes and especially the contribution given by Indian actors to developing a multi-stakeholder governance of the Internet. In addition, revulsion for 'liberal interventions' does not mean that India is uninterested in the promotion of democracy abroad, as attested to by its membership in the Community of Democracies and its sponsorship of the UN Democracy Fund. India is also strongly committed to global governance. Multilateral cooperation within formal institutions is its default policy preference when addressing issues such as piracy, maritime security, disaster relief and climate change. India is also allocating greater resources to development aid, particularly to its neighbours but increasingly to Africa as well.

Saran sees two fundamental threats to India's continuing development as a resourceful non-Western democracy. The first relates to a political discourse of exclusion, enabled by digital platforms, eventually breaking the country's longstanding national support for political, ethnic and religious pluralism. India's billion-plus population is extremely diverse and not foreign to ethnic or religious tensions. If India's deeply rooted nationalism were to be construed along exclusionary ethnic or religious lines, the post-colonial social contract supporting the country's liberal institutions would be jeopardised. In turn, this would complicate India's appeal as a non-Western liberal democracy, as well as its ambition to elevate its position above that of a developing country struggling to expand its outlook beyond its surroundings. Such an occurrence would compound the second threat identified by Saran, which is characteristically geopolitical in nature: the risk that China's simultaneous development of the new land and maritime Silk Roads, like a standard pincer move, curtails India's access to global trade networks.

What does this review of the process of repositioning of each global player tell us about the future of the liberal international order? A first conclusion is that no player aims to destroy the order. Europe and India are genuine supporters of the liberal multilateral project, even if their ability to support it is constrained by limited resources (especially in India's case) and threatened by the possibility of a strong nationalist turn of their domestic politics. Russia and China's commitment to the liberal order relates to the 'order' part of it more than to the liberal one. But even accounting for the illiberal nature and generally anti-American views of the regimes in both Moscow and Beijing, neither is willing to do away fully with liberal practices concerning, in particular, the governance of global challenges such as climate change, economic imbalances or cooperative crisis management. Given the symbiotic relationship between American power and the liberal project described in the Introduction, the US is the only player that can actually threaten the very existence of the liberal international order. However, the lingering support for liberal norms, institutions and practices in the US seems strong enough to make the prospect of a full American withdrawal from the liberal order unlikely. Nevertheless, even if no global player champions an alternative vision, as was the case with the Soviet Union and communism, the endurance of the liberal international order remains in doubt. The crucial factor is less the conflicting visions of order than the competition among great powers within the existing system, especially in areas where liberal norms and practices are weak and contested.

Regional conundrums

As the origins of each global player's dissatisfaction with the structure of the existing liberal order are different depending on the player considered, settling contentious issues has become an increasingly challenging task. To be sure, all global players are aware that some form of accommodation is needed, but as they are still in the process of global repositioning, their immediate preference goes to securing a power base from which they can 'negotiate' a new global settlement from a position of strength (national strength or regime strength, or both). This competitive pattern is especially evident in those regions of the world where order is more a matter of contestation than renegotiation: the former Soviet space in Eastern Europe and the South Caucasus, the Middle East, and the Asia-Pacific – the objects of the last three articles of this Special Issue. These regions are like atmospheric low-pressure zones around which winds gather force; as the regions themselves experience stormy weather, the surrounding areas become more volatile.

In Laure Delcour's article, *Eastern Europe and the South Caucasus* emerge as a region entirely defined by order contestation. This geographical non-contiguous, economically non-integrated and politically divided area arose only recently, after it was separated from the Central and Eastern European states that were accepted as NATO and EU candidate member states. Initially, the 'excluded' former Soviet republics (Belarus, Moldova and Ukraine; Armenia, Azerbaijan and Georgia) adopted liberal discourses and practices, yet they were only partly or superficially internalised. True, all claimed allegiance to liberal norms, sought stronger ties with the quintessentially liberal EU, and joined institutions of the liberal international order such as the UN, the Organisation for Security and Cooperation in Europe and the Council of Europe. However, the democratic addendum to these diplomatic moves was limited, with some countries experiencing some progress (Georgia, Ukraine), others stuck in troubled transitions (Armenia and Moldova) and still others never actually exiting from dictatorial rule (Azerbaijan, Belarus).

As Russia gradually but decisively withdrew its support for Western liberalism, the region's disconnect from liberal frameworks widened. In the 1990s, respect for human and minority rights came under pressure in all the places where internal conflicts had first arisen and then become 'frozen' under provisional and dysfunctional arrangements: Transnistria, Abkhazia and South Ossetia, Nagorno Karabakh. Following Russia's interventions in Georgia (2008) and Ukraine (2014), the region experienced a near-total collapse of internationalist principles, most notably the norm forbidding military intervention unsanctioned by the UN Security Council.

Regionalism has remained weak, with the former Soviet republics being continuously drawn to competing ideas of order: on the one hand, the US-backed and EU-enabled liberal model of economic integration and political cooperation; on the other, Russia's hub-and-spoke system (formalised in projects such as the Cooperative Security Treaty Organisation or the Eurasian Economic Union) enforced through a mix of coercion and elite co-optation. Even economically the region is anything but integrated, not least due to Russia taking aggressive steps (tariff and non-tariff barriers, energy price manipulation, and visa restrictions/concessions) to divert or obstruct movement of goods, capital and people along political lines, and the incompatibility between the EU's trade and economic agreements and Russia's customs union ambitions.

For Delcour, the result is an area of overlapping orders that hinders the development of shared governance of transnational issues. Eastern European and South Caucasus countries possess neither the resources nor the political will to embark on regionalisation processes that may one day produce an endogenous alternative to the competing orders the area has been dragged into. The most they can aspire to is either to become part of one of those orders or engage in constant balancing.

The *Middle East* is a region that, in theory at least, could produce an endogenous order, independent from global players and nonetheless fully capable of distributing benefits among its population. It is of considerable size demographically, full of natural resources, and relatively homogeneous in cultural and religious terms. Nevertheless, the Middle East has experienced a growing degree of conflict over the last decades, and is arguably the region where geopolitical order and political authority is most contested. The problem, Paul Salem explains, lies with the inability of intra- and extra-regional players to create synergic connections between Middle Eastern politics and the broader international system. One reason for that is liberalism's troubled relationship with the region.

Salem's arguments explaining the sources of the Middle East's imperviousness to liberalism are rooted in history rather than culture or, as Samuel Huntington's disciples contend, civilisational aspects. Between the 19th century and the first half of the 20th, the Europeans imposed – and the Americans tolerated – an imperial system of military subjugation of regional countries, co-optation of the elites and manipulation of the masses, as well as exploitation of local resources. As the US' global role became more prominent in the mid-20th century, so did its involvement in the region. Over time, and largely with European acquiescence or outright support, the US built a system of partnerships with authoritarian regimes aimed at securing American strategic interests in checking Arab nationalism, excluding left-leaning as well as Islam-rooted political options, exploiting hydrocarbon resources and supporting Israel's occupation of Arab lands.

As Western policies have undermined internationalist principles of self-determination, non-exploitation of foreign resources and non-intervention, it is not hard to see why liberalism has struggled in the Middle East. Even less controversial elements of the Western liberal tradition, such as republicanism, are losing ground, in spite of support for democracy and the rule of law being widespread in largely disempowered masses. Historically situated at the intersection of the three republics of Egypt, Iraq and Syria, the centre of gravity of Arab geopolitics has moved to the dynastic monarchies of the Arabian Peninsula. Secularism is also facing mounting challenges. Extremist groups taking inspiration from Wahhabism conceive of power only as an emanation of religious authority, and even the president of the once staunchly secularist Turkey, Recep Tayyip Erdogan, is blurring the line between state and religion. And of course, the constitution of post-1979 Iran, though republican and with elements of democracy, is predicated on the explicit rejection of religion as a private matter with which the state should not concern itself.

As for regionalism, it has made little progress – if any. In fact, Salem argues that the kind of regionalism Middle Eastern countries have engaged in has resulted in less, rather than more, cooperation. The Arab League and the Gulf Cooperation Council have at best papered over interstate differences, and at worst served to reinforce the legitimacy of the mostly authoritarian regimes in power through mutual recognition. In addition, both organisations (incidentally, now moribund) have excluded non-Arab countries such as Israel, Turkey and Iran, thereby making intra-regional rivalries even more acute. Fragmentation has increasingly run along ethnic and also sectarian lines, the latter becoming more prominent after the 2003 US-led invasion of Iraq exacerbated conflicts between Sunnis and Iranian-backed Shias. Governments have failed to devise instruments of shared governance even of intra-regional trade, which is extremely underdeveloped. With few exceptions, Middle Eastern countries have not integrated their economies. In part, history provides the explanation, as they sought rapid industrialisation through protectionism and import substitution. The over-reliance on hydrocarbons is another reason, with most countries competing for the same extra-regional markets. But political divides probably matter the most, as security and politics have regularly trumped economic sense. Today, only Turkey and the Emirate of Dubai stand out for their extensive trade and financial relations with regional players.

The interaction between the Middle East and the broader international system has been anything but beneficial for its security, stability and cohesiveness. External players have for the most part played a disruptive role, exploiting or fomenting intra-regional divisions to secure advantages they have used in a broader, global contest. The story has repeated itself cyclically, first with European imperialism, then superpower competition during the Cold War, and lastly with the US' attempt to reorganise the region around its interests (the ultimate rationale of the 2003 invasion of Iraq). With Russia's intervention in Syria and China's growing focus on the region, the Middle East is again enmeshed in bigger power games.

The region, Salem concludes, is a 'penetrated' system, not so much by liberal discourse and practices as by brute geopolitics.

There is, however, one key difference with the past. While during the age of imperialism and the Cold War the external powers competed for local resources and thus an outside-in logic was mostly dominant (some exceptions notwithstanding, such as the 1973 Yom Kippur war Egypt and Syria waged against Israel), now an inside-out logic is strongly at play, with Middle Eastern divisions reverberating negatively beyond the region. To start with, regional disintegration harms global stability through the spread of jihadism and illicit traffics, as well as by generating massive outflows of refugees. Even more worrisome is the effect on great power relations. To give just one example, the brief era of consensus over the 'responsibility to protect' norm, which lasted from the World Summit of 2005 to the Security Council resolution authorising the use of force in Libya in 2011, died in the ashes of Syria's civil war. That war has resulted in the emergence of a new regional power bloc, enabled by Russia and centred on Iran and its allies, namely the Assad regime in Syria, Shia forces in Iraq and Hezbollah in Lebanon. While the US unquestionably backs Iran's rivals Israel, Saudi Arabia and the United Arab Emirates, other players such as Europe, Turkey or China are reluctant to take sides. Yet inevitably they will, as they will have to modulate between their relations with Russia and the US and the latter's preferences in the Middle East. Different priorities will thus complicate relations not only between the US and Russia, but also the US and Europe, the West and Turkey, and eventually the US and China.

If the former Soviet space in Europe and the Caucasus is an area of overlapping orders, and the Middle East a tragic instance of order breakdown, what about the third theatre of contestation, the *Asia-Pacific*? Here, signs of an endogenously produced order are visible below and beside thin liberal frameworks.

As Richard Stubbs recalls, it was only during the winding down of the Cold War in the 1980s that the norms and practices of the liberal order started to consolidate. South Korea and Taiwan eventually transited to pluralist democracy, free of military rule and based on the rule of law, partly as a consequence of their sustained economic growth. Liberalism also seemed to sink in gradually in Southeast Asia, where regional countries moved along the hub-and-spoke system of security ties with the US to pursue greater economic dynamism and cooperation.

For decades, East Asian countries followed the 'developmental paradigm', whereby the state had a direct role in managing the economy, including through mercantilist trade policies aimed at developing a domestic industrial base protected by tariffs, subsidies and affordable credit. With Cold War barriers broken down and globalisation looming, the paradigm was no longer viable, and also tolerated less by the only superpower left. While the US supported democratisation processes in South Korea, Taiwan and elsewhere (with great ambivalence, for instance in the Philippines), it also concentrated on fostering free-market reforms – actually neoliberal supply-side policies – such as privatisations, deregulation and removal of capital controls. The elevation of the Asia-Pacific Economic Cooperation to summit level in the early 1990s on the personal initiative of US President Bill Clinton contributed to strengthening a political-economic system organised around American liberal economic ideals.

However, the project of creating a regional liberal order in East Asia was only partly successful. Stubbs lists three reasons for that. The first was the lingering developmental mind-set of local economic policymakers. The second was the devastating financial crisis of 1997-98, which discredited liberal economic policies as well as liberal agents, such as an IMF blindly insisting on recessionary fiscal adjustments and an absent US. The third and most important reason was the rise of China, which provided not only a model of an illiberal capitalist economy but also concrete help to governments in financial distress. While Asian countries did not renege entirely on liberal norms and economic practices, they sought an autonomous way of ensuring regional governance to protect themselves from external economic shocks, such as the Chiang Mai Initiative.

After the 11 September 2001 terrorist attacks in New York and Washington, the US government's approach to the region shifted to security, to the extent that counterterrorism cooperation was critical in the US' decision to move negotiations over free trade deals forward with Australia, Singapore, South Korea and Thailand. Superficially, the years immediately following 9/11 saw a consolidation of American hegemony in the Asia-Pacific, yet US commitments remained narrowly focused on bilateral relations. The US was absent from the regionalisation processes, none of which espoused distinctive liberal characters.

The Asia-Pacific had long suffered from an inability to formalise patterns of cooperation, with the Association of Southeast Asian Nations (ASEAN) being a (weak) exception. China's boom in the early 2000s changed the picture. With more and more countries redirecting trade towards and from China, and with Chinese investments flooding the region, the Asia-Pacific was experiencing an order reconfiguration whose roots and origin were endogenous. The great recession of 2008-09 further dented the US' credibility as the economic hinge of Asia's economy, and actually reinforced the perception of China – relatively unscathed by the financial storm – taking up the baton. After all, China was the critical player in the establishment of the ASEAN Regional Forum and East Asia Summit, and is now the driving force behind the project for a Regional Comprehensive Economic Partnership (RCEP). The contours of a distinctive Asian regionalisation model have thus started to emerge: economic-though not market-based, infused with superficial political dialogue, committed to state sovereignty, and enabled by China.

While China's economy is the main engine transmitting power to this nascent order, the People's Republic does not perform critical hegemonic functions, such as ensuring a stable and secure political system. For the time being, it seems more interested in expanding its influence – hence its assertiveness in the East and South China Seas – and pushing back against US clout than in assuming the role (and relative burden) of a hegemon. Exclusion of the US seems the main objective of the regional initiatives mentioned above. RCEP, in particular, has been designed to counter former US President Obama's project for a Transpacific Partnership (TPP), whose strategic aim was to consolidate US influence in East Asia through increased trade and regulatory influence. America's withdrawal from TPP, one of the first acts of nationalist President Trump, means that the region is unlikely to unfold along a liberal, US-led pattern and that liberal-leaning regional players will have to adapt to a less forthcoming environment.

The fact that TPP member states have decided to move forward anyway indicates that the region is not impervious to liberal economic practices. However, the strategy of hedging adopted by many regional countries in an attempt to balance between the US and China remains an obstacle to the promotion of liberal values and practices. What the Asia-Pacific shows today is an amalgam of ideas and practices in which free market-based elements co-exist with developmental practices of state management, US power is less normatively framed but nevertheless remains very important as a check on China's assertiveness, and political liberalism is limited to the domestic politics of certain countries and relatively weak intergovernmental institutions reveal the limited internalisation of internationalism. The Asia-Pacific is a community of countries bound by geography and therefore economic needs, but without much in common in terms of political regimes, ideals and cultural legacy.

The review of the areas of contested order attests to the limitations of the universalist ideational project. In theory, the liberal project is supposed to organise the totality of international relations but, in reality, it is invariably dependent on the geopolitical weight of its main proponents, most notably the US and Europe. The effect of this dependence, most visible in Eastern Europe and the South Caucasus and to a lesser extent in the Asia-Pacific, is that liberal norms, practices and institutions are turned into political instruments that rival powers fight with or against. Another conclusion is that the areas of contestation expose the contradictions between the normative premises of the liberal project and the actual policies of its main Western promoters, particularly in the Middle East. In a way, the case of the Middle East shows that the continued existence, and even expansion, of the liberal project is invariably linked to its 'de-Westernisation'. This process involves internalisation but also transformation of liberal norms and institutions so that they reflect political and cultural specificities and engender local ownership of regional governance. Whether the result will be a reformed liberal order, however, remains an open question. More likely, it will be a different system mixing liberal elements with non-liberal ones, as is happening in the Asia-Pacific.

Reform, conflict or adjustment

For all its faults and imperfections, the US-guaranteed liberal international order has provided the ideational glue and normative-institutional framework for three critical order-related functions: first, facilitating great power peace; second, promoting a more widespread distribution of economic gains; third, ensuring greater international representation. In order for the world of tomorrow to deliver similar results, global players, along with their partners, will have to reframe the notion of a multipolar world of unchecked competition as a concert of powers collectively guaranteeing a governance system embedded in at least certain liberal norms (peace, economic fairness, environmental protection, human security), institutions (the UN and the international financial institutions, IFIs) and practices (cooperative and inclusive rather than competitive). This is a vision of a *reformed liberal international order* resting on the ability of major competitors to reconcile diverging normative priorities, for instance sovereignty and human security, make global institutions more inclusive (for instance the Security Council and the IFIs), and fully embrace informal cooperation, ranging from the G20 to minilateral endeavours such as the P5+1 group that handled Iran's nuclear programme, as the standard back-up option for addressing emergencies and crises.

The conditions needed for this order to evolve and consolidate are manifold. The main international players will have to view their mutual relationships as not threatening perceived fundamental interests, re-internalise internationalism as part of their global identity, and re-embrace a revised multilateral order (also including regional bodies and informal initiatives) as 'legitimising' a new, accepted configuration of power. For the main international players to see their mutual relationships as unthreatening, there must be an accommodation of interests globally and regionally, meaning that areas of contestation will gradually have to turn into areas of accommodation through, possibly, greater regional institutionalisation and local ownership of whatever political, security and economic arrangement is eventually reached.

The problem is that the main international players today do not see their mutual relationships as entirely not threatening their fundamental interests. Furthermore, they are in the process of re-elaborating their adherence to internationalism along a power-infused nationalist paradigm, and increasingly see multilateral institutions instrumentally. Unsurprisingly, they are unable to reconcile their differences over the areas of contestation, and are either generating local tensions or conflict, such as in the former Soviet space west of the Urals and the Asia-Pacific, or being drawn into competition by competing local players, as has increasingly been the case in the Middle East. Thus, concerns that a multipolar (that is, less American-shaped) and less liberal (more power-driven) world will also be less orderly (that is, more prone to conflict) are anything but groundless.

Beside this scenario of *increasing conflict*, wherein the structures of the liberal order would gradually be emptied of legitimacy, authority and eventually capacity to function, another, less disheartening future is also possible. Underlying this less downbeat expectation are two fundamental conclusions drawn from the two sets of analyses included in this Special Issue – one on the global players, the other on the areas of contestation. First, global actors are in the process of repositioning themselves in the order rather than advocating a fundamentally different project organising international relations. They are (still) willing to play according to the rules of internationalism, although to a varying degree. Second, conflict is not the default outcome of order contestation, as countries in areas where liberal norms and structures are not established can play along with the interaction of outside-in and inside-out dynamics to produce endogenously elements of an order still capable of fostering interstate peace, tightening economic ties, and facilitating intergovernmental exchange. The Asia-Pacific is the main case in point, as regional players have worked out governance mechanisms that may embed not only regional rivalries, but also US-China competition (and to a lesser extent China-India competition). For sure, the same cannot be said of Eastern Europe and the South Caucasus or the Middle East. Yet, the former Soviet republics inhabiting the land 'in-between' the EU/NATO and Russia have also shown a capacity to balance between the two power blocs they are drawn to, which has the potential, if not to create a cooperative environment, at least to keep a fragile status quo of 'non-conflict' in place. As for the Middle East, the emergence of a power bloc enabled by Russia and centred on Iran and its proxies may be a first step towards the consolidation of a regional balance of power with some stabilisation potential.

This scenario of *global-regional adjustment* is what Grevi refers to when he insists on the link between an overarching system of global governance and regional subsystems in which liberal elements are alternatively supplemented or replaced by non-liberal ones. In this scenario, the liberal international order would be thinner and more fragile, yet it could still ensure a degree of interaction among global players capable of absorbing tensions originating from contested areas. Yet, the question about the future is not whether it will be defined by competition – because it will be – but whether competition will be managed or, instead, usher in an era of recurrent warfare. Today's global powers are more keenly aware of the costs of great power conflict and are therefore unlikely to march blindly into war as the European empires did in 1914. They are also more integrated economically. These are two incentives to refrain from war and address economic imbalances while avoiding beggar-thy-neighbour policies. For a multipolar world to be stable, however, the key aspect of order is its inclusiveness, based on the internalisation of the norm dictating international cooperation. The policymakers of today and tomorrow can still tap into the lingering legacy of the liberal order, which will continue to exist in normative frameworks, institutional procedures, intergovernmental and transgovernmental practices and regionalisation processes. More than the eternally shifting balances of power, it is in the transformative potential of this legacy that the hopes for a world less prone to conflict lie.

Index